QuickBooks® Online

The Ultimate Guide to All Online Plans

Thomas E. Barich
Certified QuickBooks Online ProAdvisor®

CPA911 Publishing, LLC
Jacksonville, FL

QuickBooks Online

ISBN Number 10-digit: 1-932925-63-5 13-digit: 978-1-932925-63-0

Published by CPA911 Publishing, LLC July 2014

A Note to the Reader

From the Publisher

This book was written after a recent overhaul of QuickBooks online. It is as current and up-to-date as possible. However, online applications can be updated as frequently as the publisher sees fit, and QuickBooks Online is no exception.

Therefore, you may find that some instructions and screenshots in this book differ from those in the online application. If you do, it is the result of the current (at the time you're reading this) update status of QuickBooks Online.

Acknowledgments

Cover Design: InfoDesign Services (www.infodesigning.com)

Production: InfoDesign Services (www.infodesigning.com)

Indexing: Transcription Conniption (www.transcriptionconniption.com)

Proofreading: Transcription Conniption (www.transcriptionconniption.com)

Table of Contents

CHAPTER 1:

QuickBooks Online Basics

- QuickBooks Online vs. QuickBooks Desktop
- Choosing a QuickBooks Online Plan
- Which Web Browsers Are Supported?
- Subscribing to QuickBooks Online
- Logging into QuickBooks Online
- Browser Tips
- Accounting Basics

W hile QuickBooks Online has been around for quite awhile, it is only recently that it has become a major player in the accounting software arena. According to Intuit, there are now more than one half million QuickBooks Online subscribers, and the number is increasing daily. In this chapter we're going to first determine if the service is right for you, and then move on to some of the basics needed to use it efficiently.

> **ProAdvisor NOTE:** *New subscribers to QuickBooks Online are automatically set up on the newest user interface. Existing users are being ported over to the new interface. Therefore, if you're an existing user, some of the screenshots and instructions may not yet be applicable to your service. However, once your company file is move to the new interface, everything will match (except for changes made since the writing of this book).*

Is QuickBooks Online Right for You?

The first thing you have to decide is if QuickBooks Online is going to provide you with all of the tools you need to track your company's finances. Let me begin by saying that QuickBooks desktop software users are going to find many of the same features, but in an entirely different user environment. Therefore, if you're contemplating switching, it will be a new experience, so be prepared.

Clearly, there are many benefits to using an online accounting service, so let's go over them first.

- Anywhere access to your accounting data. As long as you have an internet connection and a compatible computer, tablet, or mobile phone you can view and manipulate your accounting data wherever you are.
- Use mobile devices to access accounting information. With QuickBooks Online, you're no longer tied to your computer. You can also use your iPhone, Android

mobile phone, your iPad or your Android tablet to access your data.

- Continual updates, both minor and major. With a QuickBooks Online subscription, you never have to update your software. The updates, including minor bug fixes and major overhauls, are automatically applied to the service when available.

- Multiple platform support. Access your data using Mac or PC.

- No need for a special QuickBooks server as all users log into the service and have immediate access to the same files. Only the Essentials and Plus plans offer multiple user logins.

- Automatic backups. Your files are hosted on Intuit's servers and are backed up automatically each night.

- Use FIFO inventory valuation method. The Plus plan, which is the only plan that supports inventory tracking, uses the FIFO (First In First Out) method. Only the QuickBooks Enterprise with Advanced Inventory desktop program offers FIFO.

- Invoice automation (Essentials and Plus only). Generate and send invoices, credits, and sales receipts automatically.

ProAdvisor NOTE: *A personal observation about automatic updates. I signed up for Simple Start free trial while writing this book. I found that I was missing an option in Company Settings that all of the articles said should be there. I posted a query to the Intuit Online Community and found that someone who had signed up for a Simple Start trial version three weeks earlier indeed HAD the option. I then contacted QuickBooks Online support and was informed that I had a newer release of the service in which the option had been moved, and that the other person would eventually be updated to the new release. It makes me wonder just how automatic the updates really are.*

While there are a great many advantages to using QuickBooks Online, there are, unfortunately, some drawbacks as well.

- Cost. If you need sophisticated features such as inventory tracking, 1099 preparation, budgets, class tracking, and location tracking you'll have to sign up for the most expensive plan, Plus. All these features (and more) are available in the QuickBooks Pro desktop version.

- Multiple company files. If you have more than one company for which you track finances, you'll have to subscribe to a new plan for each company with QuickBooks Online. Using QuickBooks desktop software you can track unlimited companies.

- Advanced features such as sales orders, progress invoicing, change orders, job costing reports, and the ability to receive partial purchase orders are only available in QuickBooks desktop versions.

The bottom line is, if you only want to track a single company, need the benefits of an online service, and can live without the advanced features lacking in QuickBooks Online (see previous bullet list), the service is right for you.

QuickBooks Online Plans

QuickBooks Online currently comes in three versions (plans). As you might expect, each version offers different options at a different price. Obviously, the more options, the higher the price. You can find a handy comparison chart at http://quickbooks.intuit.com/online/compare.

ProAdvisor NOTE: *Some things that you will NOT find in any online edition are multiple currencies, job costing, price levels, progress invoicing, and memorized transactions.*

Simple Start

For the basic user with minimal needs Simple Start is the ticket. It offers income and expense tracking, but no accounts payable or inventory tracking. In addition, you're limited to a single user. Simple Start also lacks advanced features such as 1099 preparation, budgets, class tracking, and location tracking. In addition, it is limited to 20+ reports. At the time of this writing the subscription price is $12.95/month.

Here is a listing of specific features found in the other plans that are missing from Simple Start:

- 1099 Preparation (Plus only)
- Attachments – This is the Attachments center, where you can upload and store attachments for later use. While Simple Start does not have access to the Attachments center, Simple Start subscribers can still attach files to individual transactions
- Automatic Invoicing
- Budgeting (Plus only)
- Class Tracking (Plus only)
- Custom Fields
- Delayed Charges
- Delayed Credits
- FIFO Inventory Valuation (Plus only)
- Inventory Tracking (Plus Only)
- Location Tracking (Plus only)
- Multiple Users
- Purchase Orders (Plus only)
- Recurring Transactions
- The ability to enter bills

- The ability to pay bills (logical since you can't enter them)
- Time-Tracking (Plus only) – both single activity and weekly timesheet
- Vendor Credits

The bottom line here is that Simple Start will work fine for you if you want to invoice customers, track your income, expenses, and sales, do payroll, and run basic reports. If you need accounts payable (tracking bills), automatic invoicing, purchase orders, inventory tracking, and the other things on the list above, you need to move on to the Essentials or Plus plan.

Essentials

The Essentials plan, which currently costs $26.95/month, includes everything in the Simple Start plan plus the following:

- 40+ Plus Reports
- Accounts Payable (enter and pay bills)
- Automatic Invoicing
- Custom Fields
- Delayed Charges & Credits
- Up to 3 Users

Plus

Plus includes everything found in Simple Start and Essentials, but adds the following:

- 65+ Reports
- Budgets
- Class Tracking
- FIFO Inventory Valuation Method

- Inventory Tracking (on hand quantities)
- Location Tracking
- Prepare 1099s
- Purchase Orders
- Time-Tracking – single activity and weekly timesheets
- Unlimited reports-only users
- Unlimited time-tracking-only users
- Up to 5 Users

Plus is currently priced at $39.95/month.

Upgrade and Downgrade

If you have subscribed to Simple Start or Essentials you can upgrade to Essentials or Plus. If an upgrade option is available, you'll see an Upgrade icon in the upper part of the screen. As a matter of fact, if you try to access a feature not available in your version, you're automatically taken to an upgrade screen.

Downgrading is another story. If you are subscribed to Essentials or Plus, you cannot downgrade to Simple Start or Essentials. You'll have to cancel your current subscription and create a new subscription to the desired plan.

Supported Browsers

I know that I read somewhere that QuickBooks Online is browser independent. It's mostly true; however, when I tried accessing the service with the Opera browser, QuickBooks Online balked and told me to try one of the preferred browsers. For the best results it's recommended that you use Chrome, Firefox, or Internet Explorer. Clearly, the newer the version, the better. Actually, QuickBooks Online works best with Chrome, so that might very well be your first choice.

Subscribing

There are two ways to subscribe, depending on your current accounting system. If you're already using a QuickBooks desktop application (either PC or Mac) you can subscribe by exporting your desktop company file to QuickBooks Online.

ProAdvisor TIP: As of this writing, none of the U.S. versions of QuickBooks Online support multiple currencies. If you need multi-currency support you'll have to sign up for one of the international versions (http://global.intuit.com/choose-country.jsp).

Unfortunately, using this method automatically signs you up for the QuickBooks Online Plus version, from which you cannot downgrade. If that's the plan you want, check out the section entitled "Importing from QuickBooks Desktop" in Chapter 3 for detailed instructions.

ProAdvisor TIP: It you want to subscribe to a Simple Start or Essentials plan, you can subscribe on the QuickBooks Online website, and then import your desktop company data after you login to the online company. See the section entitled "Importing from QuickBooks Desktop" in Chapter 3 for more.

Subscribing online is simple. Head to the QuickBooks Online website (http://quickbooks.intuit.com/products) and click the Try It Free for 30 Days link for the plan you wish to subscribe to.

ProAdvisor TIP: Ask your accountant if he or she subscribes to QuickBooks Online Accountant. If so, you may be able to get a discount by signing up through your accountant.

You're immediately asked for basic info to create a user id (see Figure 1-1).

Figure 1-1: Start with the basics.

Once the company is created, QuickBooks Online is launched, and you're asked for the additional information shown in Figure 1-2.

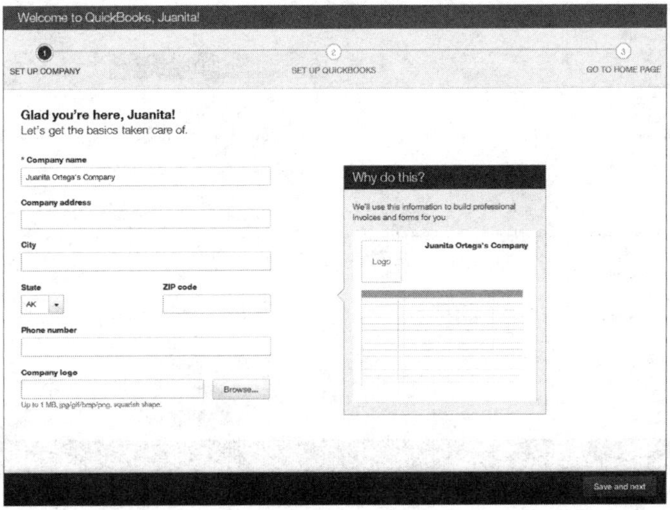

Figure 1-2: Enter your company name, address, and phone number next.

ProAdvisor TIP: *If you plan to import your desktop application data you should enter the company name (the only required field on the form) and click the Save And Next button. When you get to the third screen (Figure 1-3) be sure to answer Yes to the import data from QuickBooks question. When you click Save And Next, a dialog appears, asking if you're ready to import from QuickBooks. Click Continue to perform the import. The information in your desktop file will overwrite whatever you enter here (assuming your desktop company file already contains the information).*

As you can see in Figure 1-2 above, with the exception of the Company Name field, all other information is optional at this time. After you fill out the company information click Save And Next to move to the final setup screen (see Figure 1-3).

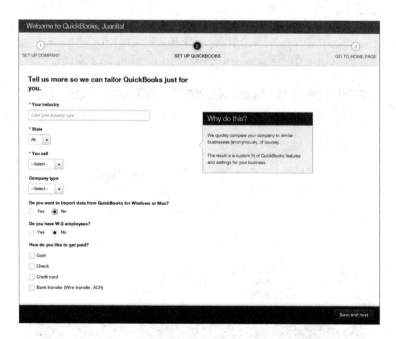

Figure 1-3: Answering questions on this page will let QuickBooks Online create a relevant chart of accounts and other necessary items.

The questions are self-explanatory, but if you have any problems, you can always change your answers later (Tools Menu (gear icon) | Settings | Company Settings). Once you're done click Save And Next to move on to the final setup page which provides some statistics on your business and a listing of features and settings customized for your particular business type. Click Save And Next to be taken to the QuickBooks Online Home page where you can begin utilizing the program.

See Chapter 3 for detailed instructions on setting up a new company and importing data from QuickBooks desktop or other applications.

Logging in

Point your browser at https://qbo.intuit.com, enter your User ID and Password, and click Sign In. It doesn't get much easier. Once you get to the login screen you might want to create a bookmark to make it easy to access.

Browser Tips

Regardless of which supported browser you're using, there are a few things you can do to improve your experience with QuickBooks Online.

One of the first things you should do is enable pop-ups. QuickBooks Online uses them, and if pop-ups are disabled on your browser, you'll go crazy trying to figure why QuickBooks Online isn't working. Check this document for instructions on turning off popup blockers in the different browsers - https://qboe.custhelp.com/app/answers/detail/a_id/2701.

Create Separate User Profiles

Since Chrome is the preferred browser, let's start there. Chrome allows you to create separate user profiles with which you can open separate company files simultaneously. This comes in handy if you need to compare data in two or more company files.

To create a new user profile in Chrome, follow these steps:

1. Click the Chrome menu icon (three horizontal bars to the right of the Address Bar) and select Settings from the menu that appears.

2. Move to the Users section and click the Add New User button to display the Create User window shown in Figure 1-4.

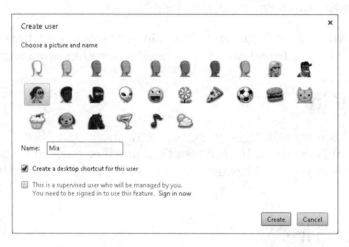

Figure 1-4: Chrome offers a variety of icons to choose from.

3. Select an icon for the new user profile.

4. Give the new user a name.

5. Check or uncheck the Create A Desktop Shortcut For This User option. When the option is enabled, a shortcut is placed on your desktop, which you can later use to open Chrome with the selected profile.

6. Click the Create button to add the new user and open a new instance of Chrome using the user profile you just created.

ProAdvisor TIP: *After you create one new user profile a user icon appears in the top left corner of the Chrome browser. To create additional users simply click the icon and select New User from the drop-down menu that appears.*

Creating a new user profile in Firefox is a little more complex. You have to first run the Profile Manager and then create your new profile. For detailed instructions go to Firefox support (https://support.mozilla.org/en-US/home) and type create user profile in the search box. Click the magnifying glass icon to start the search. The first document that appears should be Use The Profile Manager To Create And Remove Firefox Profiles. Click the title to open the document, and follow the instructions.

Open QBO Screens in Separate Browser Windows

If you want to compare screens or reports in QuickBooks Online you can do so quite easily by opening each screen in its own window. In Chrome, some links offer the option (when right-clicked) to open the related screen in a new window. Even if the link doesn't offer the option you can still click the link, copy the URL, paste it into a different browser tab, and then drag the tab below the Address Bar to create a new window. You'll find most browsers work the same.

Bookmark QuickBooks Online Windows

Since you can't customize the navigation bars to include links to specific windows it appears that you always have to follow the same path to get a particular screen each time, regardless of how many clicks it takes. For example, let's say you run several reports each morning, including the A/R Aging Summary, an A/P Aging Summary, and Time Activities by Employee Detail reports.

The best case scenario is that you click Reports | Frequently Run | <report name> to open each report. By adding a bookmark folder called QBO Favorites to your browser's bookmarks toolbar and bookmarking each report you can reduce the access clicks for each to two – click QBO Favorites | <report name>. Only saving a single click is no big deal right? Wrong. Each time you start from scratch within QuickBooks Online you have to wait for each screen to load (Reports and Frequently Run). By bookmarking the reports, you bypass those screens and go directly to the report. To add a bookmarks folder in Chrome follow these steps:

1. Click the Customize icon (three horizontal parallel bars) on the right side of the Address Bar and click Bookmarks | Show Bookmarks Bar.

2. Right click the Bookmarks Bar that appears under the Address Bar and select Add Folder from the context menu that appears. The New Folder dialog seen in Figure 1-5 opens.

3. Enter QBO Favorites (or something similar) in the Name field.

4. Make sure that the Bookmarks Bar folder is selected in the list, and click Save. The Folder is immediately added to the Chrome bookmarks bar.

When you find a QuickBooks Online window for which you want quick access, just add it to the new bookmarks folder.

Figure 1-5: Speed up your QuickBooks Online navigation by taking advantage of browser bookmarks.

If you're using a browser other than Chrome, check the browser's help files for instructions on creating folders and bookmarks.

ProAdvisor TIP: *If you find that a QuickBooks Online feature or link is not working in a separate browser tab or window, return to the original window and try it there. Some features only work in the original window.*

Clear Browser History

Clearing your browser history/temporary internet files regularly will help to maintain optimum speed. While it's true that caching web page elements initially speeds up visits to a web page, an overstuffed cache will eventually have the opposite effect as the browser spends more and more time searching the cache. For detailed instructions on clearing your history/cache check out this article - https://qboe.custhelp.com/app/answers/detail/a_id/1038.

Accounting Basics

When starting to use an accounting program of any type it's always handy to have some accounting basics under your belt.

Debits & Credits

This is the one that always confuses due to the seemingly "unnatural" use of commonly defined terms. In the English language a debit normally means a decrease, and a credit means an increase. Unfortunately, in accounting terms a debit sometimes means an increase, and other times a decrease. Likewise, a credit sometimes indicates an increase, but other times a decrease. It depends on the account type to which the debit or credit is being applied.

Here's what accountants all over the world say. Just remember that debits always appear on the left and credits on the right (double-entry accounting). They also tell you to memorize the following: by default, Assets and Expenses are debits, while Liabilities, Equity, and Income are credits. Then they show you the following table to help explain.

DEBIT	CREDIT
ASSETS	
	LIABILITIES
	EQUITIES
	INCOME
EXPENSES	

Table 1-1: Each account type belongs on its own side of the ledger

I guess I'm one of those people with a mental block, because it never used to stick with me. Finally, I realized that my common sense tells me that a credit increases and a debit decreases. Well, that holds true for Liabilities, Equity, and Income – a debit decreases each of these accounts while a credit increases each one. However, it's just the opposite for Assets and Expenses. As long as I remember that Assets and Expenses defy common sense (mine anyway), I'm okay.

Cash-Basis vs. Accrual-Basis

For income taxes purposes you must choose between a cash-basis method of tracking income and expenses, and an accrual-basis method. Most businesses file their income taxes using the cash-basis, while maintaining their books on an accrual-basis.

Cash-Basis Accounting Method

The cash-basis method is very straightforward. You account for actual money in your possession at the time of the accounting. In other words, you record income when it physically comes in – a payment received, a refund check received, a cash sale paid at the time of the sale. The same goes for expenses. You record your expenses when you actually pay them, not when the bill appears.

Accrual-Basis Accounting Method

Unless yours is a cash-only business for sales and expenses (no invoices or bills with payment terms) you will probably want to use the accrual-basis method for keeping your books. This means that income is recorded as soon as you generate an invoice. It doesn't matter when (or even if) the payment is received. Once you create that invoice, you added that amount to your Accounts Receivable (an asset) account, thus increasing your income.

Expenses are handled the same way. When you enter a bill into QuickBooks Online it immediately becomes an expense. It doesn't matter when you pay the bill, as soon as it's in QuickBooks, it's officially deducted from the related expense account.

Calendar vs. Fiscal Year

Calendar vs. Fiscal Year is a very important distinction for some businesses. It's true that most small businesses use the calendar year as their fiscal year. However, it's not an absolute must. There may be instances where it's more beneficial to run your business on a fiscal year that differs from the calendar year. Check with your accountant to see if that might be the case with your business.

Also, be sure to note that payroll and 1099 filings must be done on a calendar year basis even if your accounting is done on a fiscal year basis.

Chart of Accounts

The chart of accounts is a listing of account names. On the surface that may not seem like much, but the truth of the matter is that the chart of accounts is the keystone of your accounting system. The results of all of your transactions are ultimately linked to one or more accounts in the chart of accounts. Together, these listings and postings constitute the General Ledger which, in effect, IS your accounting system. Everything else is there to support and report on those transactional postings.

ProAdvisor NOTE: *In accounting terms, linking a transaction to an account in the chart of accounts is called posting.*

See the section entitled "Configuring an Effective Chart of Accounts" in Chapter 4 for more information.

CHAPTER 2:

Getting Around in QuickBooks Online

- Understanding the Home Page
- Using the Left Navigation Bar
- Working with the Money Bar
- Using the Top Navigation Bar
- Accessing the Tools Menu
- Monitoring the Activities Feed

Navigating QuickBooks Online is not all that difficult, especially with the improvements introduced in the latest overhaul. Sometimes the most difficult part of navigating a software or online application is using consistent terminology. To that end we are going to implement the following guidelines for the usage of QuickBooks Online terminology. You may find that others who are writing about QuickBooks Online use different terminology, but for the remainder of this book we will use the terminology found in Figure 2-1, and in the following sections.

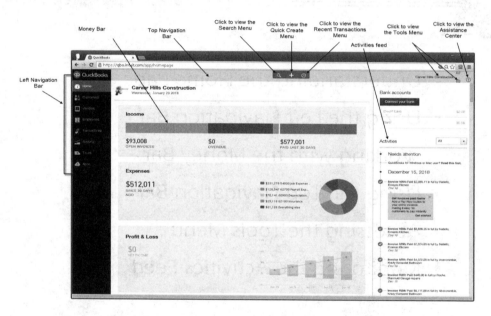

Figure 2-1: Consistent terminology is the basis for easy navigation.

In addition, there are some terms frequently used in connection with QuickBooks online that need defining before we go any further.

- Dashboards. These are windows that contain a variety of elements for displaying related information and accessing related features. In QuickBooks Online many of the centers (Customer, Vendor, Employee, etc.) can also be considered dashboards. However, to simplify matters we will refer to them as centers.

- Centers. These are the primary windows for accessing related information and features such as the Customers center, the Vendors center, and so. From the various centers you perform such actions as creating new names (customers, vendors, employees, etc.), viewing and working with existing transactions, and quite a bit more.

- Screens or Windows. I'll use these two terms interchangeably just to add a little variety to the writing. Each refers to the data appearing in a browser window.

Understanding the Home Page

The Home page, which appears by default when you log into QuickBooks Online, provides what many refer to as a dashboard interface due to the variety of elements that it contains:

- Video Tutorials. The first time you open QuickBooks Online, the section below the Top Navigation Bar offers several video tutorials that cover important topics. Click the X at the top right to remove the section from your screen.

- QuickBooks Online News/Alerts. Below the company name appears a section with announcements from Intuit ranging from news alerts to special offers. Click the X to close each instance.

- Money Bar. Below your company name and today's date (or below the news alerts if any are displayed) is the colorful Money Bar. It provides a quick glimpse at your income situation. The bar has three sections; Open Invoices (invoices not yet paid), Overdue (invoices that are past their payment date), and Paid Last 30 Days (yep, invoices paid within the last thirty days). Click a section to see a listing of the related transactions. You can continue to drill down to see more detail.

- Bank Accounts. This section is located in the top right portion of the Home page. Here you'll find all of your bank and credit cards listed. Click an account to open the account record. If it's an online enabled account you'll see the listing of recently downloaded transactions (see Figure 2). If it's a non-online enabled account the bank account register opens.

Figure 2-2: Click a listing in the Bank accounts section to see the related bank account.

- Expenses. This section provides a quick overview of your expenses with a summary of incurred expenses and a graph. Click the summary to generate a transaction report of expenses for the last thirty days. Click a section of the graph to create a transaction report displaying those transactions used to generate that particular section of the graph.

- Profit & Loss. I can't say it any plainer. This section also uses a summary and a graph to provide an overview. The summary is divided into two parts – Income and Expenses. Click the Net Income figure to display a profit and loss report. Clicking the graph generates a profit and loss report broken down by week.

- Activities Feed. Located below the Bank accounts section, the Activities feed offers a listing of items that need attention, recent transactions, upcoming tasks, and so on.

Using the Left Navigation Bar

A nice addition to the new interface is the Left Navigation Bar. It provides a handy tool that enables you to quickly and easily navigate to the major areas of QuickBooks Online. As you can see in Figure 2-3, it contains links to the primary centers as well as to transaction lists and reports.

Figure 2-3: Getting around in QuickBooks Online is easy with the Left Navigation Bar.

Click a link to be taken to the related page. In the case of the primary centers (Customers, Vendors, Employees, and Reports) a single click immediately opens the selected center. Clicking the Transactions link opens a submenu of specific transaction list links. The Taxes link behaves differently depending on whether you have a QuickBooks Online Payroll subscription. If you do, clicking the Taxes link displays a submenu of two additional links – Sales Tax and Payroll Tax. If you don't have a payroll subscription, the Taxes link takes you directly to the Sales Tax Center. The last link, Apps, takes you to the Intuit Apps center where you can purchase third party add-ons.

ProAdvisor TIP: *If you right-click any of the primary links on the Left Navigation Bar you can open the associated screen in a new browser tab or window by selecting Open Link In New Tab (or Window) from the context menu that appears. While the exact text may vary, all major browsers offer the feature.*

Working with the Money Bar

The multicolored Money Bar, which is found on the Home page, the Customers center, and the Vendors center, offers a quick overview of income or expenses (depending on where you are). Both the Home page and the Customers center Money Bars display income numbers, while the Vendors center Money Bar focuses on expenses.

ProAdvisor NOTE: *Users with restricted permissions may not see the Money Bar. See Chapter 3 for more on managing users.*

The Money Bar is not simply a visual guide to income or expenses, but also a tool for investigating the numbers further. Clicking a section of the Money Bar displays a listing of those transactions that make up the total displayed in that section. For example, clicking on the Open Invoice(s) section in the Customers center displays all open invoices, including those that are overdue. However, clicking the Overdue section shows only those open invoices that are past due (see Figure 2-4). Once the listing is displayed you can drill deeper by clicking the transaction(s) shown in the list.

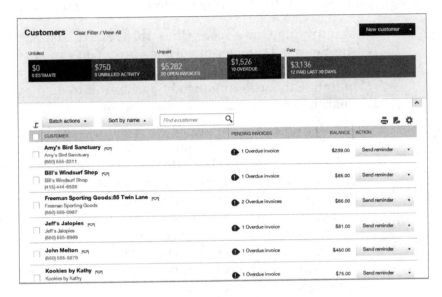

Figure 2-4: Use the Money Bar to filter out certain transactions.

When you're done viewing a selection of transactions from the Money Bar, click the Clear Filter / View All link above the Money Bar to display all transactions. Creating, editing, and using transactions is covered in later chapters on income and expense tracking.

Using the Top Navigation Bar

Located, aptly enough, at the top of the QuickBooks Online window, the Top Navigation Bar includes several vital navigational tools. As you can see in Figure 2-5, it contains a group of three icons, the company name, a gear icon, and a question mark icon.

Figure 2-5: Performing a variety of navigational tasks is done from the Top Navigation Bar.

While the Left Navigation Bar provides access to the different centers, transaction lists, and reports, the Top Navigation Bar offers entry to QuickBooks Online configuration settings, help files, and search features:

- Magnifying Glass Icon. Click this icon to display the Search Transactions dialog box. You can enter a keyword or phrase to locate transaction records that match. Click the Advanced Search link to display a Search screen with additional options.

- The X icon in the middle of the group opens the Quick Create menu shown in Figure 2-6. What you see depends on the QuickBooks Online plan to which you are subscribed. Initially the menu opens with four choices and a Show More link to expand the menu. Here you can choose to create new transactions for customers, vendors, employees, and some miscellaneous categories. However, as I mentioned earlier, those choices will be limited by the plan to which you're subscribed.

Figure 2-6: You can create new transactions from almost anywhere within QuickBooks Online by using the Quick Create menu.

- Clock Icon. For a listing of the recent transactions created, click this icon. It displays the transaction type, date, amount, and name (customer, vendor, etc.) for the last ten transactions. Click a transaction to open the transaction record. If you don't see the transaction you're looking for, click the More link at the bottom to see a list of all transactions, sorted by date in descending order (latest appearing first).

- Company Name/Gear Icon. Click the company name or the gear icon to open the Tools Menu. See the following section entitled "Accessing the Tools Menu" for more information.

- Question Mark Icon. Click this icon to display the Assistance Center (see Figure 2-7)

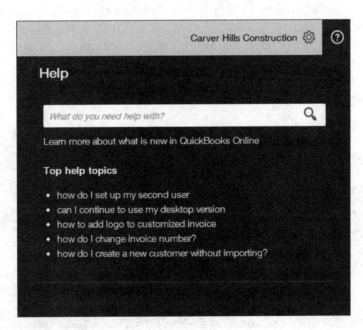

Figure 2-7: Help is only a mouse click away.

ProAdvisor TIP: *For the most accurate search results use the Advanced Search link in the Search Transactions dialog. The basic Search Transactions dialog has a few quirks that render it less than helpful unless you're aware of them. For example, if you enter text it assumes you want to search for a reference number. The same goes for entering numbers without decimals or without dollar signs. Again, it assumes they are reference numbers. The Advanced Search screen lets you choose which records to search, which fields to search, and which qualifier to use.*

Accessing the Tools Menu

The Tools Menu shown in Figure 2-8 is the QuickBooks Online control center. Here you can set preferences, work on lists, manage users, and much more. To access the Tools Menu click the company name (or the gear icon) in the top right corner of the window. The options found on the Tools Menu will vary depending upon the plan you've subscribed to, as well as any additional subscriptions (e.g., payroll) you may have.

Figure 2-8: The Tools Menu is your gateway to the inner workings of QuickBooks Online.

Figure 2-8 shows the Tools Menu for a QuickBooks Online Plus subscription.

The Tools Menu has four main categories, each with a number of links to various QuickBooks Online tools and features:

- Settings. This is where you'll find access to QuickBooks Online preferences through the Company Settings link. Click the Chart of Accounts link to set up or modify your chart of accounts. You'll also find a Payroll Settings link that lets you configure options for the payroll service. It appears even if you haven't subscribed to a payroll service plan.

- Lists. QuickBooks Online is a collection of lists, all working together to record and track your financial data. This section contains links to a page containing all lists. If you have the Essential or Plus plan you'll find additional links to specific lists as well.

- Tools. Importing and exporting tools, bank reconciliation, and the audit log are all found here. If you have a Plus plan you'll also find a link to the Budgeting tool as well.

- Your Company. This is where you can edit your billing information using the Your Account link. If you have an Essentials or Plus plan you can also add, remove, and modify user information. Since the Simple Start plan only allows for a single user the only thing you can do is add or remove accounting firms. You'll also find a couple of additional links for Feedback, Privacy, and signing out.

ProAdvisor TIP: *You can right-click any of the links on the Tools Menu to open the associated screen in a separate browser window or tab. Select the appropriate command from the context menu that appears.*

Monitoring the Activities Feed

To ensure that you are kept up-to-date on things that may require your attention, the Activities feed on the bottom right portion of the Home page maintains a listing of upcoming tasks, overdue transactions, recent transactions, and messages from your customers and your accountant. Items requiring immediate attention are flagged in red.

You can filter the list by using the drop-down menu to the right of the name Activities. From the drop-down list, you can select All (the default), Invoices, Estimates, Payments, or Expenses. As you scroll through the list you can drill down to view a transaction or other item by clicking it.

Transactions Panel

A handy new feature in QuickBooks Online is the Panel that appears in transaction windows to display additional items relevant to the transaction you're currently working on. For example, viewing an open invoice results in the Panel displaying a list of outstanding billable time for the selected customer (see Figure 2-9).

Figure 2-9: The Panel reminds you when you have outstanding items related to transactions.

To include the item in the transaction simply click Add. If you want to view the item, click Open. If the Panel is taking up unnecessary room, click the little, right-arrow tab at the top to hide it.

CHAPTER 3:

Setting Up Your Company File

- Configuring Your Company from Scratch
- Importing from QuickBooks Desktop
- Importing from Excel
- Managing Users

Whether you're a new user starting out for the first time with QuickBooks Online, a QuickBooks desktop user who has decided to switch, or a throwback to the stone age who's still using a spreadsheet, setting up a new company is relatively painless. Okay, Okay, all you spreadsheet users, stop throwing stones ... just kidding.

When you subscribed, QuickBooks Online took some basic information, and created a company for you based on that data. However, it's pretty much an empty shell waiting for you to fill with data relevant to your business. In this chapter we're going to cover the various means of adding customers, vendors, services, items, and any accounts QuickBooks Online may have missed.

ProAdvisor NOTE: *For anyone who has used a QuickBooks desktop program, you should be aware that to create multiple companies in QuickBooks Online you must have a new subscription for each company. One subscription does not support multiple companies.*

There are three avenues to getting your data into QuickBooks Online. We'll cover them all in this chapter. Of course, which method you use depends on which method (if any) you're currently using to keep track of your finances.

Starting from Scratch

If you've just signed up for a QuickBooks Online Subscription and you do not have any financial information that you want to import, you can jump right into the new company setup with a little help from this section.

Get Prepared

Maybe I was a little hasty when I said, in the opening paragraph, that "you can jump right into the new company setup." The truth is, if you want to avoid annoying time delays, frustration, and QuickBooks Online time outs (expired sessions) you should spend some time pulling together all of the information you're going to need to set up your company file before you start. Here's the short list:

- Decide how to enter historical transactions (individual transactions or totals by journal entry)
- Basic customer and vendor contact information
- Account balances.
- Products and services data.
- Payroll information (including YTD historical data).

Get to Work

Once you've gathered all of the necessary data, it's time to start building your QuickBooks Online company file.

ProAdvisor TIP: *Do not use the Opening Balance (or Balance) fields found in the forms used to create accounts, customers, or vendors. The problem is that QuickBooks Online posts these account balances to an account called Opening Bal Equity, which is only found in QuickBooks, and has no real function in an accounting system. Eventually, all postings to this account must be moved to the appropriate account by your accountant (for a fee). Save yourself time and money by adding opening balances either by entering historical transactions or by using journal entries.*

Add Customers, Vendors, and Employees

Before you start entering either current or historical transactions, it will be a lot easier if you already have your customers, vendors, and employees in the system. If you have those names in a spreadsheet you can use the import function in QuickBooks Online discussed later in this chapter. However, for the purposes of this section we're assuming that you are going to enter them manually. The mechanics for entering names into all three lists is basically the same – go to the appropriate center, click the New <name type> button (Add Employee in the Employee center), and fill out and save the form. The differences are mainly in the data that is required for each. See Chapters 6, 7, and 9 for detailed instructions on creating new customers, vendors, and employees.

ProAdvisor TIP: *If you're planning to enter your customers, vendors, and employees manually, you might want to consider creating a spreadsheet and importing it instead. The reason is twofold. First of all, it's a lot easier to add the information in the rows and columns format of a spreadsheet than in the QuickBooks Online forms. Secondly, if you have a lot of names to enter and the QuickBooks Online service or your internet connection are a little sluggish, the manual method will be frustratingly slow. For details on correctly formatting and importing spreadsheet data see Appendix B.*

Enter Historical Transactions

If you are one of those rare people who decides to start a business on the first day of your fiscal year (January 1st if you're using the calendar year), and you have no historical data to enter, you can skip this section. Everyone else, I'm afraid, has to stay and slog through it.

If you want to maintain accurate financial records you have to start with the most accurate information possible. Accounting is definitely one of those activities to which the acronym GIGO (Garbage In Garbage Out) applies. The only way to get valuable reports out of QuickBooks Online (or any other accounting system) is to input complete and accurate information from the very beginning.

Entering historical transactions individually, rather than entering totals through journal entries, provides you with a much higher level of detail. It makes it a lot easier to deal with customer or vendor queries when you have the original transactions to refer to. Therefore, you should enter historical transactions whenever possible.

For example, if you've subscribed to QuickBooks Online in February and your fiscal year begins on January 1st, it's not overly burdensome to enter all of your sales and purchase transactions for the time between. As you get further into your fiscal year (the more historical transactions you have) you might want to consider using journal entries to record the totals only. Check with your accountant so you can make an informed decision.

Unfortunately, QuickBooks Online does not offer a lot of options for entering historical data. Most of the historical transactions will have to be entered manually, with the exception of bank and credit card transactions, which can be imported from a web connect file. See Chapter 8 for information on importing web connect files and working with bank transactions. Other than that you'll have to use a third party application such as Transaction Pro Importer from Baystate Consulting (http://www.baystateconsulting.com/). Be sure to get the Transaction Pro Importer for QuickBooks Online Edition (QBOE).

To enter historical transactions by hand go to the Left Navigation Bar, click the Transactions link, and then the appropriate link in the submenu that appears. For example, click Transactions | Sales to open the Sales Transactions window (see Figure 3-1). Click the Create New button in the upper right corner of the window and select the transaction type you want to create. Fill in the data and save the transaction.

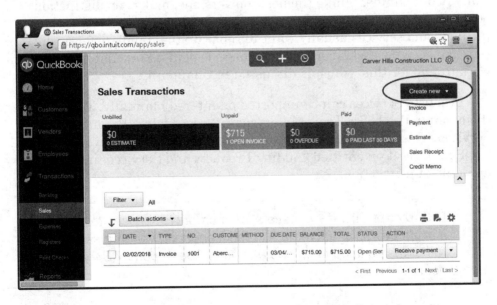

Figure 3-1: Creating new transactions in QuickBooks Online is a breeze.

Enter Account Balances

What's in your bank, who owes you what, and what do you owe others? QuickBooks Online wants to know. As I mentioned in the tip at the beginning of this section, you should never enter opening balances of any kind in the Opening Balance or Balance fields that QuickBooks Online offers you when creating accounts, customers, or vendors.

The best way to enter account balances is to add the individual, historical transactions that make up the balance. The second best way is to enter journal entries that post the amounts to the correct accounts. If you have any questions, check with your accountant. See Chapter 8 for details on entering bank account opening balances. See the Chapters 6 and 7 for instructions on creating opening balances for customers and vendors using journal entries.

Add Products and Services

If you're running a business, you're selling something. The two categories QuickBooks Online offers are Products and Services. In truth, QuickBooks Online, unlike the desktop versions, makes no distinction between the two. This is unfortunate since businesses that sell both products and services usually want to separate the numbers for each so they can see how each arm of the business is doing. Fortunately, there is a workaround for this, which is discussed in Chapter 4.

Products/Services can be imported or entered manually. To enter them manually choose Tools Menu (gear icon) | Lists | Products And Services. This opens the Products And Services window shown in Figure 3-2. See the section entitled "Adding Products and Services" in Chapter 4 for detailed instructions.

ProAdvisor TIP: *If you have a lot of products/services to enter it might be easier to create a spreadsheet and import the data rather than adding them one at a time. See Appendix B for details.*

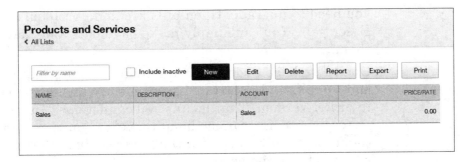

Figure 3-2: By default, QuickBooks Online comes with a single product/
service, called Sales.

Importing from QuickBooks Desktop

If you're switching from a QuickBooks desktop application (either PC or
Mac) to a QuickBooks Online subscription, you can easily port most of
your information from the desktop to the cloud. The process requires two
separate steps to complete. The first step merely provides instructions for
performing the import. If you can figure out how to export your desktop
company file you can skip the first step.

ProAdvisor NOTE: *You can only use this procedure within the
first sixty days of your subscription. After that, you'll have to
cancel your existing subscription and start a new company if
you want to import your desktop data.*

A cautionary note for Simple Start and Essentials users. As of this
writing, importing desktop data brings unsupported transactions into
QuickBooks Online. Check for the following (in your desktop file) before
starting your desktop export/import.:

- Open Bills. If you import open bills into QuickBooks
  Online Simple Start you're stuck with them. If you
  click a bill to open it so you can delete it, you're told

you need to upgrade. Open bills are not a problem in Essentials. You can simply make payments and close them.

- Open Purchase Orders. Open purchase orders that end up in Simple Start or Essentials are unsupported in either version. That means you cannot open them or receive items against them. However, you can print them so you have a copy of the PO to confirm the receipt of ordered goods.

- Unbilled Expenses are a little different. You cannot delete them or add them to a new invoice. You can, however, add them to an imported open invoice for the same customer/job. For example, if you've imported both an open invoice and an unbilled expense for ABC Hardware you can open the invoice, and add the unbilled expense. However, if you've only imported the unbilled expense you cannot add it to a new invoice for ABC Hardware. QuickBooks Online tells you to update.

The best thing to do is deal with them in your QuickBooks desktop application before starting the export to QuickBooks Online.

To get specific instructions for importing your desktop company file follow these steps:

1. Log into your QuickBooks Online account.

2. Select Tools Menu (gear icon) | Tools | Import Desktop Data to open the Import QuickBooks Desktop Data screen shown in Figure 3-3.

3. From the Select Your Version drop-down list choose the version of QuickBooks desktop from which you want to import the data.

4. Click Continue to move to the next window. The instructions for the selected QuickBooks desktop version are displayed. You can print them if you wish.

5. Log out of QuickBooks Online.

Figure 3-3: You can import from either the PC or Mac version of QuickBooks desktop.

Here's how you export the desktop data to QuickBooks Online:

1. Make sure you're connected to the Internet.

2. Open your QuickBooks desktop application.

3. From the menu bar choose Company | Export Company File To QuickBooks Online. QuickBooks launches its internal browser and begins the export process. The first screen is informational.

4. Click Continue to display the Is QuickBooks Online Right For You screen. While QuickBooks Online contains features not found in the desktop version, the same is true the other way around. Here, you're informed of the features you'll be losing by moving to QuickBooks Online.

5. This warning is only for users who are also signing up for a new subscription. If you've already subscribed to an online plan, ignore the warning and click Continue to display the login screen.

6. If you already have an Intuit ID, fill in the User ID and Password fields. If you don't have an Intuit ID, click the Need To Create A New Intuit ID? link.

7. Check the I Have Read And Agreed To The Terms Of Service option, and click the Submit button.

ProAdvisor NOTE: *What you see in the next screen depends on how you've logged in and the age of your existing online subscription. If you've logged in with an existing online company ID, AND the online company is less than 60 days old you'll see a screen similar to the one in Figure 3-4. If you don't log in to an existing online company, or you do, but the existing company is older than 60 days, a new QuickBooks Online Plus subscription is created and your desktop data is automatically uploaded.*

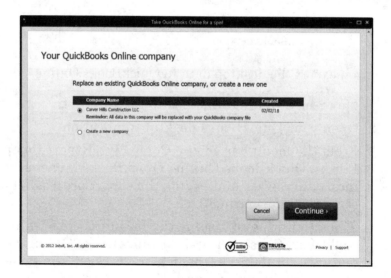

Figure 3-4: In this case you can choose to replace an existing online company or create a new subscription.

8. In this example we are going to import the data into our existing company, so select the existing company.

9. Click Continue to proceed.

10. If you're replacing an existing company QuickBooks insists that you confirm your decision. Since we're setting up our new online company with the data from our desktop company file, we definitely want to replace the existing online company. Click Yes to confirm, and the export process begins immediately.

From here you can continue to work, or close QuickBooks. As soon as the desktop data has been fully imported to QuickBooks Online, you'll receive an e-mail informing you of the fact, and providing a link to log in. The e-mail usually arrives within minutes.

Importing QuickBooks Lists from Excel

If you have a way to get your customer, vendor, and products/services lists into an Excel spreadsheet, or a CSV (Comma Separated Values) file, you can import them directly into your QuickBooks Online company. You'll still have to set up the other company information, including transactions, but importing your major lists will save a lot of time. For detailed instructions on formatting and importing lists from xls or csv files see Appendix B.

Managing Users

If you're subscribed to the Essentials plan or the Plus plan you can have multiple users accessing your online company file. If you're on the Simple Start plan only one user is permitted. However, even with Simple Start you can provide up to two accountants with access to your online file. This eliminates the need for sending files to your accountant to review and make necessary changes.

Accountant Users

In QuickBooks desktop applications you can have an External Accountant user, which permits your accountant to visit your premises and access your company file, making revisions when needed. You can also send your accountant an Accountant's Copy of the file which allows both your accountant and you to work on the same file at the same time.

Unfortunately, there are a number of restrictions on both you and the accountant that make the Accountant's Copy less than ideal.

Sending Your Accountant an Invite

All versions of QuickBooks Online, however, provide a much simpler solution. You can invite your accountant(s) (up to two) to log in to your online company as Accounting Firm users. Here's how:

1. Begin by selecting Tools Menu (gear icon) | Your Company | Manage Users to display the Manage Users window shown in Figure 3-5

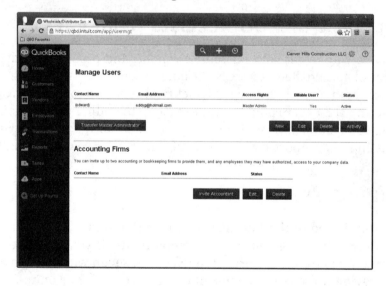

Figure 3-5: All QuickBooks Online versions allow accountant users.

2. Click the Invite Accountant button to open the Mini Interview window (see Figure 3-6). If you don't see the window, check your browser's setting and make sure pop-ups are allowed for QuickBooks Online.

3. Enter your accountant's e-mail address and name. The e-mail address is mandatory, but the name is optional.

4. Click Next to display an informational screen explaining what happens next.

Figure 3-6: Invite your accountant to access your QuickBooks Online
company.

5. Read the information and click Finish.

6. You're returned to the Manage Users screen where the accountant user has been added with a status of "Invited" (see Figure 3-7).

Figure 3-7: If your accountant doesn't respond, return here and click the
Resend button to try again.

Your job is done. Now you have to wait until your accountant (or other invitee) accepts the invitation.

Accountant Acceptance

As soon as you click that Finish button, an e-mail invitation is sent to the address you entered in the first screen of the Mini Interview. What your accountant (invitee) receives looks something like the message shown in Figure 3-8.

Figure 3-8: A single click is all it takes for your accountant to become a user in your QuickBooks Online file.

All your accountant has to do is click the Accept Invitation button to get started. Your accountant's default web browser is launched, and the QuickBooks Online Accountant page is opened. If your accountant already has an Intuit account, he or she can sign in an access your account. If not, your accountant will have to sign up for a free Intuit account.

Once your accountant has accepted your invitation and signed in to QuickBooks Online Accountant (or created a new account), the status automatically changes in your company's Manage Users screen (see Figure 3-9).

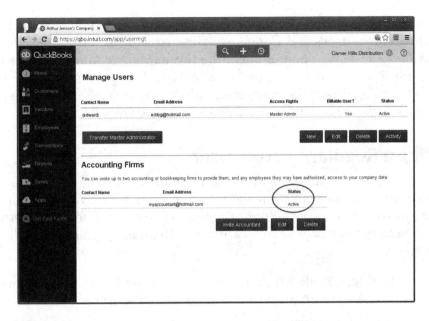

Figure 3-9: Once the invitation has been accepted, the status changes from Invited to Active.

Now your accountant can access your company data any time and make the necessary changes.

ProAdvisor CAUTION: *While it's true that you can send an invitation to anyone regardless of whether he or she is an accountant, be sure you want the invitee to have complete access to your company information. The accountant user has the same permissions/rights as the Master Administrator.*

Create Non-Accountant Users

Simple Start subscribers are limited to a single regular user, the Master Administrator. You can add accountant users, but not regular or administrator users. The only thing you can do with the Master Administrator is change the name and e-mail address, and view the Audit Log.

Essentials and Plus plan subscribers, on the other hand, can add both Regular/Custom users and Company Administrator users. Essentials subscribers can have a maximum of the three (Master Administrator plus two more). The Plus plan allows for up to five (Master Administrator plus four). Plus subscribers also have the ability to create two additional types of users – Reports Only users and Time-Tracking Only users.

Adding a Regular/Custom User

Unlike Company Administrator users, Regular/Custom users' permissions can be limited. Since your financial information is sensitive, there's no need to provide more access than is necessary to those who are assisting in maintaining your books. To create a new Regular/Custom user follow these steps:

1. Select Tools Menu (gear icon) | Your Company | Manage Users to display the Manage Users window.

2. Click the New button to display the Mini Interview window. Which Mini Interview window you see will depend on whether you have an Essentials or a Plus subscription (see Figure 3-10).

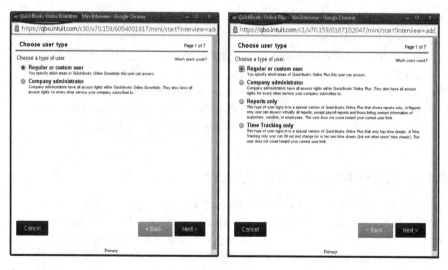

Figure 3-10: The Plus plan (on the right) offers more user types.

3. Choose Regular Or Custom User and click Next to display the Set User's Access Rights window shown in Figure 3-11.

Figure 3-11: How much access to sensitive financial information does this user need?

4. Set the new user's basic permissions from the following:

- All. Select this option if you want the user to have access to all of your financial information. The only limits you can place on this user are managing users, changing company information, or viewing and modifying subscription information.

- None. If you don't want this individual to have access to any of your financial information, but you'd like him or her to manage some of your third party add-ons, this is the option to choose. Plus users with this type of access rights can also fill out time sheets.

- Limited. This is the option that lets you fine-tune the permissions for each user. You can elect to give the user rights to access customer and sales data only, vendors and purchases data only, or both. This comes in handy when you have users whose jobs are restricted to one area or the other.

5. Click Next to view the Set User's Administrative Rights window shown in Figure 3-12. No matter which option you choose in the previous window, this window remains the same.

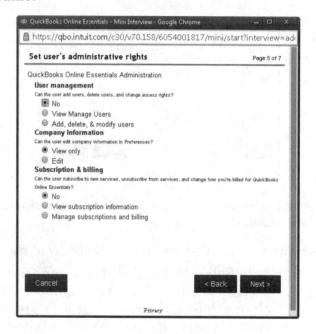

Figure 3-12: All users can have administrative rights regardless of their other permissions.

6. Set the administrative rights for this user from the following:

- User Management. You can give the user no access to the Manage Users window, the ability to simply view the Manage Users window, or the right to add, delete, and change existing users. Make the appropriate choice.

- Company Information. Selecting Edit here enables this user to open the Company Settings window and modify all company preferences.
- Subscription & Billing. You can allow this person to view or change your company's subscription information by making the appropriate choice here.

7. After you set the administrative rights, click Next to add the user name and e-mail address. The name is optional, but the e-mail address is a must.

8. Enter the necessary information and click Next to view the final, informational screen explaining what happens next, which is pretty much the same thing that happens with an accountant user. The invitee receives an e-mail invitation. When the individual clicks the [To accept this invitation] Click Here link she is taken the QuickBooks Online web page were she must sign in or create a new account. Once logged in, she has access (with whatever rights you assigned) to your company file.

Creating a Company Administrator User

Company Administrator users have access to all areas of QuickBooks Online as well as rights to other services you may be subscribed to. Therefore, be sure that the user really needs such extensive permissions.

Adding a Company Administrator user is much simpler.

1. Open the Manage Users window.
2. Click New to open the first screen of the Mini-Interview.
3. Select Company Administrator, and click Next.
4. Enter a user name and e-mail address, and click Next.
5. Now, click Finish to send the invitation.

Everything's the same on the invitee's end as it is when inviting a Regular or Custom user.

Transferring the Master Administrator Role

If you're running Essentials or Plus and have multiple users, you can choose to hand over the role of Master Administrator to another user. This might be necessary if one employee is leaving the company or moving to another area. However, the role of Master Administrator can only be transferred to an existing Company Administrator.

Here's how to make the transfer:

1. Select Tools Menu (gear icon) | Your Company | Manage Users to open the Manage Users window.

2. Invite the prospective Master Administrator as a Company Administrator (or change an existing Regular/Custom user to a Company Administrator)

3. When the invite has been accepted, or the role change has been made, return to the Manage Users window, and click the Transfer Master Administrator button to open the Transfer Master Administrator Role window (see Figure 3-13).

4. From the Transfer To drop-down list, choose the Company Administrator (if there are more than one) to whom you want to make the transfer.

5. Click Finish to send an invitation to the prospective new Master Administrator.

The role change is implemented when the new Master Administrator accepts the invitation. Until then, the roles remain as they were prior to the invitation. After the invitation has been accepted, the current Master Administrator becomes a Company Administrator the next time he or she logs in.

ProAdvisor Note: *Keep in mind that both have the same rights with one exception; the Company Administrator user can be deleted by the Master Administrator, but not the other way around.*

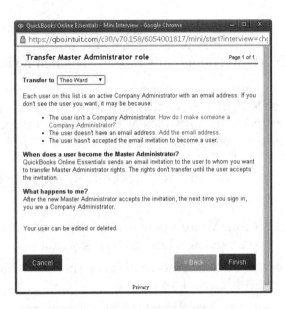

Figure 3-13: The Master Administrator role can only be transferred to an existing Company Administrator user.

ProAdvisor NOTE: *The invitee can decline the offer by clicking the "To decline these privileges," click here link. The user is taken to a special login page. As soon as the user logs in, the process is complete. A message appears informing the user that the transfer invitation has been declined, and that the current Master Administrator has been sent an e-mail informing her.*

Setting Up a Reports Only User

As mentioned earlier in this chapter, Reports Only users are available to Plus plan subscribers only. This type of user has access to one thing, and one thing only, in your company file – reports. The Reports Only user cannot access or modify any financial information or company features or settings.

The user can open all reports except payroll reports, or any customer, vendor, or employee reports that contain contact data. The user can modify, print, export, and e-mail any reports to which he has access.

ProAdvisor NOTE: *The number of Reports Only users you can have is unlimited, and does NOT count toward your five normal users allowed in the Plus subscription.*

The steps required to create Reports Only users is almost identical to those used to create Company Administrator users.

1. Select Tools Menu (gear icon) | Your Company | Manage Users to open the Manage Users window.
2. Click the New button to display the Mini-Interview dialog shown in Figure 3-14.

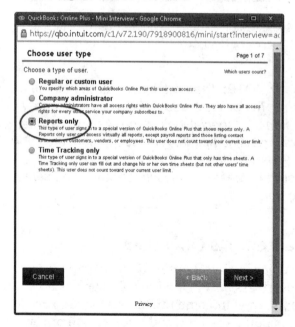

Figure 3-14: Plus subscribers can create Reports Only users.

3. Choose Reports Only and click Next.

4. Add an e-mail address (required) and a name (optional),
   and click Next.

5. Click Finish to send the individual an invitation.

The invitee gets an e-mail, accepts the invitation, logs into an Intuit
account, and views the company reports. When a Reports Only user logs
in, the only thing displayed is a Report List with links to those reports to
which the user has access (see Figure 3-15).

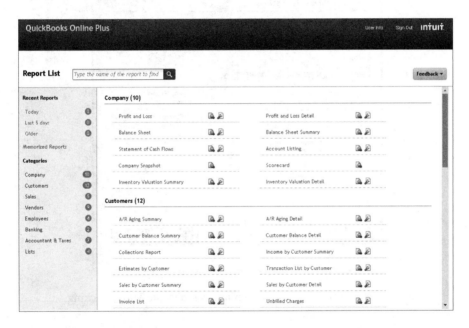

Figure 3-15: Reports Only users have access to company reports and
nothing more.

Adding Time-Tracking Users

This type of user, available only in Plus plans, is great for companies with
numerous employees. It allows each employee to log into the company
file, and fill out a time sheet for work performed. The process is similar
to that used to add Reports Only users, with one exception. The user
must be in the company file either as an employee or as a vendor (e.g.,
subcontractor). Here's how you create a Time-Tracking Only user.

1. Open the Manage Users window and click the New button to display the Mini Interview window (refer back to Figure 3-14).

2. Select Time-Tracking Only, and click Next to view the Set User's Time Sheet Options screen (see Figure 3-16).

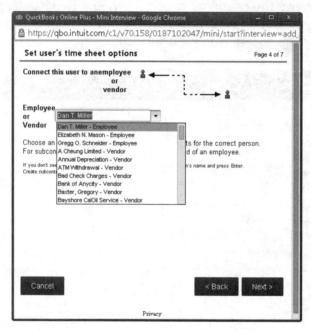

Figure 3-16: Only employees and vendors can become Time-Tracking Only users.

3. Select a name from the Employee Or Vendor drop-down list. If the name you want to add is not in the list, type in the name and click Next to display the Add Name dialog shown in Figure 3-17.

4. If you've added a new name, select Employee or Vendor from the Type drop-down list, and click Quick Add.

5. Enter the name and e-mail address and click Next.

6. Click Finish to complete the process.

Figure 3-17: You can add new employees or vendors on the fly.

As with Reports Only users, this user type does not count toward your total number of company users. When the Time-Tracking Only user logs in, the only features available to the user are the time sheets and a time report (see Figure 3-18).

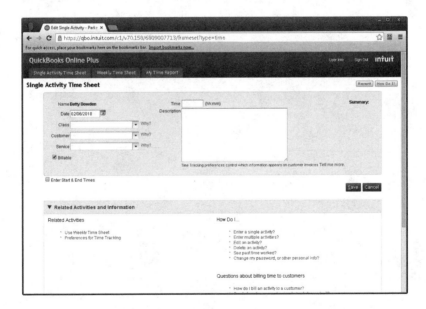

Figure 3-18: Employees and subcontractors can use weekly or single activity time sheets.

When the Billable option is checked, the time becomes available the next time you create an invoice for the customer.

CHAPTER 4:

Setting Up QuickBooks Online Lists

- Configuring an Effective Chart of Accounts

- Adding Products and Services

- Setting Up Payment Methods and Terms

- Creating Recurring Transactions

- Using Class Tracking

- Tracking by Location

- Working with the Attachments Center

Quick Books Online, like its desktop cousins, is essentially a database consisting of a large variety of lists. These lists contain names, contact information, transactions, accounts, preferences, and assorted other data. In this section we're going to cover those lists that are used in creating transactions, recording their data in the proper place, and assisting in creating useful reports.

Configuring an Effective Chart of Accounts

The Chart of Accounts is one of the most critical elements of any accounting system, including QuickBooks Online. It is the list of account names used to record the results of all of your transactions. All too often, the importance of the chart of accounts is not clearly understood. Unfortunately, this doesn't usually become apparent until a great deal of data has been input. That means lots of work (and additional fees) for your accountant.

There's an easy solution to this common problem. Follow a few simple rules when designing your chart of accounts and your record keeping will be accurate and efficient. Well, let me qualify that statement. Your record keeping will be as accurate as the information you enter into the system.

Use Naming Conventions

One of the biggest problems is that account names are frequently created on the fly, and with minimal forethought. The result is usually duplicate accounts, all of which contain postings. The solution? Create and implement a system for generating account names. Here are some guidelines.

- Names. Make sure the name clearly describes the purpose of the account. Surely, Telephone is preferable to Communication Expense.

- Use subaccounts. How many accounts do you need? You could have a single account called Auto Expenses, but will that really do the trick? Perhaps you need a parent account called Auto Expenses and subaccounts of Gas-Tolls, Insurance, Maintenance, and so on.

- Abbreviations. Limit abbreviations to a certain number of characters. If you choose four, Telephone becomes Tele, Electricity becomes Elec, and so on.

- Punctuation. It's a good idea to eliminate most punctuation.
- Word combinations. Set rules for combining words. Decide whether it will be Repairs-Maintenance, RepairsMaintenance, or Repairs&Maintenance.

The most important rule of all — once you've established your naming conventions, enforce them!

Use Account Numbers

Check with your accountant about this one, but most accountants recommend using account numbers. Without them, your chart of accounts is sorted alphabetically, which makes it difficult to get meaningful financial reports. If you want to use account numbers you must first turn them on. Here's how:

1. Select Tools Menu (gear icon) | Settings | Company Settings to open the Settings window.

2. Click Advanced in the left pane and Chart Of Accounts in the right to display the account numbers options shown in Figure 4-1.

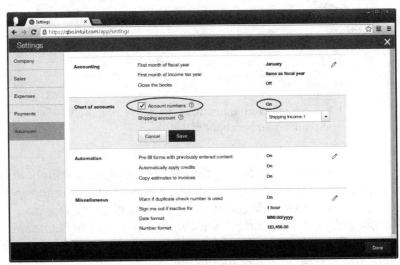

Figure 4-1: Using account numbers will help create clear reports.

ProAdvisor NOTE: *You may see additional options depending on the customize settings for your sales forms. Click the Account Numbers option to place a mark in the check box. This automatically turns on account numbering.*

---

3. Click the Save button to store the new settings.

4. Click Done to close the Settings window.

When you return to the Chart Of Accounts window you'll see that two items have been added (see Figure 4-2). The first is the Show Account Numbers option, which is enabled automatically. This option inserts the account number before the name in drop-down lists and reports. The second option is a button called Assign Account Numbers. When you click this button you can manually enter and/or modify account numbers for each account.

Figure 4-2: You can hide account numbers by deselecting the Show Account Numbers option.

ProAdvisor TIP: *QuickBooks Online only assigns numbers to standard accounts it creates. After you turn account numbering on, open the Chart of Accounts window and click the Assign Account Numbers button to view the Assign Account Numbers window. Scroll through the list, locate any accounts without numbers, and enter the numbers now.*

Modify the Default Numbering System

QuickBooks Online uses a standard four number system. Typically, a five digit account numbering scheme, using 1xxxx through 9xxxx, provides more flexibility. However the four number system should work for most small businesses. Here's the system used by QuickBooks Online.

- 1xxx for asset accounts
- 2xxx for liabilities accounts
- 3xxx for equity account
- 4xxx for income accounts
- 5xxx for expense accounts (Cost of Goods Sold)
- 6xxx for expense accounts (another specific type)
- 7xxx for expense accounts (yep, another type)
- 8xxx for other income accounts(rebates and other miscellaneous income)
- 9xxx for other expense accounts (for keeping track of penalties, late fees, and other miscellaneous expenses)

The benefit of a five number (or greater) system is that you have more room to add accounts as your business grows and expands. A four number system generally provides more than enough numbers for asset, liability, and equity accounts. It's when you get to the expense accounts that you might like to have a little more flexibility. For example, if you use the 6xxx numbers for operating expenses, you'll end up piling them on top of one another. Don't get me wrong, it will work, it will just be congested. With a five digit system you can use 60000, 61000, 62000, and so on for major categories, and then separate the smaller categories within those major categories.

ProAdvisor TIP: *When creating new accounts always be sure to leave at **least** ten numbers between to accommodate accounts you might want to add later. For example, if your operating bank account is 1000 (or 10000), and you want to add your payroll account make it 1010 (10100).*

If you want to modify your chart of accounts numbering system you'll have to do it manually, since importing a modified chart of accounts from Excel will only add duplicate accounts. To modify the chart of accounts numbering system follow these steps:

1. Choose Tools Menu (gear icon) | Settings | Chart of Accounts to open the Chart of Accounts window.

2. Click the Assign Account Numbers button to display the Assign Account Numbers screen (see Figure 4-3). If you don't see an Assign Account Numbers button that probably means you haven't yet enabled account numbers in the Company Settings preferences.

3. Click in the Number column for each account and change the number (add a zero if you're updating to a five digit system).

4. Scroll to the bottom of the list and click Save to save your changes. As the instructions at the top of the window suggest, it's a good idea to save regularly so your changes aren't lost if your QuickBooks Online session expires.

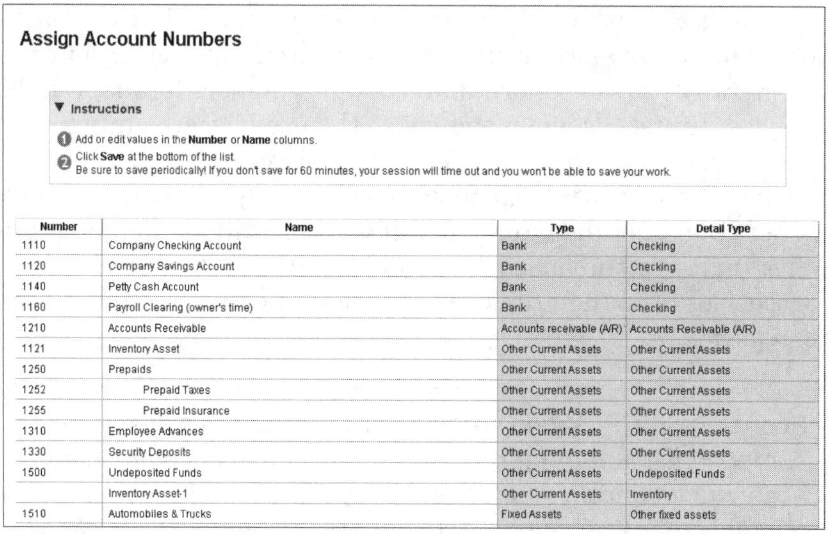

Assign Account Numbers

▼ Instructions

1. Add or edit values in the **Number** or **Name** columns.
2. Click **Save** at the bottom of the list.
   Be sure to save periodically! If you don't save for 60 minutes, your session will time out and you won't be able to save your work.

Number	Name	Type	Detail Type
1110	Company Checking Account	Bank	Checking
1120	Company Savings Account	Bank	Checking
1140	Petty Cash Account	Bank	Checking
1160	Payroll Clearing (owner's time)	Bank	Checking
1210	Accounts Receivable	Accounts receivable (A/R)	Accounts Receivable (A/R)
1121	Inventory Asset	Other Current Assets	Other Current Assets
1250	Prepaids	Other Current Assets	Other Current Assets
1252	Prepaid Taxes	Other Current Assets	Other Current Assets
1255	Prepaid Insurance	Other Current Assets	Other Current Assets
1310	Employee Advances	Other Current Assets	Other Current Assets
1330	Security Deposits	Other Current Assets	Other Current Assets
1500	Undeposited Funds	Other Current Assets	Undeposited Funds
	Inventory Asset-1	Other Current Assets	Inventory
1510	Automobiles & Trucks	Fixed Assets	Other fixed assets

Figure 4-3: Modifying accounts numbers is relatively easy in the Assign Account Numbers window.

> **ProAdvisor TIP:** *The Assign Account Numbers window also comes in handy for making name changes to multiple accounts. Normally, you'd have to open each account in the Chart of Accounts window by selecting the account, and clicking the Edit button. Then, you'd have to make the name change, save the change, and start over. By using the Assign Account Numbers screen you can make your changes right from this window, and save them all at the same time.*

Create and Edit Accounts

When you initially set up your company, QuickBooks Online creates a chart of accounts based on the type of industry your select in the subscription interview. While this chart of accounts generally contains the primary accounts you'll need, it probably won't contain every account. This means that you'll have to add some new accounts. Also, some of the accounts created may be okay, but would be better suited with a different name or number. This entails editing an existing account. Finally, there may be some accounts that you just don't need or want. Those you'll simply delete.

> **ProAdvisor TIP:** *Do not use the Opening Balance or Balance field available when creating certain account types (asset, bank, liability, and others). The amounts are posted to the Opening Bal Equity account, which is a QuickBooks invention. Eventually, your accountant will have to empty that account (more work, more money). It's better to leave the field blank, and enter opening balances by entering historical transactions or journal entries.*

Adding New Accounts

When you find that you are missing an account that you need, all you have to do is create it. Here's what you do:

> 1. Select Tools Menu (gear icon) | Settings | Chart Of
>   Accounts to open the Chart of Accounts window.

2. Click the New button to display the Account dialog box shown in Figure 4-4.

Figure 4-4: Be sure to select the correct type of account to create.

3. From the Category Type drop down list choose the appropriate account type.

4. Move to the Detail Type list and select a detail type.

5. Enter a clear, descriptive name, keeping in mind the naming convention rules you've implemented.

6. Add the account number using the QuickBooks Online system (four digits) unless you've modified it to suit your needs.

7. A description is not necessary, but can be very helpful, especially if you have multiple users.

8. If this is going to be a subaccount, check the Is Sub-Account check box.

9. Click Save to close the dialog and return to the Chart of Accounts window.

Subaccounts are extremely useful in organizing your chart of accounts. For example, rather than have separate Electricity, Telephone, LP Gas, and Water accounts, you would probably want to have a Utilities parent account with subaccounts for Elec, Tele, LPga, and Wate (using an abbreviation system of four letters). That way you can run one report to see your total utilities expenditures broken down by each different utility. Without the subaccounts you'd have to run all four reports, and total them up.

Editing and Deleting Existing Accounts

Whether it's an original QuickBooks Online account or one that you created earlier, there eventually comes a time when you need to change the information on the account. It may be a name change, a number change, or a parent/subaccount change. Whatever the reason, you can change everything about an account.

ProAdvisor CAUTION: *QuickBooks Online, unlike the desktop version, will allow you to change the Category Type of any existing account that does not have subaccounts or is not a subaccount itself. You receive a warning, but QuickBooks Online lets you proceed if you choose to do so. This is extremely dangerous. Be sure to check with your accountant before making any changes to an existing account's Category Type.*

To edit an existing account, begin by opening the Chart of Accounts window. Next, select (highlight) the account you want to modify. Now, click the Edit button to open the Edit dialog which is almost identical to the new account dialog (refer back to Figure 4-4). Make the necessary changes, and click the Save button.

ProAdvisor NOTE: *To change the Category Type of subaccounts, you must first change the Category Type of the parent account. The same goes for parent accounts with subaccounts. That means that to change the Category Type, you'll have to begin by removing all subaccounts by turning them into parent accounts. Now you can change the original parent account Category Type (since it no longer has subs). Next, you'll have to change the Category Type for all of the subs-turned-parents, to match the original parent item. Finally, convert all of the subs-turned-parents back to subaccounts.*

Deleting accounts in QuickBooks Online is easy. As a matter of fact, it may be too easy. Simply highlight the account to delete and click the Delete button. Usually, a warning is displayed letting you know the status of the account you want to delete. You may or may not be able to delete it. As always, check with your accountant before deleting any account.

Merging Accounts

If you failed to follow my earlier suggestion to implement and enforce a logical set of account naming rules, there is an "after the fact" feature that will help you eliminate those multiple accounts that have the same purpose that have appeared. You can merge accounts (and their balances) with different names into a single account.

For example, if you have both a Gas-Oil account and a Fuel account under Auto Expenses, you can meld them into one. However, there are two primary rules you must observe. First, both must at the same level and of the same parent account if they are subaccounts. Second, they must be of the same Category Type and Detail Type. If the types do not match QuickBooks Online will inform you of the fact (see Figure 4-5).

Figure 4-5: Pay heed to the QuickBooks Online warnings.

ProAdvisor CAUTION: *QuickBooks Online only warns you when the types are inconsistent. If you attempt to merge two subaccounts from different parent accounts or a parent account and a subaccount, you get no warning message because no merge is taking place. What IS taking place is an edit of the account to which you are making the changes. This can produce some very unexpected and unpleasant results, so be sure to follow the two primary rules.*

Merging accounts is simple if you follow these steps:

1. Open the Chart of Accounts window (Tools Menu (gear icon) | Settings | Chart Of Accounts).

2. Make sure the account types and levels match (see the intro paragraph to this section).

3. Open either of the accounts you want to merge. While it makes a difference in QuickBooks desktop versions, it does not matter in QuickBooks Online which account you open and edit.

4. If the account types and level are the same, change the opened account name to match the account name you want to merge it with (open Fuel account and change the name to Gas – or vice versa).

5. Click Save, and QuickBooks Online will ask you to confirm (see Figure 4-6).

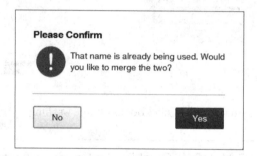

Figure 4-6: This is your last chance to change your mind.

6. Click Yes and the merge is completed.

Adding Products and Services

All three versions of QuickBooks Online allow you to enter a listing of your products and services. However, the Plus plan is the only one that lets you enter purchase information in the Product Or Service Information record. This, combined with the fact that purchase orders, bills, and inventory reports are not available in Simple Start or Essentials (bills, but without Item Details) , means that only in QuickBooks Online Plus can you actually track your inventory. In Simple Start and Essentials you can track what you sell, but that's it.

Another thing you should be aware of is that all three versions of QuickBooks Online consider products and services a single item type, differentiating them by assigning them to different income accounts. In most other accounting systems, including QuickBooks desktop applications, you can create a variety of item types such Inventory Part, Non-Inventory Part, Service, and so on). This enables you to produce reports that break down your sales in a way that you can better analyze the source of your income.

Therefore, I recommend that you begin adding products/services by creating at least two parent items and making the bulk of your products/services subitems of the parent items. For example, if you sell products and services, create a parent item called Products, and another called Services. Then create subproducts of Products called Widget, Gadget, Whatchamacallit, etc. Then create subservices of Services called Installation, Repairs, Maintenance, and so on. You can see where this is going, so create a system that serves your needs with as many parent categories as necessary.

ProAdvisor NOTE: *According to the QuickBooks Online support site, there is no limit to the number of products and services items you can have. I imported over 500 subproducts, and more than 500 subservices, and had no problems whatsoever, so I can personally vouch for that number.*

To add products/services items in *any* of the QuickBooks Online versions, follow these instructions (I'll cover the extra fields in Plus after this set of steps):

1. Select Tools Menu (gear icon) | Lists | Products And Services to open the Products and Services window.

2. Click the New button to open the (new) Product Or Service Information dialog. What you see depends on your version of QuickBooks Online (see Figure 4-7).

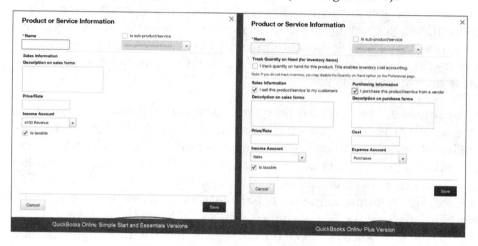

Figure 4-7: QuickBooks Online Plus (on the right) offers additional options.

3. Enter a unique and descriptive name for the product/service.

4. Enter a description that will enable both employees and customers to recognize the product easily in the Description On Sales Forms text box.

5. Enter the sales price of the item in the Price/Rate box. Do not include a dollar sign. QuickBooks Online knows that this is a currency field.

6. Assign an income account to the item by making a selection from the Income Account drop-down list.

7. If you've enabled sales tax in your company file, you can make this item taxable or non-taxable by checking or unchecking the Is Taxable option.

8. Click Save to add the new item.

For those Plus users who are creating new items, you have a few more options than the rest.

- Track Quantity On Hand (For Inventory Items). This is an option that is also found in the Company Settings. It tells QuickBooks Online that you want to keep track of your inventory by maintaining a record of those products that you have in stock. Check it if you want to track inventory.

- I sell This Product/Service To My Customers. This is a handy option for tracking non-inventory items such as supplies and job materials. Since they're not going to appear on sales receipts or invoices for customers, they don't need prices or descriptions. You may include them on a sales receipt or invoice, but probably as a single line-item called "Materials" or something similar, not as individual line-items. Remove the check mark from the option, and the sales description, price, and income account fields disappear. One caveat. If you deselect the I Purchase This Product/Service From A Vendor, the Sales Information option is automatically (re)enabled.

- Purchasing Information. These options are essential for inventory tracking. Click the I Purchase This Product/Service From A Vendor to enable them. Use the fields to record the purchase data for inventory items, and for services that you subcontract from other vendors/contractors.

See Appendix B for detailed instructions on importing items.

Setting Up Payment Methods and Terms

Both the Payment Methods list and the Terms list are minor lists when it comes to the number of items included. However, both lists are critical for maintaining accurate financial records.

Payment Methods

Payment Methods are pretty straightforward. Which forms of payment do you accept from customers? These days there are a multitude of payment methods and most businesses accept some assortment of the available payment methods. When QuickBooks Online initially sets up your company file based on your subscription interview information, it adds the most common payment methods to your Payment Methods list.

To configure the Payment Methods list follow these steps:

1. Select Tools Menu (gear icon) | Lists | All Lists to open the Lists window.

2. Click Payment Methods to display the Payment Methods window shown in Figure 4-8.

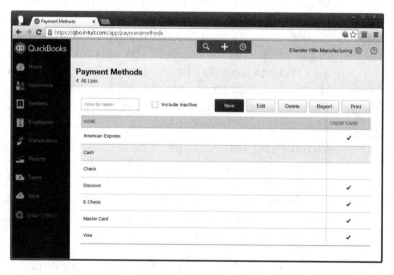

Figure 4-8: The Payment Methods list is pre-populated with the most common payment methods.

3. Chances are, you'll want to modify the original list. To delete a payment method that you do not accept, select the method in the list and click the Delete button.

4. QuickBooks Online asks if you're sure. If so, click Yes, otherwise click No.

5. To edit an existing payment method highlight the method and click the Edit button. In reality the only changes you can make are to the name and the status as a credit card.

6. To add a new method, click the New button to display the New Payment Method dialog shown in Figure 4-9.

Figure 4-9: For non-credit card methods, all you need is a name.

7. Enter the name and check the This Is A Credit Card option, if the new method is a credit card.

8. Click Save to create the new method.

Whenever you create a transaction that requires a payment (Expense, Sales Receipt, Receive Payment, etc), the methods here appear on the Payment Method drop-down list in the transaction (see Figure 4-10).

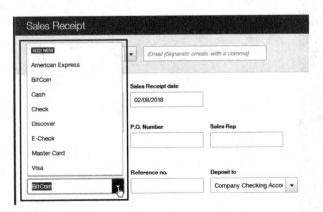

Figure 4-10: Transaction window Payment Method drop-down lists contain all of the methods on your Payment Methods list.

Work with the Terms List

Terms are the payment terms you offer your customers and the payment terms your vendors offer you. Terms indicate the amount of time to pay a bill once it's received. Additionally, terms can offer discounts for early payment. Both customer and vendor terms come from the same Terms list in QuickBooks Online. If you're running Simple Start, only your customers and invoices will have Terms fields. However, if you're running Essentials or Plus you'll see that your vendors and bills will also have Terms fields.

Creating New Terms

By default, the Terms list window in QuickBooks Online contains the most commonly used terms. This may be all you need. However, if you want to create your own custom terms, here's how you do it:

1. Select Tools Menu (gear icon) | Lists | All Lists to open the Lists window.
2. Click Terms to display the Terms list window shown in Figure 4-11.

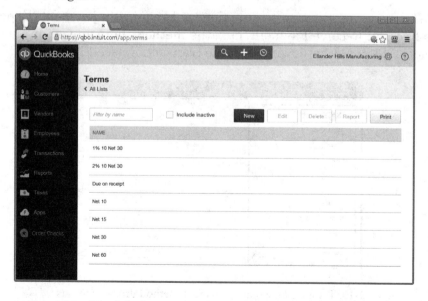

Figure 4-11: The default terms may be all you need.

3. Click the New button to open the New Term dialog box (see Figure 4-12).

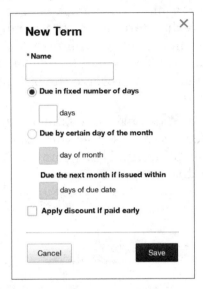

Figure 4-12: You can create as many custom terms as needed.

4. Enter a descriptive name in the Name field.

5. Choose either standard or date driven terms.

- Due In Fixed Number Of Days. This is a standard terms type that requires payment be made within a certain number of days. For example, Net 30 means that payment is due within 30 days from the invoice date. Enter the number of days from the invoice date that payment is due in the Days field.

- Due By Certain Day Of The Month. This terms type is commonly referred to as date driven. The payment is required by a certain date of the month regardless of the invoice date (well, almost). Enter the day (date) of the month in the Day Of Month field. Of course, it would hardly be realistic to expect to receive a payment on the 15th if the invoice/bill were sent out on the 10th.

Therefore, the Due The Next Month If Issued Within option should be used to make sure there's a reasonable time between the invoice date and the due date. Enter the number days after the issuance date that force the due date into the next month. This should leave sufficient time for the customer to receive the bill, pay it, and get it to you.

6. If you want to incentivize customers to pay bills in advance (or if vendors offer you such terms) you can choose the option Apply Discount If Paid Early. As soon as you do, additional options appear as seen in Figure 4-13.

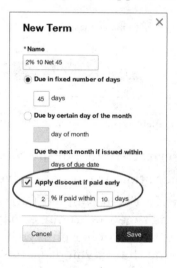

Figure 4-13: Set the discount percentage and number of days that it remains available.

7. Enter the percentage of the discount and the number of days within which the discount is in effect from the invoice date. For example, referring back to Figure 4-13, you see that we're creating 2% 10 Net 45 terms. Therefore the customer has 45 days from the invoice date to make the payment. However, if the payment is received within 10 days of the invoice date, the customer is entitled to a 2% discount.

8. Click Save to create the new terms and return to the Terms list window.

Modifying and Deleting Terms

When you need to make changes to existing terms all you have to do is return to the Terms list window and do what needs to be done.

To delete existing terms simply highlight the terms you want to eliminate and click the Delete button. QuickBooks Online asks for confirmation. When you click Yes, the terms are history unless they are the default terms for any customer or vendor.

ProAdvisor TIP: *Terms that are used as default terms for any customer (appear in the Terms field of the customer record) cannot be deleted. To delete these terms you must first remove them from all customer records.*

To edit existing terms, simply highlight the terms you want to modify, and click the Edit button.

Creating Recurring Transactions (Essentials & Plus only)

Recurring transactions, which are similar to memorized transactions in QuickBooks desktop applications, are only available in Essentials and Plus plans. They're great for things like monthly rental payments, regular invoices for client retainers, and so on. You can create Recurring transactions in one of two ways.

Use the Recurring Transactions List

The Recurring Transactions list is where all of your recurring transactions are stored. This provides quick access to recurring transactions so you can easily edit and delete them as necessary. However, it also enables you to create new recurring transactions as well.

To create a new recurring transaction, use the following steps:

1. Choose Tools Menu (gear icon) | Lists | Recurring Transactions to display the Recurring Transactions list shown in Figure 4-14.

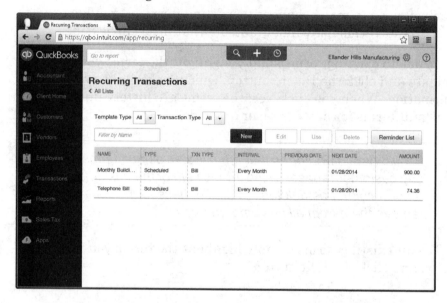

Figure 4-14: Use the Recurring Transactions list for easy access to all of your recurring transactions.

2. Click the New button to open the Select Transaction Type dialog (see Figure 4-15).

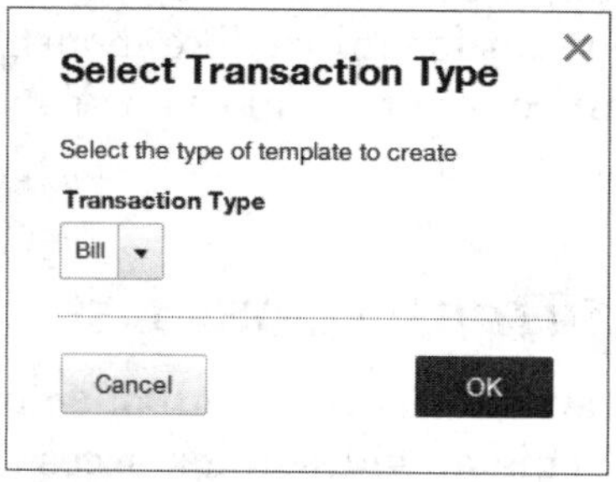

Figure 4-15: The first thing you have to decide is the type of recurring transaction to create.

3. From the Transaction Type drop-down list, choose the type of new recurring transaction you want to create. You have a wide range of transactions to choose from.

4. Click OK to open a new transaction of type selected from the drop-down list.

5. All recurring transaction templates have certain fields in common, as seen in Figure 4-16. Some transactions forms may have additional fields as well.

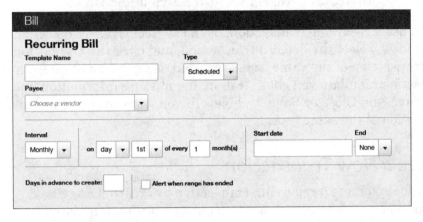

Figure 4-16: Many fields are common to all recurring transactions of the Scheduled and Reminder types.

6. While most of the fields are self-explanatory, one requires a little more explanation – Type. The Type drop-down list offers three choices:

   • Scheduled. Use this type to schedule the transaction for automatic creation. The fields seen in Figure 4-16 always appear when you select this type.

   • Reminder. If you don't want the transaction automatically created, but want a reminder to alert you when it's time to create the transaction, choose this type. The Days In Advance To Create option is replaced by a Remind Me option.

- Unscheduled. If you just want to create a template that you can use whenever the mood strikes you, select Unscheduled. All of the scheduling options disappear, and you are left with a plain transaction template.

7. Completely fill out the transaction form and click the Save Template button at the bottom. No transaction is created, simply a recurring transaction template that will create an actual transaction at the scheduled time.

To use a recurring transaction, open the Recurring Transactions list window, select the desired transaction, and click the Use button. A new transaction of the same type is created using information from the transaction template you chose. Fill in any missing information and click Save And Close or Save And New (if you want to create another transaction of the same type.

Create a New Transaction

You can also create a recurring transaction by creating a regular transaction, and saving it as a recurring transaction template.

1. Go to the Top Navigation Bar and click the Plus icon to view a listing of transaction types you can create. If you only see a handful, click the Show More link to view all available transaction types.

2. Click the transaction type you want to create to open the related transaction form.

3. Completely fill out the form and click the Make Recurring button at the bottom of the window. The Type drop-down list appears and the appropriate recurring transaction fields appear (or disappear) depending on your selection from the Type drop-down list . See the explanation of the different types in the previous section.

4. Click Save Template to create a template from the transaction.

No transaction is created, only the transaction template. If you want to create a transaction at this time, open the Recurring Transactions list window and use the template you just created.

Working with the Reminder List (Plus & Essentials only)

When Essentials and Plus users schedule a recurring transaction either to be created or to tap them on the shoulder with a reminder, that information is recorded in the Recurring Transactions list. When the time is near for the transaction to be created or the reminder to be sounded, it appears on the Reminder List. To access the Reminder List you must first open the Recurring Transactions list. Once there, click the Reminder List button to display the Reminder List window seen in Figure 4-17.

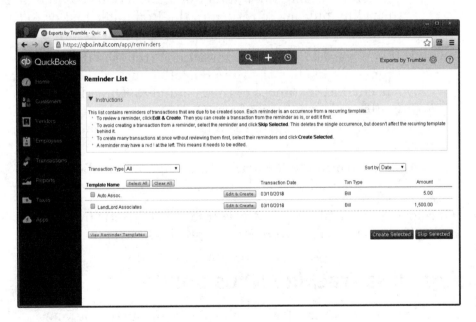

Figure 4-17: Check for recurring transaction reminders.

Using the Reminder List is relatively easy.

1. From the Transaction Type drop-down list, choose the transaction type to view. The selection is wide and includes bills, vendor credits, and everything in between. Of course the list will vary depending on your version of QuickBooks Online.

2. If a large number of reminders appears, use the Sort By drop-down list to put the list in order.

3. To work on a single transaction click the Edit & Create button on the transaction line. It opens the transaction so you can make any necessary changes and save (create) it.

4. To create multiple transactions in one fell swoop, check each transaction you want included, and click the Create Selected button. QuickBooks Online creates the transactions and displays a second Reminder List screen indicating the number of transactions created and providing buttons to return to the Reminder List or to the Home Page.

5. If you want to remove transactions from the list, check them off and click the Skip Selected button. This removes the current instances of the reminders. QuickBooks Online asks you to confirm. Click Yes to skip them. Don't worry, they'll reappear the next time the transactions are due.

6. To return to the Recurring Transaction list click the View Reminder Templates button.

Of course, you can also create the transactions directly from the Recurring Transactions list covered in the previous section.

Using Class Tracking (Plus only)

Class tracking is a great tool for breaking down and analyzing your business by different customer types, or services offered. For example, if you have retail and wholesale customers you might use two classes – Retail and Wholesale – to easily break down sales and expenses by each of these business divisions. Another example would be a contractor who does new construction, renovations, and historic restorations. Being able to separate the financial data for the different operations enables you to see what each operation is contributing to the business, and how it can be improved.

Before going any further it's important to know that only Plus subscribers have access to class tracking tools in QuickBooks Online.

Set Class Tracking Options

Unless Class Tracking is turned on in the QuickBooks Online Company Settings, you'll never see a Class field in any of the transaction forms. Therefore, it's important to ensure that the Class Tracking options are configured from the start.

1. Choose Tools Menu (gear icon) | Settings | Company Settings to open the Settings window.
2. Click Company | Categories to display the available Class Tracking options as shown in Figure 4-18.

Figure 4-18: You can customize the way Class Tracking works by setting these options.

3. Set the options as needed.

- Track Classes. This is a must if you want to use class tracking. Check the box to enable the feature.

- Warn Me When A Transaction Isn't Assigned A Class. To ensure that classes are always used, check this option. If a user tries to create a transaction without entering a class, QuickBooks Online displays the warning shown in Figure 4-19. Be advised that it won't stop the user from saving the transaction without a class assignment. This is just a reminder.

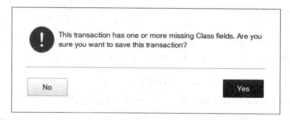

Figure 4-19: Only the consistent use of classes will provide accurate information for business analyses.

- One To Entire Transaction. This is the default option, which means that there is only one Class field per transaction. Regardless of the number of items on the transaction, one class will be assigned to everything.

- One To Each Row In Transaction. If you want to track individual line-items on a transaction, choose this option. It adds a Class field for every line-item on the transaction. This is very useful if you invoice for multiple types of work on a single invoice. For example, the contractor who may perform new construction, renovation, and restoration work for the same client, may want to send a single invoice for all three types of work. In that case, this option is an absolute must.

4. After you've set the Class Tracking options click the Save button to apply the changes.

5. To close the Settings window, click the Done button or the X in the upper right corner.

Create and Use Classes

The Classes list window, which displays your existing classes, is also where you can create new classes. Creating classes is a simple process, but one which should be thought out beforehand. Classes work best when used for a single purpose. If you want additional classifications use subclasses. For example, if you have different divisions in your company and each division services both retail and wholesale clients, you would set up your divisions as parent classes, each with a Retail and a Wholesale subclass.

To create a new class, follow these instructions:

1. Select Tools Menu (gear icon) | Lists | All Lists to display the Lists window.

2. Click the Classes link to open the Classes list window Shown in Figure 4-20.

Figure 4-20: Use the Classes list window to create, edit, and delete classes.

3. Click the New button to open the Class dialog seen in Figure 4-21.

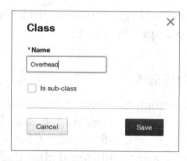

Figure 4-21: Make sure the class name is unique and descriptive.

4. Enter a descriptive name for the new class.

5. If it is a subclass of an existing class, click the Is Sub-Class option.

6. From the Enter Parent Class drop-down list that appears, select the parent class to which this should be linked (see Figure 4-22).

Figure 4-22: To create a subclass you must choose the parent class first.

7. Click Save to create the new class or subclass.

If you create a subclass it appears on the Classes list below the parent class and indented to the right (see Figure 4-23).

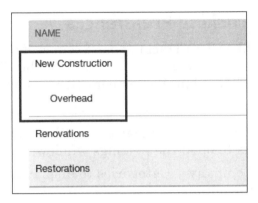

Figure 4-23: Subclasses are easy to recognize.

Editing and deleting classes is a simple matter of highlighting the class to be modified, and clicking the appropriate button (Edit or Delete).

In addition to the classes and subclasses you need for tracking the different segments of your business, you should also add two additional classes.

- Other. This provides a catchall for any transactions for which there is any confusion or question about the class assignment. You can run a report on this class at a later time and individually reclassify each transaction using the correct class.
- Overhead (or Administration). This is where you can post expenses that don't fit into other classes, but add to the cost of providing the products or services.

Tracking by Location (Plus only)

Another advantage of the Plus subscription is the ability to use Location Tracking. Location Tracking is great for businesses that have different storefronts, warehouses, or offices. You can keep track of sales and expenses for each different physical location.

Set Location Tracking Preferences

Location Tracking like Class Tracking has a couple of options that you'll want to set before starting to use the feature. Like the Class Tracking options, they're also located in the Company Settings window. Configuring them is easy.

1. Choose Tools Menu (gear icon) | Settings | Company Settings to open the Settings window.

2. Click Company | Categories to display the Location Tracking options.

3. Check the Track Locations option to enable Location Tracking and to display the other Location Tracking options as seen in Figure 4-24. If you don't see a Location drop-down list in your transaction forms, it means you haven't yet enabled Location Tracking.

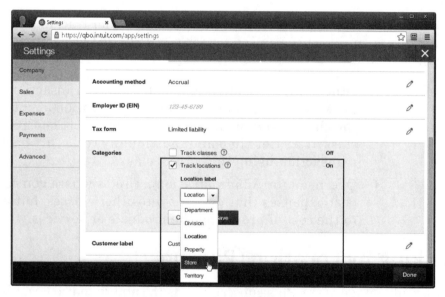

Figure 4-24: You can change the field name used in transactions forms.

4. From the Location Label drop-down list choose the terminology to use and click Save.

5. Click Done to close the Settings window.

When you create a new transaction you'll see that a Location drop-down list has been added (see Figure 4-25). Of course, if you changed the terminology in the Location Tracking options, the new terminology will be used on all of the forms. In Figure 4-25 the field is called Location because we didn't change it. However, had we chosen Store instead, the label on the field would be Store rather than Location.

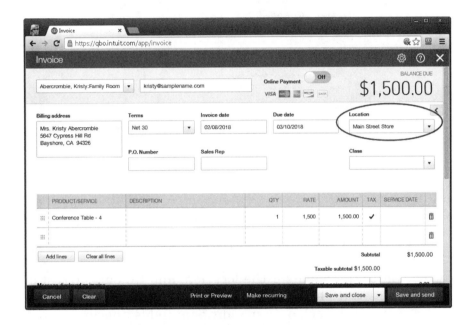

Figure 4-25: You won't see a Locations field unless you've enabled Location Tracking in the Settings window.

ProAdvisor TIP: *If you decide to close down one of your locations and incorporate its operations into another location you can merge the two locations in QuickBooks Online. Edit the location you want to eliminate, and change its name to match the location you want to keep. Click Save, and when QuickBooks Online asks you to confirm, click Yes.*

Create New Locations

To create new locations follow these steps:

1. Select Tools Menu (gear icon) | Lists | All Lists to open the Lists window.
2. Click Locations to open the Locations list window.
3. Click the New button to display the Location Information dialog shown in Figure 4-26.

Figure 4-26: You can add a lot of detail for each location.

4. Enter the name for the location, and fill out the rest of the form. The options on the form are self-explanatory. As you check each option additional fields appear for you to enter the needed information.
5. Click Save to create the location.

Editing and deleting locations are the same as in most other lists. Open the Location list, highlight the location, and click the Edit or Delete button.

Working in the Attachments Center (Plus only)

While you can add attachments to individual transactions in all of the QuickBooks Online versions, only Plus gives you the added benefit of an Attachments center where all your attachments are stored (see Figure

4-27).Attachments are great when you want easy access to documents and images related to transactions. For example, I usually attach a copy of the detailed receipt to each check I write. If there's ever a question about the check all I have to do is find the check and open the attached receipt.

Figure 4-27: The Attachments center provides easy access to all of your attachments.

Before we jump into the mechanics of the Attachment center let's see how the window can be customized. Take a look at Figure 4-27 and you'll see two gray icons above the Action column. Click the Printer icon to display the Print dialog of your browser. From there you can create a printout of the Attachments center. The other icon, the gear icon, when clicked opens a submenu of customizing options. Make selections on this menu to add or remove columns, and to change the number of rows displayed per page.

You can also see that basic information about each attachment is supplied in the list. The Linked Transactions column even contains links to transactions to which the files are currently attached. You can open the transaction by clicking the link.

Upload Attachments

Of course, the first step to using attachments in QuickBooks Online is getting them into QuickBooks Online. This is done by using one of two methods. You can locate the file on your hard drive and drag it into the Attachments box at the top of the Attachments center window. As soon as you drop it, it begins uploading.

The other method is to click the Attachments icon (paperclip), locate and select the file on your hard disk, and click Open. Either way, once uploaded, the files remain in your Attachments center until you remove them.

Use Attachments

If you refer back to Figure 4-27 you can see that there are two drop-down list buttons in the Attachments center window. You use these buttons to perform actions with or to the attachments on the list.

Batch Actions

The Batch Actions button is a real time saver if you want to perform actions on multiple attachments in one fell swoop. Here's what you do:

1. Begin by selecting all of the attachments on which you want to perform the batch action. You can select them individually by placing a check in the box to the left of each attachment, or you can click the checkbox at the very top of the list to check all of the attachments on the page.

2. Now, click the Batch Actions button to display a drop-down menu of your choices as seen in Figure 4-28.

3. Select the operation you want to apply to the selected attachments.

    • Export. Use this command to export the selected attachments to a zip file that you can save to your hard drive. You can only select attachments that are not linked to transactions. If you select any attachments linked to transactions, the resulting zip file will not open due to illegal folder names.

- Create Invoice. When you select this option, a blank Invoice form is opened with all of the selected files attached. Fill out the invoice as you would normally. You can select attachments that are linked to other transactions.

- Create Expense. Same thing here. The only difference is a blank Expense form opens.

Figure 4-28: Batch actions can speed up your work a lot.

Actions

Actions, unlike Batch Actions, are applied to a single attachment. To use an action there's no need to select the attachment first. Simply click the drop-down button (Download) in the Action column next to the attachment you want to work on. Then from the menu that appears, select an action.

- Download. What happens when you select this action depends on the file type you've chosen. For example, a PDF file opens in a separate window, and gives you the option to save it. An image file, on the other hand, simply opens a Save As dialog that offers you the opportunity to save the file to your hard drive. Since no zip files are involved, you can download attachments that are linked to transactions.

- Edit. This command opens the Edit Attachment dialog where you can change the file name and add notes.

- Delete. Not much more to say except it will remove the attachment from all transactions to which it is linked. QuickBooks Online requires confirmation.

- Create Invoice. This opens a blank Invoice form with the file attached. Fill it out and save it as you would any other invoice.

- Create Expense. Opens a blank Expense form with the attachment linked.

CHAPTER 5:

Configuring Customer-Related Preferences

- Setting Customer Preferences

- Configuring Sales Section Preferences

- Setting Sales Tax Options

- Configuring Advanced Customer Settings

Before delving into the actual customer-related preferences I would like to mention that the QuickBooks Online preferences were just significantly overhauled (of course, after I had written this chapter on the old preferences), and it appears that there are now some options missing. It's not clear whether this is a temporary situation to be remedied in a later update, or a permanent loss of some options. If you're reading this and there are more (or different) options than presented here, it means that they were added after the book was sent to the printer.

One more thing. Since no one seems to know (or cares to divulge) exactly how the QuickBooks Online update process works, you may or may not be seeing the latest preferences updates. As of this writing I have an old QuickBooks Online Plus file that is still showing the old Preferences window rather than the new Settings window used in this chapter. Any users with the old Preferences will find helpful information here explaining the options, but you'll have to search through the chapter to locate it.

Configuring Company Preferences for Customers

QuickBooks Online doesn't offer much in the way of customer-specific preferences, regardless of which version you're running. As a matter of fact, there is only one customer preference, and it's the same in all versions. It's called Customer Label and you'll find it in the Company section of the Settings window.

The very first thing to decide is what you're going to call your customers. If you're running a retail shop, "customers" is probably accurate. If you're a professional, "clients" might be a better description. A non-profit doesn't usually have customers or clients, but rather "donors." QuickBooks Online lets you decide what you want your customers to be called. Here's how you implement that decision:

1. Choose Tools Menu (gear icon) | Settings | Company Settings to display the Settings window.

2. Click Company | Customer Label to view the customer-related preference shown in Figure 5-1.

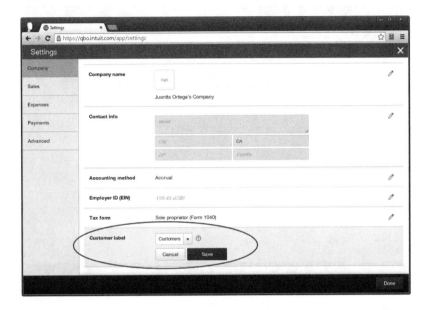

Figure 5-1: Change the customer terminology to suit your organization.

3. From the Customer Label drop-down list choose the term that best describes your customers.

4. Click Save to store the change.

Setting the Sales Section Preferences

While there are only a couple of preferences that apply directly to the customers themselves, there are a number that affect customer transaction forms. It's always a good idea to set those that are relevant to your business before you start generating customer transactions. Begin by selecting Tools Menu (gear icon) | Settings | Company Settings to display the Settings screen (see Figure 5-2).

Figure 5-2: QuickBooks Online preferences are divided into five sections.

What you see depends on the version of QuickBooks Online you're subscribed to. Essentials and Plus users will find additional options for those features found in their particular plans. If you refer back to Figure 5-2 you'll immediately see that the Preferences screen has an additional set of options for class tracking and location tracking - features only found in QuickBooks Online Plus.

Customize Forms

This option, which allows you to make modifications to invoice, estimate, and sales receipt forms, is covered in depth in the section entitled "Customizing Customer Transaction Forms" located in Chapter 6.

Sales Form Content

While the Customize Forms section lets you modify the look of the various transactional forms, the Sales Form Content allows you to modify the fields that appear on the forms, and more.

Terms

If you offer most of your customers the same terms, you can use this option to set the default, so that you don't have to enter it into each new customer record you create. Open the Settings window and choose Sales | Sales Form Content to access the option. From the Default Invoice Terms drop-down list choose the appropriate terms. For details on creating and working with terms see the section in Chapter 4 entitled "Work with the Terms List."

ProAdvisor TIP: *If you don't want any terms to appear in a new invoice form, delete the terms that appear in the Default Invoice Terms field and click Save.*

Shipping

If you ship the products you sell, and charge your customers for delivery, you should enable this option. You'll find it in the Sales Form Content section seen in Figure 5-3. Check the box next to Shipping to enable the option.

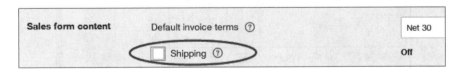

Figure 5-3: Turn this option on if you ship to customers.

The first thing that happens is that QuickBooks Online creates a Shipping Income account of the Income type. The reason is that shipping charged to customers is considered income. On the other side of the equation, you record your shipping costs, whether from a carrier or from your own delivery vehicles, as expenses. If there's a positive difference between the two, you've earned income. By the way, you can choose any account you want for shipping, or you can create a new account. You might want to check with your accountant if you're not sure.

ProAdvisor TIP: *Double-check your Chart of Accounts to see if QuickBooks Online already created an income account for shipping when you first subscribed. If so, you'll need to delete the old one, or the one that's created when you turn on the Shipping option. I found an extra income account for shipping in several of the companies I set up during the course of writing this book.*

In addition, when the option is enabled, a number of new fields are added to sales transactions (see Figure 5-4). The new fields include Shipping Address, Ship Via, Shipping Date, Tracking No., and a Shipping field for the charge just below the sales tax field (Subtotal if you don't collect sales tax).

Figure 5-4: The Shipping option, when enabled, adds shipping fields to your sales transaction forms.

The new Shipping income account is automatically configured as the default shipping income account in the Chart Of Accounts options located in the Advanced section of the Settings window (covered later in this chapter).

Custom Fields (Essentials and Plus only)

If you have an Essentials or Plus plan you have the ability to create and use custom fields on your sales transaction forms. They come in very handy when you have data that you want to track but for which QuickBooks Online does not provide the fields. For example, you might want to include a purchase order number field, a sales rep field, and so on. You're only allowed three custom fields so be sure to give it some thought before creating them.

Here's how to create custom fields:

1. Open the Settings window, click the Sales section on the left, and then choose Custom Fields to display the Custom Fields options shown in Figure 5-5.

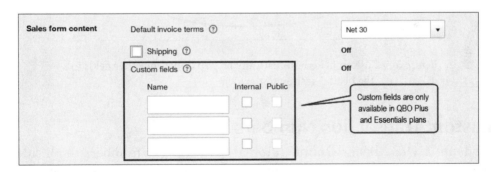

Figure 5-5: You can track additional information with custom fields.

2. Enter a unique and descriptive field name.

3. Select the Internal checkbox to have the field appear on the form in QuickBooks Online. The Public checkbox is selected automatically, which means the field will also appear on the printed and electronic forms sent to the customer.

4. If you only want the field to appear on the online form and not the form sent to the customer, deselect the Public option.

5. Enter a number in the Order column. This number dictates the position of the field (from left to right) on the sales transaction forms.

6. Click Save to create the new fields.

The custom fields that you create appear below the terms and date fields on invoices, estimates, credit memos, sales receipts, and refund receipts. If the Shipping option is enabled, the custom fields appear below the shipping fields (see Figure 5-6).

Figure 5-6: Custom fields automatically line up under the other fields in the header section of the form.

Custom Transaction Numbers

By default, QuickBooks Online automatically assigns numbers to all sales transaction forms. For some businesses this is ideal. However, others have different requirements that custom numbers help meet very nicely. For instance, you may want to use different number sets for different forms. Perhaps you want to separate (and identify) invoices by starting the numbers with an "i" (i101), and estimates an "e" (e101).

Turn on the option in Preferences by checking the Custom Transaction Numbers link in the Sales Form Content section (see Figure 5-7). Click Save and you're almost done.

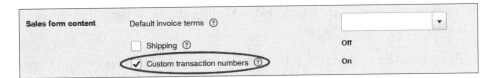

Figure 5-7: Custom transaction numbers are available in all QuickBooks
Online versions.

To start the new custom sequence you have to create a new
transaction and enter the first custom number (i.e., i2101). After you save
the transaction, the numbering sequence is reset using the new number.
Therefore, the next invoice you create will automatically display the
Invoice No. as i2102. The same numbering sequence is used for invoices,
sales receipts, credit memos, and refund receipts. Therefore, changing the
numbering sequence on any one of those forms applies to all. Estimates
are the only sales transaction form that can have a different numbering
system.

> **ProAdvisor TIP:** *To avoid having duplicate numbers you
> might want to prohibit the changing of numbers on individual
> sales transactions forms. First, enable the option and create
> new transactions implementing the new numbering system(s).
> Then, return to the Settings window and uncheck the Custom
> Transaction Numbers option. This hides the transaction
> number field, thus preventing users from changing individual
> transaction form numbers. The automatic sequence continues
> to work, but is now unchangeable.*

Service Date

Enabling the Service Date option adds an extra column to the body of
sales forms. The column is called, aptly enough, Service Date. It allows
you to enter a date on which a service was performed for each line-item
you enter. This is especially helpful for service work to ensure that both
you and the customer are in agreement over the work done. You'll find
the new column in the following forms; invoices, estimates, credit memos,
sales receipts, refund receipts, delayed credits, and delayed charges. Of

course, depending on your QuickBooks Online version, not all of those forms may be available to you.

To enable the option, open the Preferences window (Tools Menu (gear icon) | Settings | Company Settings) and click the Sales section on the left to display all of the sales options. Click in the Sales Form Content section to display the available options. Place a checkmark next to the Service Date option to turn it on (see Figure 5-8).

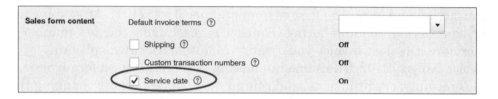

Figure 5-8: Use the Service Date to eliminate confusion.

Discounts

Customer discounts are a fact of business life. Whether you're having a sale, moving old inventory, or giving good customers a better price, you will need to offer discounts at some time. Unfortunately, the QuickBooks Online discount feature is somewhat limited. You can apply a discount to an entire sales transaction and that's it. There are no line-item discounts or price levels available in any of the online versions.

To enable discounts in sales transactions follow these steps:

1. Choose Tools Menu (gear icon) | Settings | Company Settings to open the Settings window.
2. Select Sales | Sales Form Entry to display the available options.
3. Check the Discount option to enable the feature.
4. Click Save to implement the new option.

The next time you open an Invoice, Estimate, or Sales Receipt form you'll find that a Discount field has been added (see Figure 5-9). Fill out the invoice as you would normally. To apply the discount select Discount

Percent or Discount Value from the drop-down list and enter the percent or amount of the discount in the box to the right of the list. No need to enter a percent sign or a dollar sign; QuickBooks Online knows from the choice you made in the drop-down list.

Figure 5-9: Discounting an entire sales transaction is easy when you enable the Discounts feature.

As I said earlier, there are really no good options for line-item discounting. I noticed that one member of the online community suggested creating sub-products for each discounted price. Not a bad suggestion if you only have a handful of products, but a bit cumbersome if you have a long list of products and services – especially if your products already have sub-products.

Deposits

If you accept deposits on customer purchases you can add a deposit field to the bottom of invoices to handle those customer deposits. This feature is designed for businesses that take special orders and require a deposit, as well as retailers who offer layaways.

Open the Settings window and choose Sales | Sales Form Content | Deposit. Check the Deposit option to enable the feature. The next time you open an invoice form you'll see that the Deposit field has been added to the form (see Figure 5-10).

Figure 5-10: The Deposits option adds a new field to the invoice form.

The best that can be said about this option is that it's convenient and it does the math. Unfortunately, it does not properly track the deposits in a manner that a business handling a large number of customer deposits requires. If you only take an occasional deposit and have no need to keep track of all of your customers' deposits, use it by all means. However, if you retain a lot of customer money in the form of deposits you'll want to handle it differently.

To begin, you must have (or create) a Customer Deposits liability account and a Customer Deposit product/service item. Also, make sure you've disabled the Deposits option in the Sales Form Content section.

Start with the liability account. The reason you use a liability account is that the money is not really yours yet. It still belongs to the customer until you physically hand over the product to the customer, at which time the deposit goes from being a liability to being income.

If your chart of accounts does not contain a Customer Deposits liability account, choose Tools Menu (gear icon) | Settings | Chart Of Accounts to open the Chart Of Accounts window. Click the New button and create an account of the Other Current Liabilities Category Type and of the Other Current Liabilities Detail Type. Name it Customer Deposits or something similar. Give it an appropriate number (i.e., 2200) if you're using account numbers. A description is optional, but can be helpful if you have multiple users. Do not enter anything in the Balance field. Click Save to create the new account.

Next, create the Customer Deposit item in the Products And Services list. Select Tools Menu (gear icon) | Lists | Products And Services to display the Products And Services window. Click the New button and enter a name (i.e., Customer Deposit), and description. Leave the Price/Rate blank. From the Income Account drop-down list choose the Customer Deposits account you just created. Click Save to create the new item.

To accurately track your customer deposits you'll have to create two separate transactions. First, when you receive a customer deposit you need to create a Sales Receipt to record the deposit. Open a Sales Receipt (Top Navigation Bar | Plus Icon | Show More | Customers | Sales Receipt). Enter the customer information as needed. Next, move to the first line and choose the Customer Deposit item from the Product/Service drop-down list. Press the Tab key until the cursor appears in the Amount field and enter the amount of the deposit (as a positive number). Click Save And Close to record the deposit.

When you sell the item you'll create either an invoice or another sales receipt, depending on the situation. For example, a customer who places a special order may leave the deposit (recorded on a sales receipt), and then return to pick up and pay for the item when it arrives (another sales receipt). Layaway customers, on the other hand, will need a sales receipt to record the deposit, and an invoice to record the sale (including the deposit).

ProAdvisor TIP: *When creating a sales receipt (or receiving a payment) be sure to make the right choice in the Deposit To field. The drop-down list contains all of your bank accounts and your other current assets accounts, including one called Undeposited Funds. Unless you make a separate bank deposit for each sale and/or payment you receive, you'll drive yourself crazy trying to reconcile your bank account if you allow QuickBooks Online to "deposit" every sale and payment into your bank account separately. By using the Undeposited Funds account you can make individual deposits in QuickBooks Online to match the actual deposits you make at the bank. For example, if you have five sales/payments and let QuickBooks Online "deposit" them to your bank account, your reconcile window will show five separate deposits for the day (i.e., 100, 75, 25, 50, 150). Chances are you take the money from the day and make a single deposit of $400 in your bank. If you use the Undeposited Funds account and make a single QuickBooks Online deposit of $400 it will be much simpler to reconcile those five sales/payments when your bank statement arrives with a $400 deposit for the day in question.*

No matter which sales form you use, the process is pretty much the same. Open the sales form and enter the customer information. On the first line of the form enter the item the customer is buying. If there are multiple items, use as many lines as needed. On the last line choose the Customer Deposit item and enter the original deposit amount as a negative number (see Figure 5-11). Click Save And Close to record the transaction.

Here's what's happening in QuickBooks Online when you use this method for tracking customer deposits.

The initial sale of the deposit on the sales receipt debits (adds to) the Undeposited Funds or bank account, and credits (adds to) the Customer Deposits account. Let's say you take a $500 deposit. Now you have $500 in your bank account and a liability of $500 (see Table 5-1). If debits and credits are still a little confusing, jump back to Chapter 1 and take a refresher course.

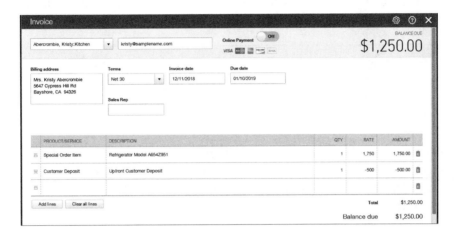

Figure 5-11: Tracking customer deposits is easy once you've created the proper account and customer deposit item.

Account	Debit	Credit
1200-Undeposited Funds	500.00	
2200-Customer Deposits		500.00

Table 5-1: Remember, customer deposits aren't yours until you make the final sale.

When you deliver the product and invoice the customer, you make the postings seen in Table 5-2:

Account	Debit	Credit
4000-Product Sales		1750.00
2200-Customer Deposits	500.00	
1100-Accounts Receivable	1250.00	

Table 5-2: When you invoice the customer you're removing the deposit from the liability account and adding it to your income (Product Sales in this case).

The postings in Table 5-2 are adding $1750 (the total sale) to your income, deducting the $500 from the liability account, and adding the balance of $1250 to both your income and A/R accounts. Even though you don't have the $1250, it's considered income because you've already earned it by selling and delivering the product.

ProAdvisor TIP: *This also works well for businesses such as accountants and attorneys who collect retainers from clients. You might want to change the liability account name from Customer Deposits to Client Retainers.*

Something to keep in mind is that these customer deposits are not yours yet. Therefore, you might want to periodically run a report on the Customer Deposits account and make sure you have that amount in your bank account in the event the orders are cancelled.

Products And Services

Here's where you'll find a pair of options to modify sales transaction forms. The first is called Show Product/Service Column On Sales Forms and displays the Product/Service column when enabled. It is on by default and, for most users, should remain enabled. Since most businesses sell either products or services, the Product/Service column is indispensable.

Track Quantity And Price/Rate is the second option in this section, and is equally indispensable to most businesses. Without the Quantity and Price/Rate fields, you have to manually calculate the totals for items sold.

Messages

This section has two parts with a number of options (see Figure 5-12). The first part includes options for customizing the e-mail messages that are sent with sales transaction forms. The second part contains the option for creating default messages on the forms themselves.

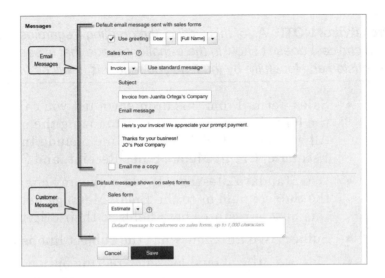

Figure 5-12: Make your forms and e-mails personalized and professional.

Email Messages

If you send any of your sales forms to customers electronically, you have the ability to customize the message that accompanies those forms before you send them. While you can always change the message information before sending any transaction, the options found here allow you to customize the default message created for each transaction type.

- Greeting. Do you want to begin the message with a formal salutation? If so, check the Use Greeting option. If not, uncheck the option.

- Greeting Format. These options only appear when the Use Greeting option is enabled. Choose the type of salutation to include at the beginning of the message. Your choices include Dear, To, and <blank>. The first two are obvious. The last removes the salutation altogether, regardless of your choice in the name drop-down list to the right. Next, choose the name format you'd like to use in the greeting.

ProAdvisor NOTE: *As of this writing, the greeting (regardless of your choices) doesn't show in the e-mail message that is sent to the customer. Hopefully, by the time you read this, it will be fixed.*

- Sales Form. From this drop-down list you can choose the form for which you are customizing the message. All versions of QuickBooks Online include Invoice, Estimate, Credit Memo, Sales Receipt, and Statement.
- Use Standard Message. If you make any changes to the Subject field or to the Email Message field, clicking this button restores both fields to their original states.
- Subject. We all know what the subject line is for.
- Message. If you enabled the Greeting option, there's no need to enter another greeting/salutation here (unless the earlier mentioned bug has not yet been fixed). Just fill in the body of the message.

ProAdvisor TIP: *You can include URLs in the message body. Use the format http:// or https://. Actually, I found that simply entering www. works fine.*

- Email Me A Copy. If you want to retain a copy of all sales forms e-mailed to customers, enable this option to have a copy sent to your company e-mail address. Note that the copy is sent as a "cc" on the original message sent to the customer, not as a separate e-mail. In other words, the customer will be aware that you were copied.

Once you've customized the settings be sure to click the Save button. As a matter of fact, if you take any amount of time customizing the settings it's a good idea to periodically click Save.

Customer Messages

Adding a message to sales transaction forms is a nice touch. Customers like to be appreciated, so saying thanks is a nice way to end an invoice or sales receipt. You can always add a customized message to each sales transaction. However, if you wish, you can also create a single message that can be added to all sales transactions.

To add a default message to invoices open the Settings window and select Sales Form Content | Messages and move to the Default Message Shown On Sales Form option. From the Sales Form drop-down list, choose the form for which you're creating the default message. Your choices are limited to Estimate and Invoices And Other Sales Forms. Enter the desired message in the text box below the drop-down list. Once you click Save, this message appears on the selected form(s).

Online Delivery

The Online Delivery section includes several options for how sales transaction forms are delivered. There are two sections, as seen in Figure 5-13; one for all forms except invoices, and another, specifically for invoices.

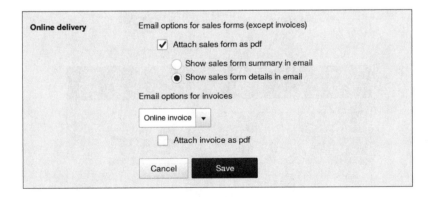

Figure 5-13: You decide how sales transactions forms are delivered to the customer.

Email Options For Sales Forms (Except Invoices)

This setting is a single option with two sub-options. The primary setting is called Attach Sales Form As PDF. For all sales documents except invoices, when turned on, it automatically attaches a PDF copy of the sales form to the e-mail. Invoices are treated differently, depending on the selections made in the next section, Email Options For Invoices.

When the option to include a PDF copy of the sales form as an attachment is turned on, two additional options appear.

- **Show Sales Form Summary In Email.** When including the sales form as an attachment you can choose to include a summary of the form contents in the body of the e-mail message as well.

- **Show Sales Form Details In Email.** Choose this option if you want the header and line-item information to show in the e-mail body as well.

As you can see in Figure 5-14, the summary option gives the recipient a quick overview of the sales form contents, while the details option provides a lot more information.

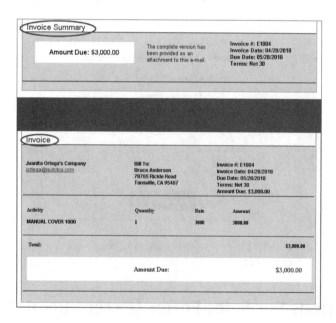

Figure 5-14: HTML e-mail comparison of the two Show Sales Form options.

Email Options for Invoices

Invoices have their own set of options to cover the unique Online Invoice (formerly EInvoicing) method of delivery. This is a special feature that places a copy of the invoice on an Intuit web site where the customer can view it and pay it (if you take any form of online payment). When the Online Invoice option is selected, your customer receives an e-mail with a link to view the invoice online. By default, the Online Invoice option is enabled, which overrides the settings in the previous section, E-mail Options For Sales Forms.

The first thing to do is make a selection from the Email Options For Invoices drop-down list. Your choices include:

- Online Invoice. As explained earlier, this option places a copy of the invoice online and an e-mail containing a link to the invoices is sent to the customer. When this option is selected an additional setting, Attach Invoice As PDF, is displayed. This setting does exactly what it says it will do. The only thing to keep in mind is that it overrides the Attach Sales Form As PDF option in the previous section.
- HTML Email. To send the e-mail in an HTML format choose this option.
- Plain Text Email. If you prefer to use plain text emails, make this selection.

When you're done, click the Save button to store your settings.

ProAdvisor TIP: *If you accept online payments, you might want to leave the Attach Invoice As PDF option turned off. The absence of a PDF copy will probably encourage customers to view (and pay) invoices online.*

See the section entitled "Using Online Invoices" in Chapter 6 for more information.

Statements

If you regularly send your customers statements to keep them updated on the status of their accounts (and to remind them of overdue invoices) you'll want to set the options in this section (see Figure 5-15).

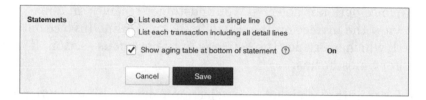

Figure 5-15: Statements options let you customize statements for customers.

The first option is called List Each Transaction As A Single Line, and is enabled by default. When this option is selected, only the transaction date and number are displayed in the statement body. To include the details of each transaction check the List Each Transaction Including All Details Lines option. You can see the different statements created by selecting one option or the other in Figure 5-16.

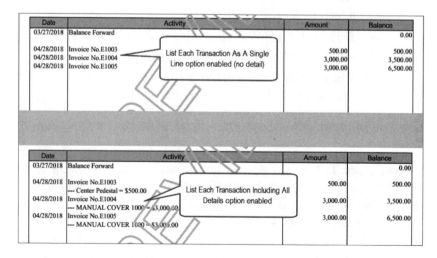

Figure 5-16: How much detail does the customer need on each statement?

The last option, Show Aging Table At Bottom of Statement is enabled by default. It's a handy option that adds an aging table to the Statement with current, and various past due amounts displayed. If you're sending statements, you'll probably want to include the table (see Figure 5-17).

Current Due	1-30 Days Past Due	31-60 Days Past Due	61-90 Days Past Due	90+ Days Past Due	Amount Due
$6,000.00	$500.00	$0.00	$0.00	$0.00	$6,500.00

Figure 5-17: The aging table provides a good reminder of the customer's account status.

ProAdvisor NOTE: *The Bill With Parent option found in the sub-customer record determines how statements are printed for customers with sub-customers (jobs). See Chapter 6 for more information.*

Setting Sales Tax Options

If you're doing business in one of the 45 states (as of this writing) in the U.S. (or the District of Columbia) that has sales tax, it's almost guaranteed that you're dealing with the issue. Even if you're in one of the states that doesn't have a state sales tax, you may be faced with city or locality sales taxes. Therefore, configuring sales tax is an important issue for most businesses and should be dealt with before setting up customers and vendors.

The Sales Tax option in the Settings window is nothing more than a link to the Sales Tax Center. Unless you're already in the Settings window, it's easier to open the Sales Tax Center by clicking Taxes | Sales Tax on the Left Navigation Bar.

When the Sales Tax Center opens for the first time, you're presented with an informational screen that asks you to configure the sales tax features. Click the Set Up Sales Tax Rates button to begin by filling out the Set Up Sales Tax form shown in Figure 5-18.

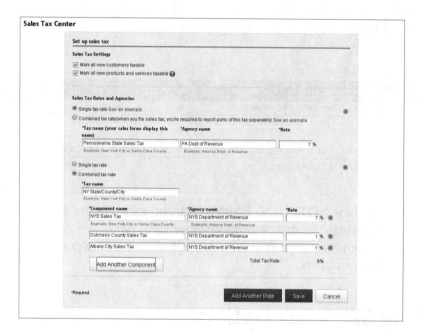

Figure 5-18: If you charge sales tax you must configure at least one sales tax rate.

1. Set the Sales Tax Settings options.

   • Mark All New Customers Taxable. If most of your customers pay sales tax (they're not nonprofit or government agencies) you should leave this option checked. Every new customer you create is automatically marked taxable. You can always change the status as needed.

   • Mark All New Products And Services Taxable. If most of the products and services you sell are taxable, check this option. It automatically marks each new product/service as taxable.

2. To configure a single tax rate, choose the Single Tax Rate option and fill in the three fields below.

- Tax Name. This is a descriptive name of your own choosing (i.e., Florida State Sales Tax).
- Agency Name. Enter the exact name of the agency to which you remit the collected sales tax.
- Rate. Enter the sales tax rate.

3. If you want to create another single tax rate click the Add Another Rate button to display another set of fields.

4. To configure a sales tax group choose the Combined Tax Rate option. The difference here is that additional fields are displayed for the different tax rates. This enables you to create one sales tax item that includes the rates for different taxing authorities. For example, if you have to collect state, county, and city sales taxes, this is the one to use.

5. Enter a name for the group, such as State/County/City Sales Tax.

6. Fill in the Component Name (i.e., Orange County Sales Tax), the name of the tax agency, and finally the tax rate.

7. Repeat for all of the necessary components (state, county, city, and so on).

8. If you need another set of component fields click the Add Another Component button.

9. When you're done, click Save to add the new sales tax rate or group.

Configuring Advanced Customer Options

The Advanced section of the Settings window contains a couple of customer-related options that you should be aware of.

Chart Of Accounts

Whether you see customer-related options in this section depends on the choices you've made in the Sales section of the Settings window. If you selected the Shipping and/or Discount option(s) in the Sales Form Content section you'll see an option for each enabled option here in the Chart Of Accounts section (see Figure 5-19).

Figure 5-19: Customer shipping charges and discounts are considered income.

From the drop-down list to the right of each option, choose the appropriate account (or create a new one). The default income accounts (Shipping Income and Discounts Given) are probably appropriate for most users. Check with your accountant to be sure.

ProAdvisor TIP: *As soon as you enable the options in the Sales Form Content section, QuickBooks Online automatically creates the default income accounts. However, when you subscribed to QuickBooks Online and created a new company, similar accounts may have been created as well. To avoid the problem of multiple accounts with the same function, double-check the Chart of Accounts and delete (or merge if they all have activity) any extra accounts you find.*

Automation

The Automation section of the Settings window provides a number of options that help to automate the process of creating customer transaction forms. As you can see in Figure 5-20, Essentials and Plus plan subscribers have more options than Simple Start subscribers.

Here are the options you'll find in the Automation section:

- **Pre-Fill Forms With Previously Entered Content.** This is a great option if your customer (or vendor, or employee) transaction forms are always the same or similar. When this option is enabled, filling out a transaction form for the customer (vendor, employee) is easy because QuickBooks Online automatically carries over most of the information from the last transaction form saved for the same customer.

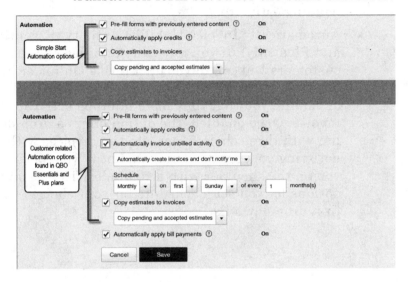

Figure 5-20: Speed up your work with these automation options.

- **Automatically Apply Credits.** In most cases, this is probably a good option to enable since it does exactly what its name says. For example if John Doe has credit of $50 from a return last month, you probably want to apply that credit toward the next sale to Mr. Doe. If that's usually the way you do business, turn this option on and QuickBooks Online will automatically take care of it. However, if you have a reason to not always apply existing credits to new sales, turn the setting off (uncheck it).

- **Copy Estimates To Invoices.** This is a great timesaver if you use estimates. Once a customer accepts an estimate you can use it as the basis for an invoice to bill the customer for the job. Otherwise, you'll have to create the invoice from scratch. Perhaps, not a terribly burdensome job – unless you're a contractor with a gazillion line-items on the estimate. As soon as you turn the option on, a drop-down list appears offering you two choices. You can limit this option to affecting accepted estimates only, or accepted and pending estimates.

- Automatically Invoice Unbilled Activity (Essentials and Plus only). If you have any unbilled charges for customers you can have QuickBooks Online either create invoices for those customers automatically, or remind you that they have unbilled activities to invoice. Once enabled, the option offers a drop-down list with three choices – create the invoices without notifying you, create them and notify you, or just tap you on the shoulder with a reminder. The remaining options let you set a schedule for your choice from the first drop-down list.

CHAPTER 6:

Tracking Customers & Income

- Understanding Accounts Receivable
- Touring the Customers Center
- Managing Customers
- Integrating PayPal into QuickBooks Online
- Customizing Customer Transaction Forms

Since very few for-profit businesses can survive without customers, tracking both your customers and the income they generate is one of the most important accounting tasks you'll face. For those businesses that extend some form of credit to their customers it will also be critical to understand the accounting concept of Accounts Receivable (A/R).

Understanding Accounts Receivable

If you sell customers items without collecting the payment at the time of the sale, it means you're extending them credit. Instead of issuing a receipt for payment at the time of the sale, you generate an invoice which the customer is to pay at a later date according to the terms you've established for that particular customer. In other words, you have Accounts Receivable, or outstanding money that's owed to you.

To begin with, Accounts Receivable is an asset account – which means that, by default, a debit increases the account and a credit decreases the account (refer back to Chapter 1 for a brief discussion of debits and credits). When you invoice a customer for a sale, you debit (increase) Accounts Receivable and credit (increase) your Income account. In real terms what happens is that your income goes up, as well as the amount of money owed to you. When you receive payment for the invoice, Accounts Receivable is credited (decreased) and your bank account (an asset account) is debited or increased, and your Income account remains untouched. Now, the amount of money owed to you is reduced, but the amount of money you have on hand (in the bank) has increased, while your income is the same. Tables 6-1 and 6-2 provide a visual reference for these transactions.

Account	Debit	Credit
4000 - Income		100
1200 – Accounts Receivable	100	

Table 6-1: When your A/R goes up, so does your income.

Account	Debit	Credit
1200 – Accounts Receivable		100
1000 – Bank Account	100	

Table 6-2: A payment brings your A/R down and your cash on hand up.

As they say in the movies "Let's follow the money." Here's what actually happens during those two transactions (Table 6-3).

Account	Invoice	Payment	Total
Money Owed To You (Accounts Receivable)	100	-100	0
Income	100	0	100
Bank	0	100	100

Table 6-3: Once you get past the accounting jargon, the math is pretty simple.

Depending on how your chart of accounts is configured, the invoice and payment postings may be a little more complex. For example, if you have two income accounts – one for sales and one for services – you would replace the single income account with the two, and split the total appropriately. The same thing applies if you add sales tax to the equation. Table 6-4 displays an invoice posting with additional accounts.

Account	Debit	Credit
4010 – Services Income		25.00
4020 – Product Income		75.00
2300 – Sales Tax Payable		7.00
1200 – Accounts Receivable	107.00	

Table 6-4: As long as you keep your debits and credits straight it's fairly easy.

Touring the Customers Center

The Customers center is your go to place for customer-related activity. As such, it offers a number of very helpful features. Take a look at Figure 6-1 and you'll see there's not much wasted real estate in the Customers center.

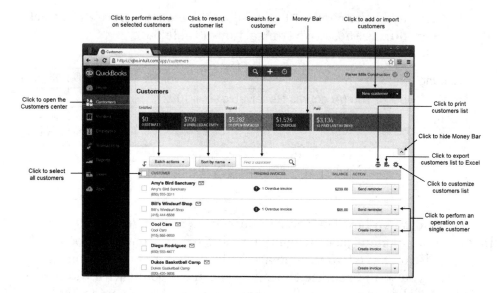

Figure 6-1: The Customers center provides quick access to customer-related activities.

To access the Customers center all you have to do is click the Customers link on the Left Navigation Bar.

Once you're in, there are a number of features that will provide you with a great deal of information and access to more. Let's take a look at those features.

The New Customer Button

Located in the top right corner of the Customers center is the New Customer button. Click it to open a blank Customer Information form to add a new customer. See the section later in this chapter about adding and removing customers.

If you click the small down-arrow to the right of the button, another command appears. It is the Import Customers command, which opens the Import Customers window. See Appendix B for detailed information and instructions on importing customers into QuickBooks Online.

The Money Bar

The multicolored, horizontal bar at the top of the Customers center is called the Money Bar. If you look closely you can see that it contains totals for a variety of customer-related transactions.

- Open Estimates. Here you'll see the total number and amount of any outstanding estimates for which invoices have not yet been created. Click this section of the bar to see a listing of the customers with open estimates. In the transaction list that opens, click the link in the Open Estimates column to see the estimate(s) for that customer.

- Unbilled Activity. The total number and amount of any unbilled charges for time and/or expenses appear here. Only appears in Essentials and Plus versions.

- Open Invoices. This one's pretty self-explanatory – the number and total amount of all open invoices.

- Overdue Invoices. Another straightforward section; total number and amount of all invoices past their due dates.

- Recently Paid Invoices. This section displays the total number and amount for all invoices paid within the last 30 days.

Click a section of the bar to see a listing of the related transactions. If you want to hide the Money Bar, click the small tab with the up-arrow at the bottom right.

Customers List Toolbar

This is the row of buttons and icons above the Customer list (see Figure 6-2).

Figure 6-2: This toolbar provides almost everything you need to work in the Customers list.

The elements found on the toolbar enable you to perform a number of actions on the Customers list:

- Batch Actions. Click this button to see a drop-down menu of commands that can be performed on one or more customers in the list. To use any of the commands you must first select the customer(s) to be affected, by checking the box to the left of the each customer's name. To select all customers check the box in the header section (to the left of Customer). The available batch actions include:

  o Send Statements. Create and send (via e-mail) statements for the selected customer(s). See the section entitled "Create Customer Statements" later in this chapter for more details.

  o Print Statements. Create a hard copy of statements for the selected customers. See the section entitled "Create Customer Statements" later in this chapter for more details.

  o Email. Send an e-mail, using your default e-mail application, to all of the selected customers. This option is not available for customers without an e-mail address in their customer records.

- Sort By Name. Click this button to display several choices for changing the sort order of the Customers list.

- Find A Customer. Enter a customer name in the text box to filter out all of the other records. Note that only the name in the Display Name As field in the customer record is searched. Let's take this example. The company name is Apex Communications, the contact name is Art Johnston, and the Display Name As field contains Apex Communications. A search for Art or Johnston will display no results. However Apex or Communications will locate the customer.

- Print Icon. Click this icon to print the complete Customers list. You don't have to select any customers before clicking the icon. The list appears in your browser's print preview window so that you can review it before printing.

- Export Icon. Click this icon to export the Customers list to an Excel spreadsheet. What happens next depends on your browser's settings. The Excel file may be automatically saved to the default download folder, or a Save As dialog may open. If a Save As dialog opens, give the file a clear and descriptive name, choose a location, and click Save to store the new file on your hard disk.

- Settings (gear) Icon. Click this icon to display options for customizing the Customers list. For example, you can add columns, set the number of rows displayed per page, and include or exclude inactive customers.

Customers List

The Customers list is, of course, the heart of the Customers center. Here you'll find a listing of all of your customers (unless you've excluded inactive customers), along with any open invoices and the total balance. To the right of each customer listing is a button that provides a number of different commands for performing operations on the customer. What you see depends on the state of open invoices and your version of QuickBooks Online.

If the customer has open invoices, the available commands are:

- Send Reminder
- Receive Payment
- Send Statement (if the customer or sub-customer has an e-mail address)
- Print Statement
- Create Invoice

If the customer has no open invoices, the available commands are:

- Create Invoice
- Create Sales Receipt
- Create Estimate
- Create Charge (Essentials and Plus)
- Create Time Activity (Plus only)
- Make Inactive

Clicking a customer or sub-customer name opens a transaction list for the selected customer (see Figure 6-3). At the top of the list is basic customer information and an Edit button to modify it. To the right is a non-interactive listing of totals for open invoices, overdue invoices, and income in the last 30 days. If the customer has sub-customers, the totals only appear for the sub-customers. The bottom half of the screen contains the transaction listing for the customer or sub-customer. This transaction listing also has a toolbar with buttons and icons that perform actions on the entire list or on individual transactions.

Figure 6-3: The customer transaction list provides a lot of information about the selected customer.

Managing Customers

Customers are an integral part of your business, which means they're an integral part of your accounting system. To ensure that you have accurate business records with which to report on and analyze your finances, you'll want to maintain good, up-to-date customer records.

Add Customers

Regardless of whether you have any customers in the Customers center, you're going to have to add new customers at some time (or you'll shortly be out of business). The way that you add new customers depends on your needs and the format of the customer information.

New Customer

If you're only adding a single customer you'll probably opt for the New Customer button. Even adding a handful is probably not worth going the through the import process. Here's how you add a new customer using the New Customer button:

1. Click the Customers link on the Left Navigation Bar to open the Customers center.

2. Click the New Customer button at the top right portion of the screen to open a blank Customer Information dialog box as seen in Figure 6-4.

Figure 6-4: Enter as much or as little information as you need.

3. Fill out the customer information you want to retain for this customer. Most of the fields are self-explanatory so I won't cover those. However there are some that require a little more explanation. Those, I'll cover here.

   • Display Name As. This drop-down list offers up to four alternative name formats for displaying in the Customers center and reports. The first is company name, if you enter one (Smith Brothers Furniture). The second is the contact name, exactly as entered in the name boxes. For example, if you enter Dr. John E. Smith Jr., that's what your second option is. The third option is simply the first and last name (John Smith). The fourth option is first and last names, but with the last name first (Smith, John).

- Print On Check As. This gives you the opportunity to use a familiar and less formal name for the Customers center and reports, but a full, legal name for using on checks. John E. Smith might be known to everyone in your organization as Johnny Smith, so you could use Johnny Smith as the customer or company name and enter John E. Smith in the Print On Check As name. To use the display name as the payee on the check, click the Use Display Name option.

- Is Sub-Customer. Sub-customers are called jobs in QuickBooks desktop applications. They serve to better organize and track sales to customers with multiple locations or divisions. Contractors who sub for general contractors can track all of the work for each general contractor, broken down by individual jobs (sub-customers). A distributor can easily track sales for customers with multiple locations. Check the box and choose the parent customer from the drop-down list below the option. If you want to include all sub-customer transactions in the parent customer's statement, select Bill With Parent. If you want a separate statement created for the sub-customer, choose Bill This Customer.

Be sure to fill in any needed information in the other tabs located below the Print On Checks As field.

- Other Details tab. This is just a single text box into which you can add notes for the customer.

- Tax Info tab. If you have enabled sales tax in your company file you'll see a This Customer Is Taxable option as well as a drop-down list from which to choose the Default Tax Code. For tax-exempt customers a Tax Resale No. field is provided.

- Payment And Billing tab. Preferred payment method and preferred delivery method are configured here, as well as the terms. There is also a field for entering the customer's opening balance. I strongly urge you to ignore this field and enter the opening balance using historical transactions or a journal entry.

Once you've entered all of the information you require, click Save to add the new customer/sub-customer to QuickBooks Online. New customers appear in the Customers center without an indent. New sub-customers appear indented below the parent customer.

To edit a customer, click the Edit button that appears to the right of the customer name. This opens the Customer Information dialog. Make the necessary changes. You cannot delete customers with activity or sub-customers, but you can make them inactive (hide them). To do so, open the Customer Information dialog and click the Make Inactive button at the bottom of the dialog box.

Generate Customer Invoices

You have a couple of options for creating customer invoices. If you're in the Customers center you can scroll through the Customer list, select the customer, and choose Create Invoice from the drop-down list to the right of the customer listing.

The other option is to use the Quick Create Menu (the plus sign on the Top Navigation Bar). Click the plus sign and select Invoice from the menu that appears (see Figure 6-5).

Figure 6-5: You can create an invoice from most QuickBooks Online screens using this method.

Regardless of which method you use, a blank invoice form slides down (see Figure 6-6). Actually, if you open the invoice from the Customers center, the invoice already contains the customer name and any related information from the customer record (Customer, Email, Billing Address, and Terms). The fields contained in the invoice form will vary, depending on which options you've enabled. See Chapter 5 for more information on setting transaction form options.

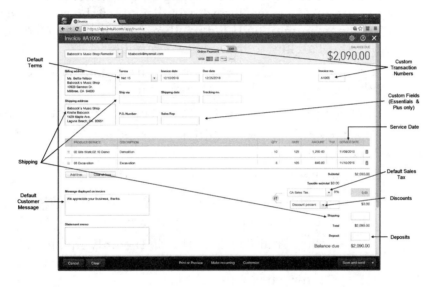

Figure 6-6: All transaction form options are enabled in this company file.

Filling out an invoice is a pretty straightforward task.

1. Select a customer from the Choose A Customer drop-down list.

2. From the Terms drop-down list choose the terms for this customer if they don't appear automatically.

3. By default, today's date is used for the Invoice Date for the first invoice you create during this session. If you want to use another date, change it. Once you change the date, QuickBooks Online will continue to use it for invoices, estimates, credit memos, sales receipts, refund receipts, delayed credits, and delayed charges (the last

two only in Essentials and Plus) until you change it again, or end the session.

4. The Due Date is automatically calculated from the terms. If you have no terms for the customer, QuickBooks Online assumes the Due Date is the same date as the Invoice Date.

5. Click in the Product/Service field on the first line to select a product or service. Depending on the information in the product/service record, some or all of the remaining information may be filled in. If not, fill it in as needed. Use the Tab key to move between fields.

6. If you want to delete a single line-item, move to the last column and click the trash can icon.

7. Click the Add Lines button to increase the number of lines.

8. To remove all of the line-item information, click the Clear All Lines button.

9. Enter a customer message if you want one.

10. Select a sales tax to apply if you collect sales tax.

11. Click one of the "Save And" buttons:

   - Save And Close. If this is the only invoice you're creating and you want to save it and deal with it later, click this button.

   - Save And New. If you want to create another invoice, click the down arrow next to the Save And Close button to display the Save And New button. When you click it, the invoice is saved, and a new, blank invoice form is opened.

   - Save And Send. If the customer has a valid e-mail address click this button to save the invoice and send a copy to the customer via e-mail. This changes the status of the invoice from "Open" to "Open (Sent)." When the customer views the invoice online (if Online Invoices is turned on) the status changes to "Open (Viewed)."

That's all there is to it.

Adding a PayPal Link to Sales Transaction Forms

While there is no way to accept PayPal payments directly in QuickBooks Online, you can add a link and instructions to your sales transaction forms and the e-mail messages that accompany them. If your customer has a PayPal account he can click the link, log in, and send money to pay the invoice, estimate (if a deposit is required to accept), or statement. For optimum results it's best to customize both the transaction form and the e-mail message that goes with it. Therefore, this is a two step process.

ProAdvisor NOTE: *This is an all or nothing option. In other words, you can't choose which transaction forms the PayPal instructions appear on. Once you create a footer, it automatically applies to invoices, estimates, sales receipts, and statements. The e-mail message, on the other hand, can be added or removed depending on the transaction form being sent.*

Step one, customizing the transaction form footer:

1. Open a blank invoice form and click the Customize button at the bottom to display the Add Personality To Your Forms window shown in Figure 6-7.

2. Click the Footer tab and move to the Footer text box.

3. Enter the text you want to appear at the bottom of each invoice, estimate, and statement. For example, you might enter something like this: **PAYPAL PAYMENT Instructions: Log into your PayPal account at www.paypal.com and send money to: <u>payments@ ourcompany.com</u>**

4. Click Save to add the new footer to all new forms.

ProAdvisor NOTE: *If you've haven't been updated to the latest QuickBooks Online version, your sales forms may not have a Customize button at the bottom. In that case, choose Tools Menu (gear icon) | Settings | Company Settings | Form Delivery | Customize Forms, and select Footer from the Content section.*

Figure 6-7: Make sales transaction forms look and work the way you want them to.

Step two, customizing the e-mail message:

1. Select Tools Menu (gear icon) | Settings | Company Settings to open the Settings screen.

2. Click the Sales section on the left and the Messages section on the right to view the default e-mail message settings.

3. From the Sales Form drop-down list select Invoice.

4. Move to the Message text box and insert the same PayPal text and link wherever you feel it is appropriate (I put mine below the company name).

5. Return to the Message For drop-down list and repeat the process for estimates and statements.

6. Click Save to store the changes.

The new PayPal instructions will appear in all e-mail messages sent with invoices, estimates, sales receipts, and statements.

You can also download your PayPal transactions into QuickBooks Online by adding your PayPal account as an online bank account. See the section entitled "Integrating PayPal into QuickBooks Online" found later in this chapter.

For information on receiving PayPal payments and properly posting the PayPal fee expense, see the section later in this chapter entitled "Receive PayPal Payments."

Using Online Invoices

This is a great option, which is enabled by default in all QuickBooks Online versions. It generates an e-mail to the customer with a link to an online site where the customer can view and pay the invoice.

If you are signed up for QuickBooks Payments, this is a great way to get paid quickly. When the Online Invoices option is turned on, your customer receives an e-mail with a link to view the invoice online, similar to the one shown in Figure 6-8.

Figure 6-8: With Online Invoices enabled, all invoice messages sent via
e-mail contain a link to view the invoice online

When the customer receives the e-mail all she has to do is click the View Invoice Now link to visit the Intuit site that hosts the online invoices. As you can see in Figure 6-9, the e-mail is displayed along with a history of the invoice on the right, a message box to communicate with the sender, and a couple of buttons to process the invoice.

Figure 6-9: Use Online Invoices for quick delivery and quick payment.

The client can print, save, or pay the invoice using the icons and Pay Now button in the top right corner of the window. If you haven't yet enabled online payments, the Pay Now button is grayed out.

To send a memo back to you, the customer enters a note in the Send A Message box and clicks the Send button. Below the message box is the history of the Invoice.

Creating Delayed Charges (Essentials & Plus only)

Delayed charges are very handy for recording customer charges before you're ready to invoice them. If you perform a series of jobs for a customer or provide a number of products, you can record each one on a delayed charge as you complete or deliver it. When you're ready to invoice the customer, you create the invoice and add all of the delayed charges. Since delayed charges are non-posting entries, none of your accounts is affected. Delayed charges can exist forever without changing your financial data.

Another nice thing is that both invoice automation and recurring invoices will pick up delayed charges. It's automatic when you check the Automatically Invoice Unbilled Activity option in the Advanced section of the Preferences window (Tools Menu (gear icon) | Settings | Company Settings), but must be enabled on recurring invoices. Simply check the Include Unbilled Charges When These Invoices Are Created option.

ProAdvisor TIP: *You can use delayed charges as backorders for inventory items currently out of stock. If a customer places an order for out-of-stock items, create a delayed charge for the items. When the inventory comes in, create the invoice and add the delayed charge. All of the backordered items will be added to the new invoice.*

Once you add a delayed charge to an invoice it is used up (doesn't appear when you create additional invoices), but it remains on the customer's transaction list. This is not a real problem, since it doesn't affect your books. However, if you use a lot of delayed charges, they may start cluttering up your transaction list. In that case, you can delete the used delayed charge transaction forms since they no longer serve a purpose.

To create a delayed charge select Quick Create (Plus icon) | Customers | Delayed Charge. If you only see a short menu with four items, click the Show More link. When the Delayed Charge form opens you'll see that it's very similar to an invoice form. Fill out the customer and product or service information and click the Save And Close button to record it.

If you have recurring charges that you want applied to regular invoices, you can create recurring delayed charges by clicking the Make Recurring button at the bottom of the Delayed Charge form. To see unused delayed charges run the Unbilled Charges report found in the Review Sales section of All Reports.

Using Recurring Invoices (Essentials & Plus only)

If you're a professional and you bill your clients regularly for retainers, recurring invoices are ideal. You can create a recurring invoice template that QuickBooks Online sends automatically or that you send manually when the client's retainer fund has been depleted. Recurring invoices are also perfect for service providers that bill on a regular basis, such as lawn or pool maintenance services.

ProAdvisor TIP: *If you generally collect retainers from your clients, you should create an Other Current Liability account called Retainers Held, and a service item called Client Retainers linked to the Retainers Held account. That way, you can track those retainers (which are not your money until you perform services) separately. When you invoice the client, use the Client Retainers item (as a negative number) to record the payment from the Retainers Held account.*

Creating recurring invoices is easy. See the section entitled "Use the Recurring Transactions List" in Chapter 4 for detailed instructions.

Receive Payments

This is the good part, when the money starts rolling in. To ensure that your records are accurate, you'll want to take extra care when receiving payments. If you receive payment at the time of the sale, you use a Sales Receipt form, which is covered in the next section. In this section we're going to cover receiving payments on open invoices.

There are two ways to receive payments. If you're in the Customers center, locate the open invoice and choose Receive Payment from the Action drop-down list to the right. Anywhere else in QuickBooks Online click the Plus icon on the Top Navigation Bar and select Customers | Receive Payment. You may have to click the Show More link to display all the choices.

ProAdvisor TIP: *If you're running QuickBooks Online Essentials or Plus you should check to make sure all delayed credits have been applied before receiving a payment, since delayed credits are not applied automatically, nor do they make an appearance in the Receive Payments window.*

If you open the Receive Payment window from within the Customers center, the customer and all outstanding transactions for the customer are automatically included in the form. For this exercise we're going to open a blank form using the Plus icon.

1. From the Choose A Customer drop-down list select the correct customer or sub-customer name. All of the open invoices for the customer appear.

2. Change the Payment Date if needed.

3. Select the payment type from the Payment Method drop-down list.

4. Optionally, enter a Reference No. (i.e., the check number).

5. Choose the account to which you want the payment deposited. This is a very important choice. Unless each payment is being automatically deposited to your bank account separately, you'll want to choose Undeposited Funds so you can create QuickBooks Online deposits that match the physical deposits you make into your bank. Otherwise, reconciliation will be a bear.

6. Enter the amount of the payment in the Amount Received field. QuickBooks Online automatically applies the payment to earliest invoices. For example, if the first three invoices are $1,000, $2,000, and $3,000 and you enter a payment $5,000, QuickBooks Online will pay off the first two invoices and apply the remaining $2,000 to the third, leaving it with a balance of $1,000.

7. If you want to apply the payment differently, deselect (uncheck) the invoices QuickBooks Online has paid automatically, and select the outstanding invoices against which you want to apply the payment. You can also click the Clear Payment button to start over.

ProAdvisor CAUTION: *When you deselect and reselect invoices to pay, QuickBooks Online automatically places the full amount due in the Payment field. If you do not change it, QuickBooks Online assumes you want to create (and apply) a credit for the difference between the Amount Received and the total of the open invoices checked.*

---

8. Click Save And Close to apply the payment.

Receive PayPal Payments

One of the biggest concerns PayPal users have is matching the actual bank deposits with the PayPal transactions. The problem arises due to the fact that the sale is recorded for the total amount, while the deposit reflects the total amount minus the PayPal fee. Fortunately, the solution is relatively simple.

Start by using the Receive Payments form to record the PayPal deposit. Enter the amount of the actual PayPal deposit (total minus fee). The important thing to remember here is to select Undeposited Funds from the Deposit To drop-down list. Finish filling out the form and save the payment.

The next step is to create a deposit. From the Quick Create menu (Plus icon) select Other | Bank Deposit to open the Deposit form. Choose the PayPal deposit in the Select Existing Payments section. Now, move to the Add New Deposits section where we'll enter the fee, and fill out the first line-item as follows:

- Received From. Select PayPal from the drop-down list.

- Account. From this drop-down list you'll want to choose the expense account you use for PayPal fees.

- Description/Payment Method/Ref No. These fields are optional.
- Amount. Enter the amount of the PayPal fee as a negative number.

Click Save And Close to record the deposit.

The final step, if you've downloaded the transaction from your bank, is to match the transaction.

Create Sales Receipts

Sales to customers where the payment is received at the time of the sale are called cash sales, regardless of the form of payment. Therefore, a cash sale could involve a payment by check, credit card, or debit card, and still be considered a cash sale, simply because the customer paid at the time of the sale. In QuickBooks Online you record a cash sale with a Sales Receipt form.

1. Choose Quick Create (Plus icon) | Customers | Sales Receipt to open a blank Sales Receipt form. If you don't see the Customers section, click the Show More link. The Sales Receipt form is similar to the Invoice form, with a couple of major differences – the Sales Receipt has a Payment Method and Deposit To field, both of which are missing from the Invoice form.

2. Select the customer from the Choose A Customer drop-down list.

3. Choose a method of payment from the Payment Method drop-down list, and enter a Reference No. if needed (i.e., check number).

4. Unless this payment will be deposited in your bank account by itself, choose Undeposited Funds from the Deposit To drop-down list.

5. Enter the item(s) being sold in the body of the form. Click the Add Lines button if you need to enter additional items.

6. Click Save And Close to create the Sales Receipt (see Figure 6-10).

Figure 6-10: Use the Sales Receipt form to record cash sales.

Work with Estimates

For some businesses, such as contractors and service providers, estimates are an integral part of the business. For those users, the ability to create estimates in QuickBooks Online is a big plus. They enable you to give prospective customers a quote for services that you're offering to perform for them. Fortunately, estimates are available in all online versions. To make the feature even more practical, QuickBooks Online offers several options that let you fine-tune estimates. For details on setting options for estimates see Chapter 5.

ProAdvisor NOTE: *Each new estimate is marked as "Pending" until its status is updated by using the Update Status command or until an invoice is created from it.*

Generating Estimates

Creating estimates is easy. Like most transaction forms, estimates can be generated from the Customers center, the Sales Transactions list, or the Quick Create menu. For this exercise we'll use the Quick Create menu since it's available in most QuickBooks Online windows.

1. Click the Plus icon on the Top Navigation Bar to view the Quick Create menu (see Figure 6-11).

Figure 6-11: Use the Quick Create menu for easy access to most transaction forms.

2. Click Estimate to open a blank estimate form.

3. Choose a customer and complete the form. Filling in the form is almost the same as filling out an invoice form. However, there are two fields that merit a mention here:

   • Estimate Status. By default, all new estimates are marked "Pending." Therefore, you shouldn't have any need to change the status until after the estimate is sent and accepted or rejected. However, the field is available, and by clicking the small down-arrow next to Pending, you can view (and select) a different status for the estimate (see Figure 6-12).

   • Expiration Date. This is an important field to fill in, since it limits the amount of time available for the prospective customer to accept the estimate.

Putting a date in the field accomplishes two things. First, it gives the client an incentive to respond in a timely fashion. Second, it ensures that you are not bound by the estimate at some distant date when your costs have risen.

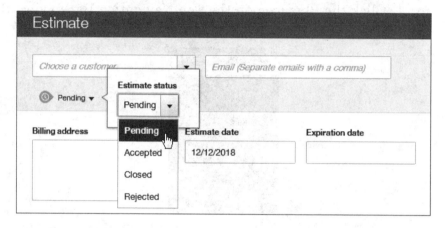

Figure 6-12: You can change the estimate's status as needed.

4. Click Save And Close to complete the process.

Creating Invoices from Estimates

When your customer accepts your estimate and you perform the work, you'll want to bill the customer for the work performed. Generating an invoice from an estimate is pretty easy in QuickBooks Online.

Open the estimate and use the Copy To Invoice button located at the top of the estimate, to the left of the invoice amount (as seen in Figure 6-13). Otherwise, you can locate the estimate in either the Sales Transactions or Customers center window and select Start Invoice from the Action drop-down list. Either way, a new Invoice form is opened and all of the information from the [Accepted] estimate is transferred. Edit the information as needed and save the invoice.

ProAdvisor CAUTION: *If you have imported your company file from a QuickBooks desktop application you may run into some strange anomalies, such as a missing Copy To Invoice button until you change the status to Accepted and save and reopen the estimate. Another weird thing I noticed with an imported company was the appearance of a Class field on estimates after I made copies of them. They appeared in Simple Start and in Essentials, even though neither version supports classes. The fields in these versions were non-functioning.*

Figure 6-13: Once the estimate status has been changed to Accepted you can convert it to an invoice.

After you convert the estimate to an Invoice, the estimate status is automatically changed to Closed.

Progress Invoicing from Estimates

Unfortunately, QuickBooks Online does not support progress invoicing. In other words, there's no way to automatically create a partial invoice from an estimate if only part of the job has been completed. However, here's a workaround that I use to implement progress invoicing. It's not ideal, but it does work in all three QuickBooks Online versions.

1. Open the estimate from which you want to create a partial invoice.

2. Click the Copy To Invoice button to transfer the data from the invoice to a new invoice form.

3. Move to the line-items and change the quantities. The example in Figure 6-14 is for a 50% billing. I've cut the quantities in half to achieve this.

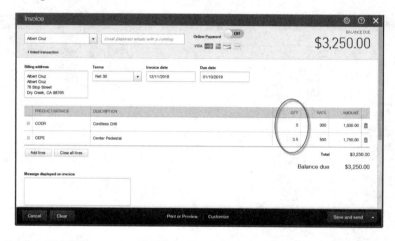

Figure 6-14: Change the quantities on the invoice to reflect the partial work done or materials delivered.

4. Click Save And Close. The invoice is saved and the original estimate reappears, with its status changed to Closed (see Figure 6-15).

5. Change the status of the estimate to Pending (click Closed and select Pending from the Estimate Status drop-down list that appears).

6. Move to the line-items and change the quantities to reflect the remaining amounts. In our example, you would cut them in half since we just invoiced the customer for 50%. However, if you had billed the customer for 25%, you would change the estimate to reflect the remaining 75%.

7. Click Save And Close to save your changes. QuickBooks Online reminds you that this transaction is linked to another (the invoice) and asks if you want to change it anyway. Answer in the affirmative.

Figure 6-15: The original estimate is intact, but the status is changed to Closed.

Now when you return to the Customer Transactions list you'll see that you have a pending estimate for the balance and an invoice for the partial charge (see Figure 6-16). When you are ready to bill the customer again, open the pending invoice and repeat the process (or invoice for the total and leave the estimate status at Closed).

DATE	TYPE	NO.	CUSTOMER	METHOD	DUE DATE	BALANCE	TOTAL	STATUS	ACTION
12/11/2018	Estimate	1005	Albert Cruz		12/11/2018	$0.00	$3,250.00	Pending	Start invoice
12/11/2018	Invoice	1004	Albert Cruz		01/10/2019	$3,250.00	$3,250.00	Open	Receive payment

Figure 6-16: Our progress invoicing workaround leaves you with a new invoice and a pending estimate for the balance due.

Generate Credits and Refunds

Every business has to deal with customer returns, overcharges, and an occasional complaint that results in the customer being issued a credit or a refund. The difference is simply whether or not you hold onto the amount and apply to existing or future invoices (credit memo), or if you hand the money directly back to the customer (refund).

Credit Memos

When it comes to credit memos, Simple Start users have but a single option, while Essentials and Plus users have two choices. All versions of QuickBooks Online support basic credit memos, which are automatically applied to existing (or newly created) invoices. Only Essential and Plus utilize delayed credits, which can be retained and applied at a future date.

ProAdvisor TIP: *You can change the default setting for automatically applying credits. Choose Tools Menu (gear icon) | Settings Company to open the Settings window. Click the advanced section on the left and the Automation section on the right. Click the Automatically Apply Credits and deselect the option.*

Credit memos work the same in all three versions of QuickBooks Online. When you create a credit memo QuickBooks Online looks for open invoices for the customer. If it finds one or more, it automatically applies the credit memo to the earliest open invoice and keeps moving (date-wise) until it's all used up. For example, let's say you have two open invoices, one for $200 and another for $800. Now you create a credit memo for $500. If the earlier invoice is $200, QuickBooks Online will pay it off and apply $300 to the $800 invoice, leaving a balance of $500. If the larger invoice is the earlier, QuickBooks Online will pay off $500, leaving a balance of $300, and the $200 invoice untouched.

Basic Credit Memos

When you create a credit memo in QuickBooks Online, the program looks for open invoices for the customer. If it finds any, it automatically applies the credit to one or more invoices, depending on the dates and the amounts. Credit memos are automatically applied to existing open invoices for the customer. If no open invoices exist, the credit is retained until an invoice is created, at which time it is applied automatically.

If you have sub-customers, the scenario changes somewhat, depending on the sub-customer settings.

- Sub-customer with "Bill With Parent" option selected. A credit memo created for the parent customer will also be applied to sub-customers with the Bill With Parent option selected until the credit is used up. If a credit balance remains, it will be applied to newly created invoices for the parent or sub-customer with the Bill With Parent option enabled. A credit memo created for this sub-customer will apply only to this sub-customer, not to the parent.
- Sub-customer with "Bill This Customer" option selected. The only credit memos that will be applied to this type of sub-customer are those created specifically for this sub-customer.

ProAdvisor NOTE: *I noticed that sometimes a credit memo balance would not be applied to new invoices immediately, but at a later time after another invoice was created. This may a bug, a design flaw, or yours truly having senior moment. Keep your eyes peeled.*

Creating Credit Memos is a straightforward process.

1. Click the Plus icon on the Top Navigation Bar and select Customers | Credit Memo. If you don't see Credit Memo,

click the Show More link. A blank Credit Memo form opens (see Figure 6-17).

2. From the Choose A Customer drop-down list select the appropriate customer.

3. Change the Credit Memo Date as needed.

4. Move to the line-items and enter the item(s) for which the credit is being given.

5. If you need more lines click the Add Lines button.

6. Enter a message, memo, and/or attachment (optional).

7. Click Save And Close to complete the process.

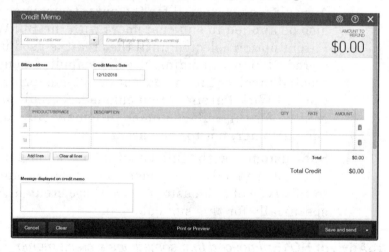

Figure 6-17: Credit memos are available in all three QuickBooks Online versions.

Delayed Credits

Delayed credits, which are really retained credits, can only be created in Essentials and Plus versions. Delayed credits are stored for future use even if the customer has currently outstanding invoices. The nice thing about delayed credits is that you – not QuickBooks Online – decide when and where to apply the credit.

Creating a delayed credit is easy. As a matter of fact, the process is almost exactly the same as creating a regular credit memo described in the previous section. Of course, you have to select Delayed Credit instead of Credit Memo. The only physical differences are the form name, "Delayed Credit", and the inability to send the form to the customer.

This makes sense, since the form is retained on the customer's account until you decide to apply it. Therefore, sending it at this point would serve no purpose.

Actually, there is another difference. Unlike the regular credit memo, you can make a delayed credit a recurring transaction. See the section entitled "Use the Recurring Transactions List" in Chapter 4 for detailed instructions.

Create Customer Statements

If you invoice your customers, statements are a great way to ensure that both you and your customers agree on the state of their accounts. It's also a nice way to remind them that they have balances due in case it may have slipped their minds. All three versions of the QuickBooks Online support customer statements.

ProAdvisor TIP: *The first time you create customer statements, you might want to check each customer's current balance to ensure it's accurate. The easiest way to do this is to run a Customer Balance Summary Report by selecting Reports | All Reports | Manage Accounts Receivable | Customer Balance Summary.*

To create a customer statement follow these steps:

1. From the Top Navigation Bar click the Plus icon to open the Quick Create menu.

2. Now, select Other | Statement to display the statement criteria dialog box seen in Figure 6-18.

Figure 6-18: Choose the statement type and criteria to generate customer statements.

3. Choose one of the three statement types.

- Balance Forward. Use this statement type to provide the customer with a listing that includes the balance forward (open balance from previous period), along with all activity between the statement dates you set. It shows the original amount and the current balance of each transaction. This is the statement you generally send when your customer has a balance that needs to be paid. It includes an Amount Due and an Enclosed field in the header section, along with a dotted (cut along this) line, and a message to detach and send the header portion. Along the bottom it contains an aging table showing amounts past due, and the days they are in arrears.

- Open Item. If you want to give your customer a listing of open transactions, this should be your choice. It does not include a balance forward, simply a list of invoices and credit memos with an open balance. It shows each transaction with the original amount and the amount received (invoice) or used (credit).

- Transaction Statement. For those customers that need a complete listing of transactions for the period, use the Transaction Statement. It lists all invoices and credits regardless of their "open" status. Like the Open Item Statement, it displays each transaction with the original amount and the amount applied (invoice) or used (credit). No balance forward is included.

4. Choose the statement date(s) from the Set Statement Dates section. For Balance Forward and Transaction Statement types you can enter a statement date as well as a date range for included transactions. For an Open Item type, you can set a statement date only, since all open transactions are included regardless of date.

5. Set the optional criteria in step three.

- Balance Forward. You can choose to filter customers for whom statements are generated by setting a customer balance greater than a certain number. You can also select only customers that do not have a current statement dated the same as the statement you are working on.

- Open Item. Here you have the same two choices offered on the Balance Forward statement type, plus one additional option; you can filter customers based on the number of past due invoices they have.

- Transaction Statement. For this statement type there are no additional criteria to set.

6. If you're sure that you want to send statements to the customers based on the options you've set in the above steps, check the Create And Send Statements Now Without Showing Me The List Of Customers option.

7. Click OK.

What happens next depends on your action in the previous steps. If you select the Send Statements Now option, the Statements Created window shown in Figure 6-19 appears. If you want a hard copy of the statements, click the Print Statement button to open the Print Invoices And Other Sales Forms windows where you can set the print options and statements to print.

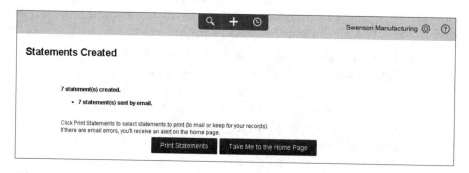

Figure 6-19: Either print a hard copy or return to the Home Page.

If you did not select the option to send statements now, the Statements window opens (see Figure 6-20). Here you select/deselect customers to receive statements, preview the statements, and/or edit the e-mail addresses. You can also change the statement criteria. When you're done, click the Create/Send Selected Statements to generate the statement(s).

When the Sending Forms By E-mail dialog box opens, check the appropriate options and click Finish to send the statement(s) and display the Statements Created window (refer back to Figure 6-19).

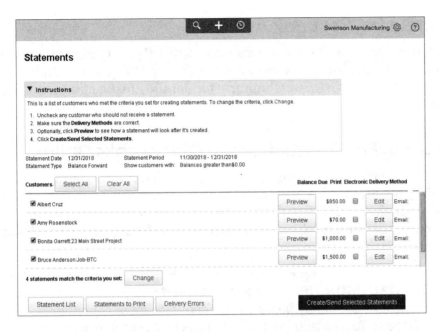

Figure 6-20: It's always a good idea to review the statements before sending them.

Integrating PayPal into QuickBooks Online

If you want to integrate your PayPal account into QuickBooks Online you must first understand the process involved. At the time of this writing there is no automatic integration. Therefore, incorporating PayPal into QuickBooks Online requires several steps.

- Set up PayPal as a QuickBooks Online bank account.
- Enter PayPal transactions in QuickBooks Online as Sales Receipts or Invoices.
- Download and match PayPal transactions in the PayPal bank account.
- Transfer money from the PayPal bank account to your operating bank account (if/when you do the same from PayPal online).

Create a PayPal Bank Account

You can create a PayPal bank account in QuickBooks Online by importing the data or by adding a new bank account to the QuickBooks Online Chart Of Accounts list. See Chapter 8 for detailed instructions on both methods.

Enter PayPal Transactions in QuickBooks Online

Entering PayPal transactions as sales receipts or invoices is the same as entering any other sales receipt or invoice, with one exception. You must account for the PayPal fee which is deducted from each transaction. If you don't, you won't be able to match the entered transactions with the downloaded transactions.

PROADVISOR TIP: *You should also add a Payment Method type for PayPal payments so you can track them separately. Choose Tools Menu (gear icon) | Lists | All Lists to display the available QuickBooks Online lists. Click the Payment Methods link to open the Payment Methods list. Click New, enter "PayPal", and click Save.*

Create a PayPal Fees Expense Account and an Item

You need a PayPal Fees item added to your Products And Services list. In addition you need an existing expense account to link it to. If you already have a Merchant Account Fees account or something similar, you can use that – or you can create a separate expense account just for PayPal fees. Either way, see the section entitled "Adding New Accounts" in Chapter 4 for more on creating accounts.

Once the expense account is created you can add the PayPal Fees item. For detailed instructions on creating new items see the section entitled "Adding Products and Services", found in Chapter 4. Just make sure the item is linked to the expense account for PayPal fees.

Tracking the PayPal Fee

There are actually two ways you can deal with the PayPal fee. Which you use depends on your needs. The easiest way to track the fee is by making it part of the QuickBooks Online transaction, using the PayPal Fee item. Unfortunately, this means that both the original amount of the sale and the fee appear on the customer's transaction form. Many users prefer to send an invoice or sales receipt that displays only the amount of the sale, with no indication of the PayPal fee. To do this requires adding the fee when the money is deposited.

Record the Fee with the Sales Transaction

If you don't send the customer a copy of the QuickBooks Online sales transaction you can simply deduct the fee right on the sales transaction form. This is ideal if you send the PayPal form to the customer, and only use QuickBooks Online to track the sale. Enter all of the line-items that comprise the sale. On the final line use the PayPal Fees item and enter the fee amount as a negative. The total sale amount is recorded as income (using the income account(s) associated with products/services included in the sales transaction), and the fee is added to the expense account associated with the fee item. The accounting is accurate.

For example, if you sell a widget for $50 and a gadget for $50 and your PayPal fee is $3.50 here's what you do:

1. Open the sales transaction form (either a sales receipt or an invoice).
2. Choose the PayPal bank account from the Deposit To drop-down list.
3. Enter the widget on the first line and the gadget on the second line.
4. Move to the third line and choose your PayPal Fee item from the Product/Service drop-down list.
5. Move to the Amount field and enter the PayPal fee as a negative number.

6. Click Save And Close, and you're done.

Your transaction should look something like the form shown in Figure 6-21. If you use this method, you can then download and match transactions directly from your PayPal account with ease since the fee has already been subtracted.

Figure 6-21: Enter the PayPal fee as a negative number.

Record the Fee with the Deposit

If you want the full amount of the transaction to show on the sales transaction form you create, you can ignore the PayPal fee until you make the deposit. The trick to this method is using the Undeposited Funds account in the transaction form rather than the PayPal bank account.

Let's use the widget and gadget example from the previous section to illustrate this method. Enter the sales information as indicated in the earlier example, and leave out the PayPal Fee item. Then, from the Deposit To drop-down list, select the Undeposited Funds account instead of the PayPal bank account.

For an invoice, just enter the sales info as you would on any other invoice, and ignore the PayPal fee. If you use an invoice instead of a sales receipt, the payment received must be deposited into the Undeposited Funds account (select Undeposited Funds from the Deposit To drop-down list in the Receive Payment form).

The next step is to create a deposit to the PayPal bank account using the Deposit form:

1. Choose Quick Create (Plus icon) | Other | Bank Deposit to open the Deposit form.

2. Select the PayPal bank account from the Choose An Account drop-down list.

3. In the Select Existing Payments section choose the correct transaction.

4. Move to the first line of the Add New Deposits section.

5. Skip to the Account field and choose the PayPal Fees expense account from the drop-down list.

6. Tab to the Amount field and enter the PayPal fee as a negative number.

7. Click Save And Close to record the deposit.

When you download your PayPal transactions into the QuickBooks Online PayPal bank account you'll be able to easily match the deposit to the original PayPal transaction.

Moving the Money into Your Operating Account

As you move money from your online PayPal account into your regular bank account you'll have to do the same in QuickBooks Online. It's a simple matter of making a transfer.

1. Choose Quick Create (Plus icon) | Other | Transfer to open the Transfer screen.

2. From the Transfer Funds From drop-down list select the PayPal bank account.

3. Select the operating account from the Transfer Funds To drop-down list.

4. Enter the amount you're moving from PayPal into your regular bank account in the Transfer Amount field.

5. Enter the date the actual transfer took place.

6. Optionally, enter a memo.

7. Click Save And Close to record the transfer.

Now, both accounts should be accurate.

Recording a PayPal Refund

Refunds are just another fact of business life and have to be dealt with on occasion. When they're PayPal refunds they require a little more work, but are not all that difficult to handle. The procedure is comprised of three steps:

- Create a credit memo
- Create a journal entry
- Download and match the PayPal refund transactions

The credit memo is just an ordinary credit memo issued to the customer for the full amount of the sale. Only the sale information should be included in the memo, regardless of how the original sale was made. Do not include the PayPal fee in the credit memo, as this will be handled later on. See the section earlier in this chapter, entitled "Generate Credits and Refunds" for detailed instructions.

The credit memo credits your Accounts Receivable account with the refund amount. Since the refund was already given to the customer via PayPal, you have to clear the amount from the Accounts Receivable account. This is done with a journal entry:

1. Choose Quick Create (Plus icon) | Other |Journal Entry to open a blank Journal Entry form.

2. Move to the first line and select the Accounts Receivable account from the Account drop-down list.

3. Enter the refund amount in the Debits column, and select the customer from the Name drop-down list (you

have to have a customer name when using the Accounts Receivable account in a journal entry).

4. Move to the next line and select the PayPal bank account from the Account drop-down list. QuickBooks Online automatically inserts the refund total in the Credits column.

5. Change the Credits amount to the amount of the PayPal fee and enter a memo indicating this entry is for the fee.

6. Enter the customer name in the Name field.

7. Move to the third line and enter the PayPal bank account in the Account field. QuickBooks Online automatically inserts the refund amount, minus the previous line's amount, into the Credits column. Leave it, and enter the customer name in the Name field.

8. Click Save And Close to record the journal entry, which should look something like the one in Figure 6-22.

Figure 6-22: This journal entry cleans out the Accounts Receivable account.

You're almost done. There's only one thing left to do – download and match the PayPal transactions.

1. On the Left Navigation Bar select Transactions | Banking to open the Bank And Credit Cards Screen.

2. Make sure the PayPal bank account is the active account.

3. Click the Update button to download recent transactions from PayPal online. You'll see two transactions for the refund – one for the fee and one for the total minus the fee (see Figure 6-23). Together they should equal the total amount of the refund (and the credit memo you created).

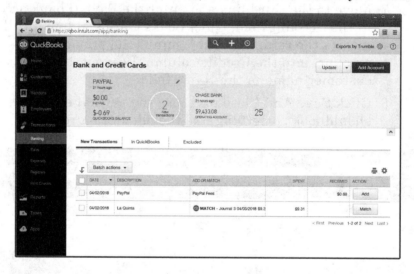

Figure 6-23: PayPal transactions can be matched and added like other downloaded transactions.

4. Click the fee transaction listing to display additional fields and choose PayPal Fees (or whatever you named them) from the Category field.

5. Click Add to record the transaction in QuickBooks Online.

6. You'll see that the transaction for the remainder of the refund has been matched to the journal entry for the

same amount. Click Match to add this transaction to QuickBooks Online.

Now, you're done. The customer's account, the Accounts Receivable account, and your PayPal bank account are all in sync and are accurate.

Customizing Customer Transaction Forms

Since not all QuickBooks Online users have the same needs, it's nice to know that customer transaction forms can be modified to suit your particular requirements. However, before going any further we need to clarify that the customizing forms options have changed in the recent QuickBooks Online update.

Unfortunately, the change is to fewer options rather than more. Since everyone will eventually be updated to the newest version, we are not going to cover the earlier options. Suffice it to say that you still have the older incarnation of QuickBooks Online if you see a Customize Forms link in the Form Delivery section of the Company Settings (Tools Menu (gear icon) | Company Settings).

ProAdvisor NOTE: *Only invoices, estimates, sales receipts, and statements can be customized, and not all to the same extent. Also, changes made to one form type apply to all (where possible) customizable form types. For example, if you add a footer to the invoice form, the same footer text will appear on estimates, sales receipts, and statements.*

There are two ways to customize sales transaction forms. You can choose Tools Menu (gear icon) | Settings | Company Settings to open the Settings window. Then click the Advanced section on the left and the Customize Look And Feel button in the Customize section on the right. The second option is to customize the forms directly from within a form, which is what we're going to do here. For this exercise we'll use an invoice form.

1. From the Quick Create menu (Plus icon), select Invoice to open a blank form.

2. Click the Customize Form button found at the bottom of the form. This opens the Add Personality To Your Forms window shown in Figure 6-24. As you can see, it contains four tabs – Style, Header, Columns, and Footer, each of which contains options for the related section of the form.

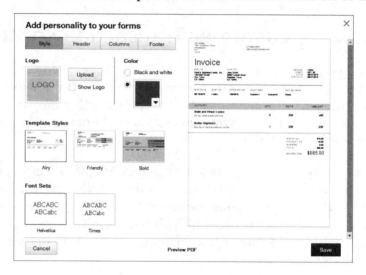

Figure 6-24: You can customize all sections of the transaction form.

3. Move to each tab and set the options as desired. For the most part, the available options are self-explanatory. However, there are a few things that may need a little more clarification.

- Style. The options here are straightforward. You can add your logo, change the form template, color, and the fonts used on the form. The changes here apply to invoices, estimates, and sales receipts, but not to statements.

- Header. Check the field to include it in the header of the form. The first four fields can be modified by clicking the pencil icon that appears when you move your cursor to the right of the field name. All changes made here are saved and used as the defaults for these forms in the future. One

more thing. Essentials and Plus users who have
turned on Custom Fields will see their custom
fields listed, and may select or deselect them. If
you want to change the form name that appears
in the header section, modify the names in the
Form Names section. You can also turn on custom
transaction numbers by checking the option at
the bottom of the window.

- Columns. The only thing of interest here is
  the fact that changes made to the Description,
  Date, and Amount field names are applied to
  statements as well as the other forms. Actually,
  there's one more thing. If you check the Account
  Summary option, a short summary of the
  customer's account is inserted into the Invoice
  (see Figure 6-25).

Figure 6-25: Adding an account summary to your invoices kills two birds
        with one stone.

- Footer. The Message To Customer On Invoices field is duplicated for invoices, sales receipts, and estimates. If you prefer to use a different customer message on estimates, go to Company Settings, click the Sales section on the left and the Messages section on the right. Move down to the Default Message Shown On Sales Forms and choose Estimate from the Sales Form drop-down list. Enter the message in the text box below the drop-down list.

4. When you've made your changes, click Save to store them and return to the form you were working on.

The changes are applied to all forms that are printed or sent after the customizations are made. This applies to existing forms as well.

CHAPTER 7:

Managing Vendors & Expenses

- QBO Version Differences
- Setting Vendor-Related Preferences
- Navigating the Vendors Center
- Creating Vendors
- Managing Expenses and Bills
- Understanding Accounts Payable (A/P)

All businesses rely, to some extent, on vendors. Some businesses have more vendors than customers. A large manufacturer may purchase parts, services, and supplies from a wide array of vendors, while a single consultant may only purchase office supplies and utilities from a handful of suppliers. Whichever category you fall into (or something between), you'll need to familiarize yourself with the QuickBooks Online tools for handling vendors and tracking expenses.

QuickBooks Online Version Differences

Before exploring the Vendors center let's briefly go over the vendor tracking differences found in the three QuickBooks Online versions.

- Simple Start. With Simple Start you can track your vendors and your expenses. What is missing, however, is the ability to record and track bills, purchase orders, and vendor credits.
- Essentials. The ability to track bills and vendor credits is added, but purchase orders are still lacking.
- Plus. If you need real accounts payable functions, Plus is your best choice. It provides tracking for vendors, expenses, bills, vendor credits, and purchase orders.

There are additional differences that will be covered, where appropriate, in the following sections of this chapter.

Setting Vendor-Related Preferences

This is one area where the differences in the three QuickBooks Online versions come quickly into view. To access the vendor-related options, select Tools Menu (gear icon) | Settings | Company Settings to display the Settings window seen in Figure 7-1. You'll find vendor-related preferences in two different areas of the Settings window.

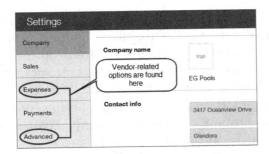

Figure 7-1: Only Essentials and Plus users have options in the Expenses section.

Advanced Settings

The Advanced section of the Settings window offers several preferences for vendors and vendor-related transactions. You'll find one in the Automation section, and the others in the Miscellaneous section. If you're a Plus subscriber you may also have a vendor-related option in the Chart Of Accounts section (see Figure 7-2).

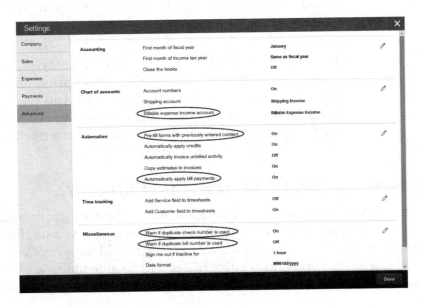

Figure 7-2: Advanced section vendor options available to a Plus user.

- Pre-Fill Forms With Previously Entered Content (All versions). This option, which is found in the Automation section, is a great option if your vendor (or customer, or employee) transaction forms are always the same or similar. When this option is enabled, filling out a transaction form for the vendor (customer, employee) is easy because QuickBooks Online automatically carries over most of the information from the last transaction form saved for the same vendor.

- Warn If Duplicate Check Number Is Used (All versions). This is a good option to keep checked at all times. It tells QuickBooks Online to warn you when you attempt to assign a check number that has already been used. The preference is located in the Miscellaneous section.

- Warn If Duplicate Bill Number Is Used (Essentials & Plus only). This is the same concept as the previous option, however, applied to bills rather than checks. This option is also located in the Miscellaneous section.

- Billable Expense Income Account (Plus only). Located in the Chart Of Accounts section, this option only appears if the Track Billable Expenses And Items As Income setting is enabled in the Expenses section. It lets you choose which income account to use for billable expenses treated as income.

Expenses Settings (Essentials and Plus only)

If you're a Simple Start subscriber and you access the Expenses section of the Settings window, QuickBooks Online simply suggests you upgrade if you need access to these settings. Essentials users will have access to one Bills And Expenses option. Plus subscribers will be able to use all Bills And Expenses settings, as well as Purchase Orders options (see Figure 7-3).

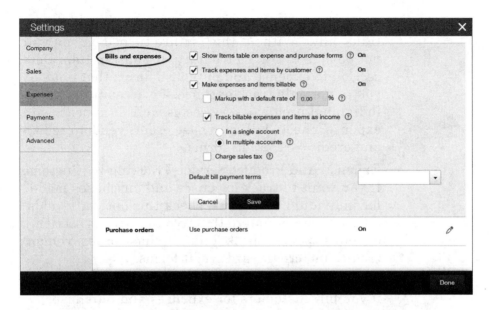

Figure 7-3: Plus subscribers will see all these options, while Essentials users only one (Default Bill Payment Terms), and Simple Start users, none.

Bills And Expenses

While Simple Start users have expenses, they do not have access to the bills features. Although this section is labeled Bills And Expenses, it really only pertains to bills (which of course, are also expenses). Here's what Essentials and Plus subscribers will find.

- Default Bill Payment Terms (Essentials & Plus only). The drop-down list in this option contains all of the terms in the QuickBooks Online Terms list (both preconfigured terms and custom terms you've created). Select one to apply to new Bill transaction forms that you create. However, note that if a vendor with its own default terms is selected in a transaction, those terms will override the selection you make here.

- Show Items Table On Expense And Purchase Forms (Plus only). Without this feature turned on you will not be able to track inventory. It adds an Item Details section to expense and purchase forms that enable you to not only track expenses by account, but by individual products/services as well. It appears on expense, check, bill, purchase order, vendor credit, and credit card credit forms.

- Expense And Product/Service Tracking By Customer. If you want to track expenses and purchases made for individual customers, check this option. It adds a Customer column to the Account Details section of your expense, check, bill, purchase order, vendor credit, and credit card credit forms.

- Make Expenses And Items Billable. Check this option if you bill customers for expenses and purchases. When enabled, this option automatically adds those billable expenses to the customer's next invoice. It also inserts a Billable column in the Account Details section of expense, check, bill, vendor credit, and credit card credit transaction forms. When checked, the following options appear as well:

  o Markup Rate. This is a handy option that lets you create automatic markups on billable expenses. Perhaps you add a 10% "handling charge" on all items you purchase for a customer job. Use this option to automate the process. Check the I Mark Up And The Rate Varies. The Default Rate Is option. Then enter the percentage by which to mark up all billable items. As soon as you check the option, another option appears – Markup Income Account. Select the correct income account to which you want the markups posted. A Markup % column is added to the Account Details section of expense, check, bill, vendor credit, and credit card credit forms.

o   Track Billable Expenses And Items As Income. Here, you have three choices. Use a single income account (the Billable Expenses Income account created automatically), use multiple accounts, or don't bother to track the billable expenses income at all (deselect the Track Billable Expenses And Items As Income option). When you choose the In Multiple Accounts setting, you can use multiple income accounts. Enabling this option adds a Use For Billable Expenses option, plus an Income Account drop-down list, to your expense accounts in the Chart Of Accounts. That way you can add different income accounts for different expenses.

o   Charge Sales Tax. If you have sales tax turned on in your company file, this option adds a Tax column to the Account Details section of the expense, check, bill, vendor credit, and credit card credit forms. You can decide which billable expenses are taxed and which are not.

Purchase Orders (Plus only)

Plus subscribers also have access to the purchase order feature, which is a big help when it comes to tracking inventory. As a matter of fact, some suppliers require purchase orders. Purchase orders are not posted to any accounts, and therefore have no effect on your financial numbers. See Chapter 10 for more on purchase orders.

To get the most out of purchase orders you should set the purchase order options available in QuickBooks Online Plus (see Figure 7-4).

Figure 7-4: You can add some nice customizations to purchase orders.

The first thing you have to do is turn purchase orders on. Check the Use Purchase Orders option to enable purchase orders. When the option is deselected, all access to purchase orders is removed. That includes access from both the Quick Create (Plus icon) menu and the Action menus in the Vendors center. When the setting is enabled, the following additional settings appear:

- Custom Fields. This option affords you three custom fields that appear only on the purchase order transaction form.

- Custom Transaction Numbers. This setting allows you to design your own numbering system that applies to purchase orders only.

- Default Message On Purchase Orders. Enter the message text you want to automatically appear on all purchase orders. You can, of course, modify it as you wish on each purchase order you create.

Navigating the Vendors Center

Like all QuickBooks Online centers, the Vendors center offers one-stop shopping for related activities. As you can see in Figure 7-5, the Vendors center is very similar to the Customers center. Let's begin by taking a look at what the Vendors center has to offer.

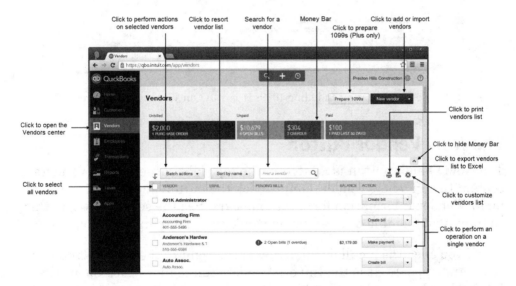

Figure 7-5: The Vendors center provides access to vendor-related activities.

The Prepare 1099s Button (Plus only)

Only QuickBooks Online Plus offers the ability to prepare 1099s for your subcontractors. Clicking the Prepare 1099s button opens the

1099 wizard seen in Figure 7-6. Using the wizard, you can select the eligible vendors, assign accounts, preview the data, and file electronically.

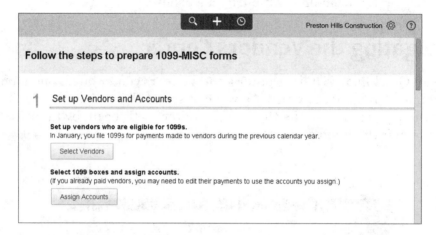

Figure 7-6: Preparing and filing 1099s is easy in QuickBooks Online Plus.

The New Vendor Button

The New Vendor button is located in the top right corner of the Vendors center. To add a new vendor, simply click the button and fill out the blank Vendor Information form that appears. See the section later in this chapter about adding and removing vendors for more information.

If you click the small down-arrow to the right of the button, another command appears. It is the Import Vendors command, which opens the Import Vendors window. See Appendix B for detailed information on importing vendors.

The Money Bar

The multicolored, horizontal bar at the top of the Vendors center is called the Money Bar. If you look closely you can see that it contains totals for a variety of vendor-related transactions. Keep in mind that purchase orders are only available in QuickBooks Online Plus. Therefore, users running Simple Start or Essentials will only see a Money Bar with three sections.

- Open Purchase Orders (Plus only). Here you'll see the total number and total amount of any outstanding purchase orders which have not yet been converted to invoices. Click this section of the bar to see a listing of the vendors with open purchase orders. Click the link in the Open Purchase Orders column to see the purchase order(s) for that vendor.

- Open Bills. This one's pretty self-explanatory – number and total amount of all open bills. Although this section appears in QuickBooks Online Simple Start, it holds no information since Simple Start does not support vendor bills.

- Overdue Bills. Another straightforward section. Total number and amount of all bills past their due dates. The same applies here; Simple Start does not support vendor bills, so there will be no useful information here.

- Paid Last 30 Days. This section displays the total number and amount for all expenses and bills paid within the last 30 days. For Simple Start users, this is the only section of the Money Bar that will provide useful information since it displays expenses activity as well as bills activity.

Click a section of the bar to see a listing of the related transactions. If you want to hide the Money Bar, click the small tab with the up-arrow at the bottom right of the Money Bar.

Vendors List Toolbar

This is the row of buttons and icons above the Vendor list (see Figure 7-7).

Figure 7-7: This toolbar provides almost everything you need to work in the Vendors list.

The elements found on the toolbar enable you to perform a number of actions on the Vendors list:

- **Batch Actions.** Click this button to see a drop-down menu of commands that can be performed on one or more vendors in the list. To use any of the commands you must first select the vendor(s) to be affected, by checking the box to the left of the each vendor's name. To select all vendors, check the box in the header section (to the left of Vendor). The available batch actions include:

    - **Email.** Send an e-mail, using your default e-mail application, to all of the selected vendors. This option is not available for vendors without e-mail address in their vendor records.

- **Sort By Name.** Click this button to display several choices for changing the sort order of the Vendors list.

- **Find A Vendor.** Enter a vendor name in the text box to filter out all of the other records. Note that only the name in the Display Name As field in the vendor record is searched. Let's take this example. The company name is Apex Communications, the contact name is Art Johnston, and Apex Communications is in the Display Name As field. A search for Art or Johnston will display no results. However Apex or Communications will locate the vendor.

- **Print Icon.** Click this icon to print the complete Vendors list. You don't have to select any vendors before clicking the icon. The list appears in your browsers print preview window so you can review it before printing.

- **Export Icon.** Click this icon to export the Vendors list to an Excel spreadsheet. What happens next depends on your browser's settings. The Excel file may be automatically saved to the default download folder or a Save As dialog may open. If the Save As dialog opens, give the file a clear and descriptive name, choose a location, and click Save to store the new file on your hard disk.

- Settings (gear) Icon. Click this icon to display options for customizing the Vendors list. For example, you can add columns, set the number of rows displayed per page, and include or exclude inactive vendors.

Vendors List

The Vendors list is, of course, the core of the Vendors center. Here you'll find a listing of all of your vendors (unless you've excluded inactive vendors), with any open bills (Essentials & Plus only) and the total balance. To the right of each vendor listing is a button that provides a number of different commands for performing operations on the vendor. What you see depends on the state of open bills and your version of QuickBooks Online.

If the vendor has open invoices the available commands are:

- Make Payment
- Create Bill (Essentials & Plus only)
- Create Expense

If the vendor has no open invoices, the available commands are:

- Create Bill (Essentials & Plus only)
- Create Expense
- Write Check
- Create Purchase Order (Plus only)
- Make Inactive

Clicking a vendor name opens a transaction list for the selected vendor (see Figure 7-8). At the top of the list is basic vendor information and an Edit button to modify it. To the right is a non-interactive listing of totals for open and overdue bills. The bottom half of the screen contains the transaction listing for the vendor. This transaction listing also has a toolbar with buttons and icons that perform actions on the entire list or on individual transactions.

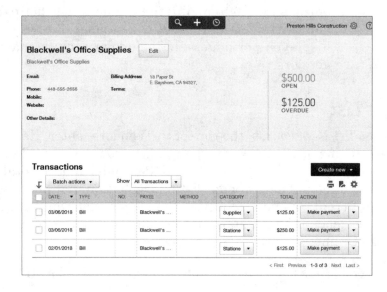

Figure 7-8: The vendor transaction list provides a lot of information about the selected vendor.

Working with Vendors

Vendors are an integral part of your business. Accurately keeping track of vendors and expenses allows you to analyze the profitability of your business, and make decisions to help reduce costs and boost profits.

Create New Vendors

Some vendors stay with you for a long time. Others come and go. Even if you import your initial list of vendors, the time will come when you need to add a new vendor. The process is quite simple.

New Vendor

If you're only adding a single vendor, you'll probably opt for the New Vendor button. Even adding a handful is probably not worth going through the import process. Here's how you add a new vendor using the New Vendor button:

1. Click the Vendors link on the Left Navigation Bar to open the Vendors center.

2. Click the New Vendor button at the top right portion of the screen to open a blank Vendor Information dialog box as seen in Figure 7-9.

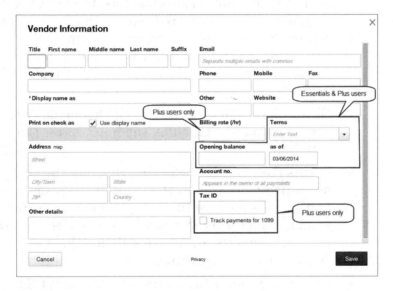

Figure 7-9: The QuickBooks Online Vendor Information form available to Plus users is more complex than the others.

3. Fill out the vendor information you want to retain for this vendor. Most of the fields are self-explanatory, so we won't cover those. However, there are some that require a little more explanation. Those we'll cover here.

- Display Name As. This drop-down list offers up to four alternative name formats for displaying in the Vendors center and reports. The first is the company name, if you enter one (Compton Manufacturing). The second is the contact name exactly as entered in the name boxes. For example, if you enter Dr. Paul J. Compton Sr., that's what your second option is. The third option is simply the first and last name (Paul Compton). The fourth option is first and last names, but with the last name first (Compton, Paul).

- **Print On Check As.** This gives you the opportunity to use a familiar and less formal name for the Vendors center and reports, but a full, legal name for using on checks. Paul J Compton might be known to everyone in your organization as Johnny Compton, so you could use Johnny Compton as the vendor or company name and enter Paul J. Compton in the Print On Check As name. To use the display name as the payee on the check, click the Use Display Name option.

- **Billing Rate (/hr) (Plus only).** If the vendor provides services that are billed by the hour, enter the hourly rate here.

- **Terms (Essentials & Plus only).** Click the small down-arrow located to the right of the drop-down list and select Add New to create terms for this (or any) vendor. The terms selected in this list become the default terms for all future bills for this vendor unless you modify the individual bill.

- **Opening Balance (Essentials & Plus only).** Another of those QuickBooks Online fields that you should ignore. It's always better to enter historical transactions to create the opening balance whenever possible.

- **Tax ID (Plus only).** You'll only find this field in QuickBooks Online Plus, for the simple reason that only Plus supports 1099 preparation and filing. To provide a vendor with a 1099 form you must have the vendor's Tax ID number (either a social security or EIN number).

- Track Payments For 1099 (Plus only). Check this option if you want QuickBooks Online to track this vendor for 1099 filing.

Once you've entered all of the information you require, click Save to add the new vendor to QuickBooks Online.

To edit a vendor, open the vendor Transactions list and click the Edit button that appears to the right of the vendor name. This opens the Vendor Information dialog. Make the necessary changes. You cannot delete vendors with activity, but you can make them inactive (hide them). To do so, open the Vendor Information dialog and click the Make Inactive button at the bottom of the dialog box.

Managing Expenses and Bills

Before going any further, it's important to understand the differences between the QuickBooks Online versions when it comes to dealing with expenses and bills. There are significant differences that affect what you will see and what you will be able to track.

The biggest difference is that only Plus offers inventory tracking. Both Simple Start and Essentials let you track your expenses (i.e., utilities, insurance, shipping, etc). The expense form found in all three QuickBooks Online versions provides an Account Details area where you can record individual expenses along with their associated expense accounts. The same goes for bill transaction forms found in Essentials and Plus.

However, in Plus only, both expense and bill forms contain an additional section called Item Details. It is here that you can record individual Products/Services items. This means that you can track inventory products purchased for resale and services that you subcontract.

Track Expenses

As mentioned above, all three versions of QuickBooks Online offer an expense form that you can use to track your business expenses. Filling it out is a simple task as long as you have your chart of accounts set up properly.

ProAdvisor NOTE: *The extra columns seen in the QuickBooks Online Plus expense form (Figure 7-11) are available when the Bills And Expenses options are enabled. Plus users will find them in the Expenses section of the Settings window (Tools Menu (gear icon) | Settings | Company Settings).*

---

1. From the Top Navigation Bar select Quick Create (Plus icon) | Vendors | Expense to open a blank Expense form (see Figures 7-10 and 7-11).

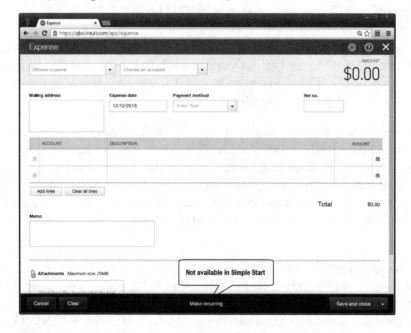

Figure 7-10: This is the expense form that QuickBooks Online Simple Start and Essentials users will see.

2. Select a vendor from the Choose A Payee drop-down list.
3. If you have multiple bank accounts, make the appropriate selection from the Choose An Account drop-down list.

Figure 7-11: An expense form with all the trimmings from QuickBooks
Online Plus.

4. Modify the Expense Date, Payment Method, and Ref No.
   fields as needed.

5. Move to the Account Details Section.

6. From the Account field choose the expense account for the
   first line-item expense.

7. Enter a description to clarify the details of the expense.

8. Enter the amount of the expense.

9. Continue adding expense items. If you need more lines
   click the Add Lines button.

10. Enter a Memo and add an attachment if so desired.

11. Click Save And Close to record the expense.

Plus users can fill in these additional fields:

   ● Billable. If you are going to bill a particular customer
     for this expense, check the Billable box. If you

uncheck the box you can still track the expense for a particular customer by selecting the customer name from the Customer drop-down list.

- Markup %. If you set a default markup percentage in the Make Expenses And Items Billable option, it appears here. You can always override the default by entering a percentage while filling in the form. The amount of the expense is increased by the percentage amount when added to the customer's invoice.

- Tax. If this is a taxable expense for which you're billing the customer, check the Tax box.

- Customer. Open the drop-down list and choose the customer to whom you want to bill, or for whom you want to track the expense.

Understand Accounts Payable (A/P)

Accounts payable is what you owe your vendors for the goods and services you purchase to run your business. If you pay for those goods and services at the time you purchase them you have no Accounts Payable. For example, Simple Start users do not have the ability to track bills. Therefore, they cannot track accounts payable in QuickBooks Online. Essentials and Plus users, on the other hand, can track accounts payable by recording vendor bills and vendor payments.

To better understand accounts payable it will help if you are familiar with the postings made in QuickBooks Online (Plus and Essentials). The first thing to remember is that accounts payable is a liability. As mentioned in Chapter 1, liabilities are, by default, credit side accounts. This means that a credit increases accounts payable, and a debit decreases accounts payable. Since expenses are debit side accounts, their postings are the opposite. In other words, a credit decreases an expense account, while a debit increases an expense account. Let's take a look (Table 7-1) at the postings for a vendor telephone bill that includes both phone and internet service.

Account	Debit	Credit
6300-Telephone	125.50	
6305-Internet	49.00	
2100-Accounts Payable		174.50

Table 7-1: Accounts Payable tracks money you owe.

One thing to keep in mind is that not all vendor bills are expenses. For example, a major equipment purchase may be posted to a fixed asset account rather than an expense account. If you send a vendor an upfront deposit on a large purchase you'll post that to a current asset account (it's still your money until you receive the item), not an expense account. When in doubt, check with your accountant.

Enter Bills (Essentials & Plus only)

When you make a purchase from a vendor and receive the bill, you must record it. Once you do, QuickBooks Online keeps track of all of the particulars – who, when, and how much.

ProAdvisor NOTE: *If you have an open purchase order for the vendor (Plus only) it will appear in the bill window so you can enter the data automatically and close it.*

To create a new bill follow these steps:

1. Click the Plus icon on the Top Navigational Bar to open the Quick Create menu.

2. Click the Show More link to expand the menu.

3. Click Vendors | Bill to open a new Bill transaction form (see Figure 7-12). If you're running QuickBooks Online Plus, your Bill transaction form will have an Item Details section, and may have more columns (refer back to Figure 7-11).

Figure 7-12: A Bill transaction form is very similar to an Expense transaction form.

4. Select a vendor from the Choose A Vendor drop-down list.

5. If need be, change the Terms, Bill Date, Due Date, and Bill No. fields.

6. Move to the first line and choose the appropriate account (usually an expense account).

7. Enter a description to help identify the item at a later time.

8. Enter the amount of the expense.

9. Continue to enter line-items until you're through. If you need more lines, click the Add Lines button.

10. Click Save And Close to record the bill.

Take a look at Table 7-2 to see the postings QuickBooks Online automatically makes for the bill we've just created (refer back to Figure 7-12).

Account	Debit	Credit
6200-Office Supplies	125.50	
6260-Freight-Shipping	13.50	
2100-Accounts Payable		139.00

Table 7-2: Double-entry bookkeeping demands that both sides balance.

Make Some Bills Recurring Bills (Essentials & Plus only)

If you have bills that recur on a regular basis, such as a rent payment to the landlord, a mortgage payment to the bank, or a retainer due to your accountant, you'll be glad to know you can track them in QuickBooks Online Essentials and Plus. Recurring bills in QuickBooks Online are similar to QuickBooks desktop memorized transactions. Once you've recorded a recurring bill, QuickBooks Online will remind you when it's time to pay it, and even fill it out for you.

1. Create the Bill following the steps outlined in the previous section.

2. Click the Make Recurring button at the bottom of the form.

3. The Template Name and Payee fields are filled out using data from the bill.

4. From the Type drop-down list choose one of the three available types:

   • Scheduled. If the bill is due the same time every month, and is for the same amount each month, this is probably your best choice. QuickBooks Online will create it on whatever schedule you set up here, and let you know when it's due.

- Reminder. If you just want to be reminded that the bill is upcoming, select Reminder. Instead of creating the bill automatically, QuickBooks Online just taps you on the shoulder when it's due.

- Unscheduled. This is handy for those bills that recur, but not on a precise schedule or for the same amount. The only thing QuickBooks Online does is save the template so you can recall it later and have it filled out for you when you need it.

5. If you selected Unscheduled in the previous step, you're done. Click Save Template to store the recurring bill for later use.

6. If you chose Scheduled or Reminder, move to the Interval section and make the appropriate selection from the Interval drop-down list.

7. Fill in the interval details, which will vary depending on the interval chosen from the list.

8. Enter a Start Date – the first date on which the next payment is due.

9. If there's an end date (i.e., loan with a finite number of payments) enter it in the End field.

10. The next field is the days in advance to create the bill or reminder (depending on your choice from the Type drop-down list). Enter the number of days required.

11. If you've set an End date for the bill, check the Alert When Range Has Ended option to have QuickBooks Online remind you that the recurring bill is about to end.

12. Click Save Template to record the recurring bill (see Figure 7-13).

Once you create a recurring bill it seems to disappear from QuickBooks Online altogether. It's not accessible from the Vendor center or from the individual vendor's transaction list. Fortunately, it can be accessed; you just have to know where to look for it. You'll find it on the Recurring Transactions list. Choose Tools Menu (gear icon) | Lists |

Recurring Transactions. Here you can highlight the transaction and use it (create a new transaction), modify it, or delete it.

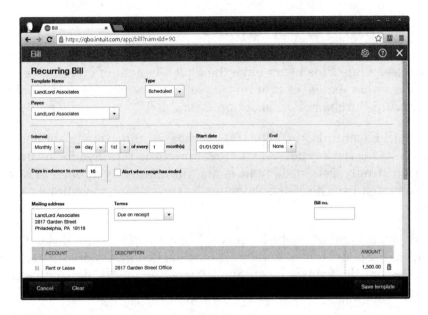

Figure 7-13: Let QuickBooks Online (Essentials and Plus) worry about creating recurring bills.

ProAdvisor NOTE: *The Recurring Transaction list is not just for recurring bills. It houses all recurring transactions, including bills, invoices, checks, estimates, and more.*

Another thing you'll find in the Recurring Transactions list is a button that opens the Reminder List. See the section entitled "Working with the Reminder List" in Chapter 4 for more information.

Add Vendor Credits and Refunds (Essentials & Plus only)

Your vendors may issue you credits and/or refunds for a variety of reasons. Common examples are the return of defective or damaged merchandise, an erroneous charge, or an item missing from an order.

How you process a vendor credit depends on your version of QuickBooks Online.

Working with Vendor Credits

The first thing to note is that vendor credits in Essentials are limited to expenses, while Plus users have the added benefit of creating vendor credits for either expenses or items (as long as the Show Items Table On Expense And Purchase Forms option is enabled).

In both Essentials and Plus, the credit is automatically applied to open bills for the vendor. Any leftover credit is retained for future use. Interestingly, retained credit is not automatically applied to new bills. You must use the Make Payment feature to apply retained credits.

To open a Vendor Credit form (see Figure 7-14) choose Quick Create (Plus icon) | Show More | Vendors | Vendor Credit. As mentioned earlier in this section, the form will contain different elements, depending on your QuickBooks Online version and the options you have enabled.

Filling out the Vendor Credit form is pretty straightforward. It's a lot like the expense form and the bill form. As with those two, there are a couple of things Plus users will have that Essentials users won't.

If you're using Essentials your only choice is to enter expenses. If you're using Plus, you can move to the Account Details section to enter expenses, or to the Item Details section to enter products/services (the Show Items Table On Expense And Purchase Forms option must be enabled to see the Item Details section).

Plus users may have additional columns in both sections, depending on the state of the Bills And Expenses options located in the Expenses section of the Settings window. See the section entitled "Setting Vendor-Related Preferences" earlier in this chapter for more information.

Handling Vendor Refunds

When a vendor gives you a refund, no vendor credit is involved. Unlike a vendor credit, a vendor refund doesn't affect the vendor's account in any way. It's not applied to the current balance, it isn't retained to apply to future balances, and it has no affect on your A/P balance.

Figure 7-14: QuickBooks Online Essentials offers a basic Vendor Credit form.

The first thing to *not* do is create a vendor credit. A vendor credit plays no part in recording a vendor refund. Simply deposit the refund into your bank account using the Deposit transaction form (Quick Create (Plus icon) | Other | Bank Deposit). Leave the Received From field blank. You can make a note of the vendor and the reason in the Description field. Enter the original expense account in the Account field. Fill out the rest of the form as needed and save it.

ProAdvisor TIP: *If you receive a refund from a prior fiscal year you may want to make the deposit to an Other Income account rather than the expense account. This will prevent the refund from distorting this year's expenses. Check with your accountant to be sure.*

Pay Bills

Eventually, those bills that you've entered into the system need to be dealt with. Fortunately, QuickBooks Online provides all of the tools you need to handle bill payments with ease. Keep in mind that Simple Start users cannot record bills in QuickBooks Online so they do not have the ability to make bill payments. For them, all bills have to be direct disbursements (writing a check). Essentials and Plus users, on the other hand, can make both bill payments and direct disbursements.

ProAdvisor TIP: *Be sure not to confuse bill payments and direct disbursements. A bill payment is a payment generated (using the Pay Bills feature) for a vendor bill that is already in the QuickBooks Online system. A direct disbursement is a payment made to a vendor for a bill that is not in the system. For example, writing a check to a delivery man standing at your door is a direct disbursement. If you write a check (rather than use the Pay Bills feature) to pay a bill already in the system you'll end up with incorrect postings that will eventually have to be tracked down and corrected by you or your accountant.*

Direct Disbursements (Writing Checks)

Users of all three versions of QuickBooks Online have the ability to create direct disbursements. If you're using Simple Start, it's the only method you have for paying bills. Whether you create a direct disbursement out of need (Simple Start users) or convenience, the process is the same. You write a check.

1. From the Top Navigation Bar choose Quick Create (Plus icon) | Vendors | Check to open the Check transaction form seen in Figure 7-15.

2. Select a vendor (or other name) from the Choose A Payee drop-down list.

3. If you have multiple bank accounts, choose the correct one from the Choose An Account drop-down list.

4. Modify the Expense Date and Check No. fields as needed.

5. Move to the first line-item and enter the expense account in the Account field.

Figure 7-15: Use the Check transaction form to make a direct disbursement.

6. Enter a note in the Description field to help you identify the transaction at a later date.

7. Enter the amount of the expense in the Amount field.

8. Repeat for all of the expenses to be paid using this check. If you need more lines click the Add Lines button.

9. Add a memo and/or an attachment as needed.

10. Click Save And Close to create the check.

ProAdvisor NOTE: *Plus users (who have the ability to track inventory) may also find an Item Details section on the check that can be used to record inventory or other products/services paid for by the check. In addition, they may have additional columns depending on their Billing And Expenses settings in the Settings window.*

Essentials and Plus users also have the added convenience of being able to create recurring checks. Both will find a Make Recurring button at the bottom of the Check transaction form.

If you refer back to Figure 7-15, you'll see that the form contains two additional buttons at the bottom.

- Print Check. If you're writing a manual check from your physical checkbook, ignore this button. However, if you want QuickBooks Online to print the check for you, this is the way to start. Clicking the Print Check button opens the Print Checks Setup window where you can choose the check type, the bank account, and other settings. You can also elect to do batch printings by recording each check and then clicking the Print Check button on the last check. At the bottom of the Print Checks Setup window is a listing of all of the recently created checks. Select all of the checks to print and click Print. If a manually written check is on the list, select it and click Remove Selected to remove it from the list.

- More. Once the check is created you can return to it and use the More button to void it. You'll also find commands to copy or delete the check, as well as commands to open the transaction journal and the audit log.

ProAdvisor TIP: *While it's tempting to delete a check (or other transaction) that you no longer need, it's rarely a good idea. You should always void a check rather than delete it to ensure that there is a record of the transaction. For one thing, it will save you a lot of time when reconciling your bank account if you don't have to wonder what happened to a missing check number.*

Using the Pay Bills Feature (Essentials & Plus only)

If you've recorded bills in QuickBooks Online you must pay them using the Pay Bills feature. Using a check to pay a bill already in the system will make a mess of your postings, which your accountant will be happy to fix (for a fee, of course).

When you're ready to pay bills here's what you do.

1. From the Top Navigation Bar choose Quick Create (Plus icon) | Vendors | Pay Bills to open the Pay Bills window seen in Figure 7-16.

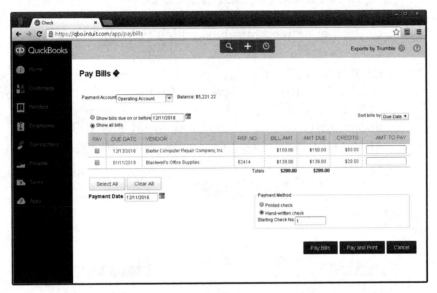

Figure 7-16: Display open bills in the Pay Bills window.

2. If you have multiple bank accounts, make the appropriate selection from the Payment Account drop-down list.

3. Either enter a Show Bills Due On Or Before date, or select Show All Bills to view the open bills.

4. Select the bills you want to pay with this check. If you have multiple bills from the same vendor you can elect to pay them with a single check by selecting them all. However, you can select them individually and pay each one separately. The choice is yours. Use the Select All and Clear All buttons to make easy work of the selection process.

5. Once you select a bill to pay, the Amt To Pay field is automatically filled in with the balance due on the bill. You can change it if you want.

6. Set the correct Payment Date. This is the date you want to appear on the check, regardless of when the check is actually printed/written.

7. Choose the appropriate Payment Method. If you select Printed Check, the Starting Check No. is changed to "To Print." If you select Hand-Written Check it's changed to the next check number, which you can change if necessary.

8. Click Pay Bills to create the bill payment and display a second Pay Bills window (see Figure 7-17). The number of bills paid is displayed and several buttons offer you the opportunity to return to the original Pay Bills window or to print the checks, or to view the Bill Payment List report.

Figure 7-17: QuickBooks Online offers a quick summary of bills paid.

If you want to print the check(s) now, click the Pay And Print button to open the Print Checks Setup window discussed in the previous section on direct disbursements.

Track Petty Cash Expenses

While the major expenses are usually taken care of with direct disbursements or bill payments, the minor and immediate expenses are frequently paid for with cash or debit cards. These are considered petty cash expenses, and keeping track of them is just as important as the other expenses.

The first thing you need to do is create a Petty Cash account of the Bank type. It doesn't matter that it's not a real bank account; it's handled in the same manner. Choose Tools Menu (gear icon) | Settings | Chart Of Accounts to open the Chart Of Accounts window. Click the New button and select Bank from the Category Type drop-down list. Choose Cash On Hand as the Detail Type, and enter Petty Cash in the Name field. Give it a number if you're using account numbers. Don't enter a Balance. We'll add that next by making a deposit.

First, create a vendor called "Cash." Next, write a check to Cash from your operating bank account and post it to the Petty Cash account you just created, by selecting the Petty Cash account from the Account drop-down list in the Account Details section. That will take care of the petty cash balance. QuickBooks Online credits (decreases) the operating bank account and debits (increases) the petty cash account.

Tracking Cash Disbursements

When you pay for expenses out of petty cash, you record them in QuickBooks Online using a check. Since you're probably not going to track every payee paid from the petty cash account, you should create a vendor named Petty Cash that you use for all petty cash expenditures.

Keep in mind that you don't have to write a check for every expense paid from petty cash. You can keep the receipts and write a check weekly or monthly, depending on the number of receipts you have.

ProAdvisor TIP: *To avoid problems with your petty cash account you should implement a strict rule that no reimbursements are made to employees (or owners) without a receipt. This will ensure that receipts are collected and stored. It's also much easier to face a tax audit when you have the receipts.*

To write the check, open the Check transaction form, select the Petty Cash vendor you created, choose the Petty Cash account from the Choose An Account drop-down list, and fill out the check for the expense. Since you'll never receive a statement from the bank, you can either use the automatic check numbers or you can enter PC or something else in the Check No. field.

Issuing Petty Cash Advances

If you're in the habit of authorizing advances from the petty cash box, you'll want to record them to ensure that the money in the petty cash account and in the petty cash box always match. The easiest way to handle this is to create a Petty Cash Advances account of the Other Current Assets type. When you give an advance from the petty cash box, have the recipient sign an IOU and then post the advance to the Petty Cash Advances account using a check from the Petty Cash bank account.

When the recipient returns with receipts (and possibly change) use a journal entry to return the advance to the petty cash account and then write a check to record the expenses. To record the journal entry, choose Quick Create (Plus icon) | Other | Journal Entry to open the Journal Entry window. Debit the Petty Cash bank account for the amount of the advance, and credit the Petty Cash Advances account for the same amount (see Figure 7-18). Now the petty cash accounts are straight, and you can put the receipts in the receipts envelope and add them to your next weekly or monthly check.

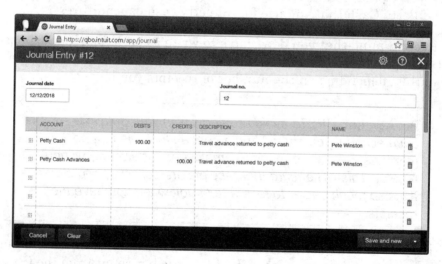

Figure 7-18: Move the money back into the petty cash account so you can write checks against it.

If you (or your accountant) prefer to make a single journal entry to take care of everything, you can include the expenses on the journal entry.

In that case, you credit (decrease) the Petty Cash Advances account and debit (increase) all of the expense accounts involved. However, if you do it this way, be sure to mark the receipts as "Entered" so you don't include them in the weekly or monthly check. One more thing. If there's money left over you'll have to account for that on the journal entry as well. In that case, the last entry should be a debit (increase) to the Petty Cash bank account for the amount of money returned to the cash box.

Replenishing the Cash

Petty cash boxes are usually in a constant state of flux, needing a periodic refill. This is done by writing another check (to Cash) from the operating bank account and posting it to the petty cash bank account.

Track Debit Cards

How you track debit card transactions depends on how you make them. If you make an ATM withdrawal, it's the same as writing a check; simply record it in QuickBooks Online as a check, posting it to the appropriate expense account. If not all of the cash is used, you'll have to record it as a cash advance and track it as petty cash.

If you use the debit card as a credit card to make purchases, record the transactions as checks without numbers (use ATM as the check number). Like any other check, the amount is posted to the proper expense account.

CHAPTER 8:

Banking with QuickBooks Online

- Creating Bank Accounts
- Entering Opening Balances
- Importing Bank Account Data
- Downloading Transactions
- Handling Bounced Checks
- Reconciling Bank Accounts

One of the most important financial tasks facing any business owner is managing the bank account(s). Unless you're still hiding your money under the mattress, the bank account is where most, if not all, of your cash is stored. QuickBooks Online banking features make the chore of maintaining and tracking bank accounts a breeze.

Creating Bank Accounts

Regardless of whether you plan to use online banking or not, the first thing you must do is create a bank account in your Chart Of Accounts window. If you don't want or need direct online access for your bank account, create the bank account in the Chart Of Accounts window and enter all of your transactions manually. If you're going to use online banking, you might as well create the bank account in your Chart Of Accounts window to save time when making the online connection. It's true that you can create a new QuickBooks Online bank account during the online setup process, but it's easier if the account is already in place in QuickBooks Online.

ProAdvisor NOTE: *Once you import one bank account, all other bank accounts (including non-online banking accounts) show up in the Bank Accounts section of the Home page.*

1. Choose Tools Menu (gear icon) | Settings | Chart Of Accounts to open the Chart Of Accounts window.
2. Click the New button to display the Account dialog (see Figure 8-1).
3. From the Category Type drop-down list choose Bank.
4. Select the bank account type from the Detail Type list.
5. Enter the account name, give it an appropriate number (if you're using account numbers), and provide a description if so desired.
6. Do not enter a balance. This should be done either by a deposit or a journal entry. See the section later in this

chapter entitled "How to Enter Opening Balances the
Right Way."

7. Click Save to create the new bank account.

Figure 8-1: Don't use the Balance field. Use a journal entry instead.

How to Enter Opening Balances the Right Way

It's very tempting to use the Balance field to record your bank account
opening balance when creating a new bank account in the Chart Of
Accounts window. However, you'll make your life easier by avoiding that
temptation.

First of all, if you're going to import your bank account data by using
online banking, the balance will be imported automatically. If you're
not going to use online banking, using the Balance field will only create
additional work for you.

The problem with all of the Balance (or Opening Balance) fields in
QuickBooks Online is the fact that they all post to an equity account
called Opening Bal Equity.

This is an account that only exists in QuickBooks products. It's
a temporary resting place for all these opening balances. However,

since they cannot stay there forever, they must be moved to the correct accounts eventually. That means that either you or your accountant (for a fee, of course) will have to create a whole bunch of journal entries and make the correct postings.

To correctly enter the opening balance for any bank accounts not online, you should use a journal entry.

1. Open the quick Create (Plus icon) menu and select Other | Journal Entry to display the Journal Entry window.

2. Enter the date of your last, reconciled statement.

3. Move to the first line of the journal entry and select the bank account from the Account drop-down list.

4. Tab to the Debits column and enter the opening balance. Remember, the opening balance will be the ending balance from the last, reconciled statement.

5. Leave the Name field blank and move to the next line.

6. From the Account drop-down list choose an equity account such as Owner's Equity or Retained Earnings. Check with your accountant, who will probably have a preference.

7. Once you enter the account, QuickBooks Online automatically fills in the same amount and the same memo from the line above (see Figure 8-2).

8. Click Save And Close to record the journal entry.

The only thing left to do is record all of the unreconciled transactions, which includes all outstanding checks, deposits, and fees. For these you can use the Check window (Quick Create (Plus icon) | Vendors | Check) and the Deposit window (Quick Create (Plus icon) | Other | Bank Deposit).

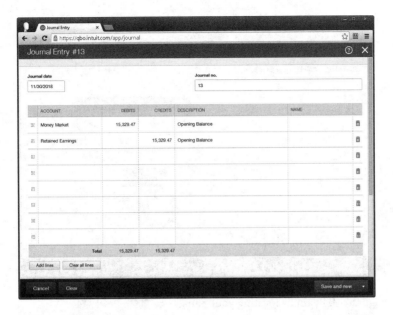

Figure 8-2: Use a journal entry to record your bank account opening
balance.

Import Bank Account Data

The most convenient way to bring transaction data into your QuickBooks
Online bank account is to use online banking and import the data directly
from your bank.

1. Click Transactions | Banking in the Left Navigation Bar
   to open the Bank And Credit Cards window, and then
   click the Add Account button. This opens the Import
   Transactions From Your Bank Or Credit Card window
   shown in Figure 8-3. You can also use the Connect Your
   Bank button on the Home page. If you've already added
   one account this way, the button disappears and a
   Connect Another Bank link appears instead.

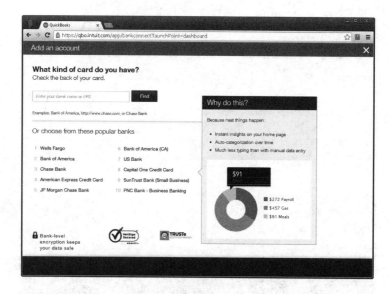

Figure 8-3: Begin by locating your bank.

2. Enter your bank name or its URL in the text box and click Find to locate it online. Select the correct name that appears to display the login screen (see Figure 8-4).

Figure 8-4: Have your User ID and password ready.

3. If you clicked one of the names in the list of "popular" banks, the login screen opens automatically.

4. Enter the required information and click Log In.

5. QuickBooks Online connects to your bank, and the Select The Accounts You Want To Connect screen seen in Figure 8-5 appears.

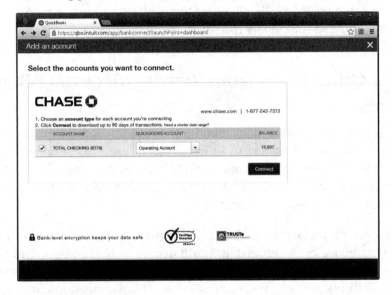

Figure 8-5: Link the online account to an existing bank account or create a new QuickBooks Online account.

6. If you have multiple accounts under the same login they're all displayed.

7. Check the account(s) you want imported into QuickBooks Online.

8. From the QuickBooks Account drop-down list choose the existing QuickBooks Online account to link to the online bank account. If the account does not already exist in QuickBooks Online, choose Add New and create a new account.

9. Click the Connect button to import the account data into QuickBooks Online.

10. Once the import is completed, QuickBooks Online displays a success screen to let you know.

11. Click the I'm Done. Let's Go! button to return to work in QuickBooks Online.

> **ProAdvisor TIP:** *You can create a PayPal bank account using this same method. Simply enter "paypal" in the search field in step 2 above and follow the online instructions.*

Prevent Other Users from Viewing/Accessing Bank Accounts

Essentials and Plus subscribers who have multiple users logging into QuickBooks Online may want to limit access to banking information. Unfortunately, the ability to limit users' rights is itself rather limited. You cannot pick and choose which areas users can access, the way you can in the QuickBooks desktop versions.

When you create users with limited rights in QuickBooks Online you have to choose between giving them access to Customers And Sales or Vendors & Purchases. Users who have Vendors & Purchases access also have banking access. You cannot refine the permissions any further. Users with Customers And Sales access only are prevented from working with checks, accounts, and bank registers.

See the section entitled "Managing Users" in Chapter 3 for more on setting user permissions.

Downloading Transactions

To use online banking with QuickBooks Online you have two choices. You can either connect your account directly to your online banking account and download transactions, or you can upload a Web Connect file to QuickBooks Online.

Update Account Information

If your QuickBooks Online bank account is connected to your bank (called Direct Connect in QuickBooks desktop applications) you can download transactions directly into QuickBooks Online.

1. Select Transactions | Banking from the Left Navigation Bar to open the Bank And Credit Cards window.

2. Click the Update button located in the upper right portion of the window. This opens the Update Your Accounts dialog (see Figure 8-6).

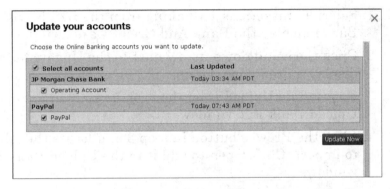

Figure 8-6: You can update as many of your connected accounts as desired.

3. Select the accounts you want to update. By default, all accounts are selected. Deselect those accounts you do not wish to update.

4. Click the Update Now button to begin the download. When the update is finished, the dialog box indicates the number of transactions downloaded and the current bank balance.

5. Close the dialog (X in the upper right corner) to return to the Bank And Credit Cards window.

Now you can begin matching and adding the new transactions. See the section entitled "Match and Add Downloaded Transactions" later in this chapter.

Upload a Web Connect File

If you choose not to connect your QuickBooks Online bank account directly to your bank account you can still automate the process of downloading transactions as long as your bank offers the Web Connect service.

Follow your bank's instructions for downloading account activity into a Web Connect (.qbo) file. Set the date range of transactions you want included and download the file. Now, go to QuickBooks Online and follow these instructions:

1. Select Transactions | Banking from the Left Navigation Bar to display the Bank And Credit Cards window.

2. Click the small down-arrow next to the Update button to display a drop-down menu.

3. Choose File Upload from the drop-down menu to open the Upload Bank File window.

4. Click the Browse button in step 2 and locate the .qbo file to import. Click Open to add it to the Upload Bank File window.

5. Click Next to display the second Upload Bank File screen (see Figure 8-7).

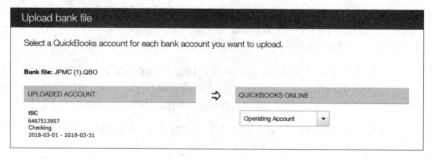

Figure 8-7: Upload the .qbo file to the correct account.

6. From the drop-down list on the right, select the
   QuickBooks Online bank account into which you want the
   .qbo file imported.

7. Click Next to begin the upload.

When the upload is complete, click the I'm Done. Let's Go! button to
return to the Bank And Credit Cards window where the newly imported
transactions appear in the New Transactions list.

Match and Add Downloaded Transactions

Once you've imported transactions from your bank account, the next step
is to match them to existing transactions in QuickBooks Online and add
them to the bank account register. QuickBooks Online offers three options
for dealing with downloaded transactions, all of which are covered in the
following sections.

Match Transactions

Theoretically, you are entering transactions into QuickBooks Online
as they occur. Therefore, when you download your online banking
transactions, the QuickBooks Online transactions should already exist.
Since you certainly don't want duplicate transactions in your bank
account register you have to match the incoming transactions with the
appropriate existing transactions.

QuickBooks Online compares certain data to automatically match
a downloaded transaction with an existing transaction. It compares the
date, payee, and amount fields. It auto-matches transactions with the
same amounts, dates, and payees. However, if the amounts are the same
and one other field (date or payee) is also the same, it still considers the
two transactions a match. For example, if an existing transaction and a
downloaded transaction have the same payee and the same amount, but a
different date, QuickBooks Online considers them a match. The same goes

for transactions with the same dates and amounts, but different payees (see Figure 8-8). If the amount is different, but the payee and the date are the same, QuickBooks Online will not suggest them as a match, but will offer them as possible matches when you open the transaction and click Find Match (or Find Other Matching Transactions).

ProAdvisor TIP: *If you find that your deposits aren't matching, it may be the result of depositing sales receipts and/or received payments directly into your bank account rather than into the Undeposited Funds account. For example, if you make three cash sales (sales receipts) and deposit them directly to your bank account, QuickBooks Online will show three deposits. However, you probably add all three to a single deposit to take to the bank. Therefore, your bank shows only a single deposit for all three. If you use the Undeposited Funds account and create a single deposit using the Deposit window (Quick Create (Plus icon) | Other | Bank Deposit) in QuickBooks Online, the downloaded deposit should match the QuickBooks Online deposit.*

If QuickBooks Online declares two transactions a match, but they're really not, you can click the transaction to display additional options (refer back to Figure 8-8). You can search for other possible matches by clicking the Find Other Matching Transactions button, click Add to add the transaction, or click Transfer if the transaction is a transfer. See the following sections for more information.

When a downloaded transaction that is marked Match, is designated correctly, click the Match button to match it to the transaction in the QuickBooks Online bank account register.

If you accidentally match transactions that are not really a match, you can easily unmatch them. Click the In QuickBooks tab, locate the transaction, and click the Undo button in the Action column. The transaction is unmatched and returned to the New Transactions tab.

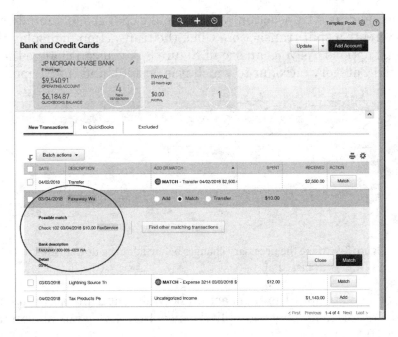

Figure 8-8: Transactions with the same dates and amounts are a match.

Add Transactions

When you cannot find an existing transaction that corresponds to a downloaded transaction, you can add it to the register. This feature is for transactions that do not exist in the QuickBooks Online bank account. Transactions that you've forgotten to enter, or that you haven't gotten around to entering may fit the bill. In reality, it's always better to go back into QuickBooks Online, enter the transaction, and then return to the Bank And Credit Cards window to make the match.

ProAdvisor TIP: *If you find that you are plagued with duplicate transactions in your bank register, review the way you're matching and adding downloaded transactions. If you add a downloaded transaction (rather than match it), and the transaction already exists, you're creating a duplicate transaction.*

When adding a transaction, you can make changes to a number of fields or create a split transaction. Click the transaction to display the additional options. As you can see in Figure 8-9, you can change the Payee, the Category (account to which it is posted), and the Memo.

Figure 8-9: Make the necessary changes before adding a downloaded transaction.

If you need to split the transaction between multiple accounts click the Split button to display the Split Transaction dialog box shown in Figure 8-10.

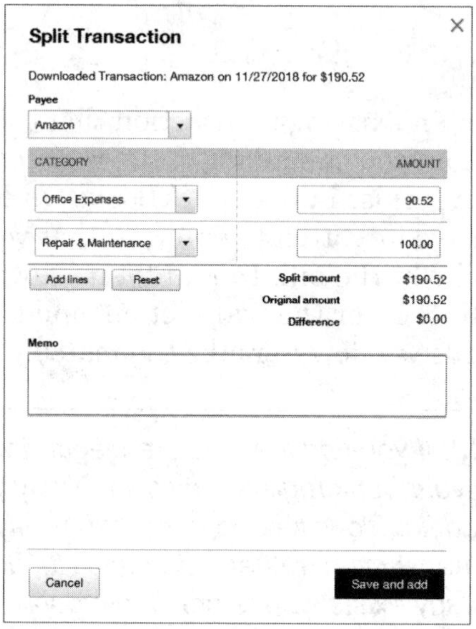

Figure 8-10: Splitting a downloaded transaction is easy.

Transfer Transactions

If a downloaded transaction is actually a transfer you made, but failed to enter, you can use the Transfer options seen in Figure 8-11 to add it to the register. Click the downloaded transaction and choose Transfer. Select the account from which it was transferred, enter a memo if so desired, and click Transfer.

Figure 8-11: You can add transfers by using the Transfer options.

Excluding Transactions

If a downloaded transaction has already been added to the account register and cleared, you don't want to match it or add it, but rather, get rid of it. The way you do that in QuickBooks Online is to exclude the transaction.

In the New Transactions list, select the transactions to exclude (place a checkmark next to each one). Then, click the Batch Actions button and choose Exclude Selected from the drop-down list that appears. Excluded transactions appear on the Excluded tab, where they can be re-added to the New Transactions tab by undoing them (click the Undo button).

Merging Existing Bank Accounts

If you've accidentally added the same bank account to QuickBooks Online twice, or had one bank buy out another, you may find that you need to merge two existing QuickBooks Online bank accounts into one.

Before you can perform the merge you must do a couple of things. First, make sure both accounts are of the same Category Type and Detail Type. Only identical bank account types can be merged.

You can merge an online banking bank account with a non-online banking bank account. However, you cannot merge two accounts that are both set up for online banking (including Web Connect). Therefore, if both are connected, you must disconnect one of them. Go to the Chart Of Accounts list and edit the bank account you want to disconnect. Check the Disconnect This Account On Save option located at the bottom right of the Account dialog box, and click Save (see Figure 8-12).

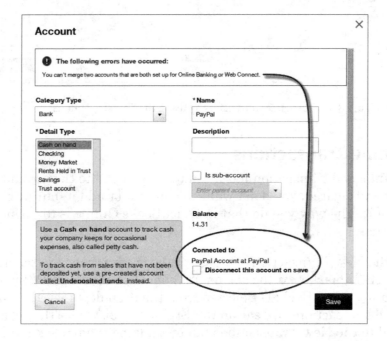

Figure 8-12: QuickBooks Online prevents the merging of two online banking bank accounts.

ProAdvisor CAUTION: *Transactions in the bank accounts will NOT be merged. Therefore, if you have entered the same transactions in both bank accounts, they will be duplicated and you'll have to remove them manually.*

Once the bank accounts are prepared, the process is fairly easy. Open the Chart Of Accounts window (Tools Menu (gear icon) | Settings | Chart Of Accounts). Select the bank account that you want to eliminate (merge into another) and click the Edit button to display the Account dialog. Change the name to match the name of the bank account you want to keep. Click Save to merge the two. QuickBooks Online immediately informs you that there's another account with the same name, and asks if you want to merge them (see Figure 8-13). If you're sure that you want to merge them click Yes. Otherwise click No.

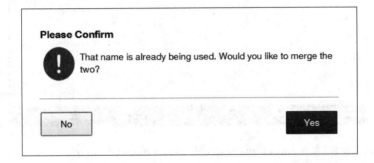

Figure 8-13: Merging bank accounts is an easy way to eliminate duplicate accounts.

Transferring Funds between Accounts

If you have multiple QuickBooks Online bank accounts, you may find that you need to transfer money between them on occasion. This will definitely be the case if you maintain separate operating and payroll bank accounts. To transfer money between them you have two options. You can either use the Transfer feature, or you can write a check from one account and deposit it in the other. The difference between the two methods is that the first – the transfer – has no effect on your financial reports.

Use the Transfer Form

Since the Transfer feature does not affect your financial reports it's the preferred method. In addition, as you can see in the following steps, it's the simplest method.

1. Choose Quick Create (Plus icon) | Other | Transfer to open the Transfer screen (see Figure 8-14).

Figure 8-14: A funds transfer cleanly moves money from one account to another.

2. Select the source account from the Transfer Funds From drop-down list.

3. Select the target account from the Transfer Funds To drop-down list.

4. Enter the amount to transfer in the Transfer Amount field.

5. In the Memo field enter a brief description of the transfer for future reference.

6. Add an attachment if so desired, and click the Save And Close button to record the transfer.

If you open the bank registers, you'll see that the transactions are marked Transfer in both accounts. Since they are both asset accounts, the source has been credited with the amount and the target has been debited, leaving your total assets unchanged. Remember, crediting an asset account reduces it, while debiting increases it.

Write a Check

Writing a check from one account and depositing in the other is an acceptable, if more complicated, way of transferring funds. The problem with this method is that you need to be sure you don't affect your financial reports. The best way to handle this is to create a separate "virtual" bank account for handling the transfers. Make it a checking account and call it FundsTransfer or something similar. You'll also need to create a payee to use for the transfers. Unfortunately, since QuickBooks Online does not offer an "Other Names" category, you'll have to create a vendor to use. Name the new vendor Cash, or use the bank's name.

Write the check to the new payee from the source account, but post it to the FundsTransfer bank account (select FundsTransfer from the Account drop-down list). After you make the actual deposit, return to QuickBooks Online and enter the deposit into the target account register. Here you'll also select the FundsTransfer account from the Account drop-down list. To double-check that everything is done correctly, run a balance sheet report. Your FundsTransfer account should have a zero balance.

Handling Bounced Checks

Bounced checks are a fact of business life. Even the best of customers sometimes miscalculates, enters the wrong date, or otherwise causes a check to be returned to you. Dealing with it properly ensures that your financial records remain accurate.

To this end, you need to do the following:

- Reduce the bank account to which the check was deposited by the amount of the check.
- Enter all bank charges incurred as a result of the bounced check.
- Remove the payment applied to the invoice so that it is once again due.
- Recover the money from the customer.

Adjust Account Balances for Bounced Checks

You must remove the amount of the check from your bank account and adjust the offset account that received the posting. To do this, you either make the adjustment in the bank register or you create a journal entry. Which you use depends on how the original check was processed.

For example, if you deposited a check for an invoice or sales receipt directly into your bank account you'll want to use the register. See the steps outlined in the next section entitled "Using the Bank Register." If, on the other hand, the check was posted to the Undeposited Funds account, and later deposited with other checks, you should use a journal entry, which is covered in the section entitled "Using a Journal Entry" later in this chapter.

Using the Bank Register

If you deposited the check directly into the bank instead of using the Undeposited Funds account, you can adjust the bank account and the offset account from the bank register.

To access the bank register click Transactions | Registers on the Left Navigation Bar to display the Registers window. Then highlight the account register to view, and click the Go To Register button. If the deposit was a payment for an invoice, its listing in the bank register has a type called Received Pmt. To void it, highlight the transaction and click the Edit button. This opens the original payment transaction. Click the More button at the bottom of the screen and select Void from the pop-up menu that appears. When asked if you're sure, click Yes.

The invoice that was paid returns to its balance due before the payment and the payment is retained with a zero amount. Voided is entered into the Memo field. If you want, you can open the payment and add additional information to the Memo field to indicate that the reason was a bounced check.

The Accounts Receivable account is also adjusted (the amount is added back). The invoice will show up as unpaid if you send a statement to the customer. You should also invoice the customer for any bounced-check charges you incurred (see "Invoicing Customers for Bounced Checks" later in this chapter.)

If the deposit was a sales receipt, its listing in the bank register has a type of Sales Receipt. Highlight it and click the Edit button to display the original sales receipt. Click the More button at the bottom of the window and choose Void from the menu that appears. Click Yes when asked if you're sure. The amount of the transaction changes to 0.00, the bank balance is adjusted, and the Memo field displays Voided.

Using a Journal Entry

If you used the Undeposited Funds account, create a journal entry to remove the amount of the bounced check from the bank. The alternative is to remove the original deposit from the Undeposited Funds account, which affects the Make Deposit transaction you created. If that deposit contained other payments, you have to recreate the entire deposit. Therefore, a journal entry is easier and less prone to mistakes.

To create a journal entry to adjust the amounts, choose Quick Create (Plus icon) | Other | Journal Entry, which opens the Make General Journal Entry window. Then, take the following steps:

1. Click in the Account column and select the bank into which you deposited the payment.

2. Move to the Credit column and enter the amount of the bounced check.

3. Use the Memo column to write yourself a note (e.g., Jackson Ck #2345 bounced).

4. Click in the Name column and select the customer whose check bounced.

5. On the next row, click in the Account column and choose one of the following accounts:

   • If the deposit was a payment for an invoice, select the Accounts Receivable account to which the invoice was posted.

- If the deposit was a sales receipt, select the income account to which the sales receipt was posted.

6. QuickBooks automatically fills in the amount in the Debit column.

7. Click Save & Close.

Don't forget to invoice the customer to collect the amount of the bounced check (see "Invoicing Customers for Bounced Checks" later in this section).

Record Bank Charges for Bounced Checks

If your bank charged you for a returned check, you have to enter the bank charge. To do so, start by opening the register for your bank account. Then, fill out the fields as follows:

1. Click the Date field in the blank line at the bottom of the register and enter the date that the bank charge was assessed.

2. Delete the check number that's automatically entered.

3. Tab over to the Payment field and enter the amount of the service charge for the returned check.

4. In the Account field, assign this transaction to the expense account you use for bank charges.

5. Click the Save button in the register window to save the transaction.

Your bank account balance is reduced by the amount of the service charge. You should charge the customer for this, and in the following sections, I'll cover the steps needed to accomplish that.

Invoice Customers for Bounced Checks

If you have to re-invoice your customer after a check bounces, you don't submit an invoice for the same item because you don't want to increase the activity for that item—this is a replacement for a previously entered transaction.

Instead, you have to create a specific item for bounced checks and another item for service charges. Then, use those items in the invoice. Those tasks are covered in the following sections.

Creating an Item for a Bounced Check Replacement

If you want to issue an invoice for the bounced check, you need an item for bounced checks. Open the Products And Services list window by selecting Tools Menu (gear icon) | Lists | Products And Services. Click the New button to open the New Item dialog. Then fill out the fields using the following guidelines:

- The item Name is Returned Check (or another phrase of your choice).
- The Description is optional.
- The Price/Rate field is blank (you fill in the amount when you create the invoice).
- The item is not taxable (if you collect sales tax).
- Link the item to an income account.

The income account can present a problem if you have multiple income accounts to track different types of revenue. The Returned Check item must be linked to the same income account as the original transaction. Therefore, if you have multiple income accounts you'll have to create a Returned Check item for each account and link it accordingly. For example, if you have a Product Sales income account and a Services income account you'll need two separate Returned Check items – Returned Check Products, linked to the Product Sales income account, and a Returned Check Services, linked to the Services income account.

When you voided the check, you also removed the amount from the income account. When the customer pays the invoice for the bounced check, the same income account has to be credited.

The easiest way to handle multiple income accounts is to create subaccounts for each of the income accounts. Using the above example, you would open the Chart Of Accounts window, create a new account called Returned Checks – Product Income, and make it a subaccount of the Products Sales income account. Then repeat the process for the Services account.

Create an Item for Service Charges

If you plan to charge the customer for the service charge you incurred, and possibly add one of your own, you'll need an item for that. To create an item for invoicing customers for the bank service charges you incur when their checks bounce, use the following guidelines:

- The item Name is RetChkChg (or something similar).
- The Description is optional.
- The Amount is blank (you fill it in when you create the invoice).
- The item is not taxable.
- The Account is an Income account you create specifically for this purpose.

Create the Invoice

The way you create the invoice depends on the original transaction. If the original transaction was a sales receipt, you'll want to create an invoice that includes both the items from the original sales receipt plus the service charges for the bounced check. To make it clear that this is the result of a bounced check either call the customer and explain, or add a note to the invoice.

If the original transaction was an invoice, you do not want to recreate that invoice. Doing so will mess up your bookkeeping and reports. Remember, the original invoice is still active in QuickBooks Online. You only voided the payment for that invoice, not the invoice itself. To create an invoice for a bounced check invoice follow these steps:

1. Enter the name of the customer who gave you the bad check.

2. Enter the date on which the check bounced.

3. Click in the Product/Service column and select the item you created for returned checks.

4. Enter the amount of the returned check.

5. If necessary, add another line-item for the service charge that you incurred for the bounced check, using the item you created for service charges.

6. Save the invoice and send it to the customer.

Voiding Disbursements

Sometimes you have to void a check that you've written—you made a mistake in preparing the check, you decided not to send it for some reason, or you sent it but it never arrived. Whatever the reason, if a check isn't going to clear the bank, you must void it.

To void a check, open the register of the bank account you used for the check and find the check's listing. If the check was written as payment for a vendor bill (Essentials and Plus only), its transaction type is Bill Pmt. If the check was a direct disbursement, its transaction type is Expense.

Select the check's transaction line and click the Edit button to open the original transaction. Now, click the More button at the bottom of the transaction window and choose Void from the menu that appears.

If the check you're voiding was a bill payment, QuickBooks displays a warning that your action will change previous transactions. This means the vendor bill, which had been paid, will be changed to unpaid and the Accounts Payable account will be increased by the amount of this check. Since those are exactly the results you're looking for, click Yes to continue.

If the check you're voiding was a direct disbursement, QuickBooks asks for confirmation and then voids the check. The expense account to which you posted the check is credited with the appropriate amounts (the original posting was a debit). The check amount is changed to 0.00, and the text Voided appears in the Memo field.

QuickBooks lets you delete a check instead of voiding it, which is a terrible idea. Deleting a check removes all history of the transaction, and the check number disappears into the ether. This is not a good way to keep financial records. Voiding a check keeps the check number, but sets the amount to zero, which provides an audit trail of your checks.

(The ability to delete a check is a terrific feature for an embezzler who wants enough time to cash the check and run before you learn about the check in your next bank statement.)

Reconciling Bank Accounts

Reconciling bank accounts is one of those important tasks that is all too often left for another day. However, if you want to ensure your finances are accurate and healthy, you should make an effort to do it every month – as soon as your bank statement arrives. In this section, we'll go over the steps required to reconcile your bank accounts in QuickBooks.

Business owners should always go over the bank statement and the bank register and compare them. Unlike the other reports discussed in this chapter, you don't view the bank statement to check figures and analyze them. Instead, this is a security check.

Unfortunately, statistics show that the rate of embezzlement in small businesses is much higher than you'd guess (and higher than embezzlement rates in large businesses). Even worse, a large percentage of embezzlers are family members who work in the family business.

According to a recent report from the Association of Certified Fraud Examiners, businesses lose 5% of their annual revenues to fraud, and small businesses are especially vulnerable. The median loss suffered by small businesses was estimated at $140,000.00 per business, which is higher, on average, than the amounts large companies lose.

According to the U.S. Chamber of Commerce, check tampering and fraudulent billing (the most common small-business fraud schemes) destroy many small businesses. The American Management Association estimates that one-third of small-business bankruptcies – and at least twenty percent of business failures – are due to employee theft.

Examine the Bank Statement

The bank statement contains check numbers (without names) for checks you sent to vendors, and payee names for electronic transfers. Pictures of the checks (both front and back) are often included in the statement or can be ordered from the bank.

Look for vendor names that appear frequently. Look for vendor names that only appear occasionally to which the amounts seem to be unusually large. Look for vendor names that aren't familiar to you, and check for those vendor records in your accounting system. What's the address and telephone number, and what do you buy from them? Call the vendor if the name isn't familiar to you.

Look for bank transfers between bank accounts and make sure all of the banks listed for these transfers are yours.

Compare checks on the statement to the bank register and be suspicious of a check that was entered into the register months earlier than the check cleared; this indicates a back-dated check. A back-dated check is designed to be hard to spot, because the last time you checked the bank register, it didn't exist. This is especially suspicious if the check date in your system is for the previous year and the check was cashed this year (business owners hardly ever create reports for the previous year, so they don't see back-dated transactions).

Prepare to Reconcile

Select Transactions | Registers from the Left Navigation Bar to Open the registers window. Highlight the bank account you're about to reconcile and click the Go To Register button to open the account register. If the bank statement shows deposits or checks (or both) that are absent from your bank register, add them to the register. If you miss any, don't worry. You can add transactions to the register while you're working in the Reconcile window, but it's usually quicker to get this task out of the way before you start the reconciliation process.

Interest earned and standard bank charges don't count as missing transactions, because the bank reconciliation process treats those transactions separately. You'll have a chance to enter those amounts during bank reconciliation.

Adding Missing Disbursements to the Register

The way you add missing disbursements to the register depends on whether the disbursements were checks or non-check withdrawals, such as electronic payments or debit card withdrawals.

To enter a check, you can add the data directly to the register, or use the Check window (Quick Create (Plus icon) | Vendors | Check) and enter the check number, payee, and amount.

To enter a disbursement that isn't a check, add the data directly to the register. QuickBooks automatically enters the next check number, which you should delete and replace with an appropriate code (such as EFT for Electronic Funds Transfer, ATM for a debit card withdrawal, or DM for a bank Debit Memo). You don't need to enter a payee for a debit card withdrawal, because usually that's a cash purchase at a store that you're not tracking as a vendor. However, entering the store's name will provide you a better audit trail. Enter the expense account (or petty cash account if you're refilling the petty cash box).

Adding Missing Deposits to the Register

You may see deposits on the bank statement that don't appear in your check register. This almost always means you forgot to make the deposit in QuickBooks. Check the Undeposited Funds account to see if you entered the deposits when they arrived, but neglected to use the Deposit window.

Choose Quick Create (Plus icon) | Other | Bank Deposit and see if the deposits are there (the odds are quite good that they are). Select the deposits that appear on your statement and deposit them into the appropriate bank account. If you have multiple undeposited monies listed, deposit the funds in groups that match the deposited totals on the statement.

For example, your bank statement may show a deposit of $145.78 on one date and a deposit for $3,233.99 on another date. Both deposits still appear in the Deposit window. Select one of the deposits, process it, and then repeat the procedure for the other deposit. When you reconcile the account, your transactions reflect the transactions in your bank statement.

If a missing deposit isn't in the Undeposited Funds account, you have to create the deposit – which may have been a customer payment of an invoice, a cash sale, a transfer of funds between banks, a payment of a loan, or a deposit of capital.

For customer invoice payments or cash sales, fill out the appropriate transaction window. If you deposit the proceeds to the Undeposited Funds account, don't forget to take the additional step of depositing the funds in the bank so the transaction appears in the reconciliation window. If you deposit the proceeds directly to the bank, the transaction appears in the reconciliation window automatically.

The fastest way to enter deposits unconnected to customers and earned income – such as a refund check or the proceeds of a loan – is to work directly in the bank account register. Enter the deposit amount and post the transaction to the appropriate account (you can skip the payee, but, again, entering the payee will provide a better audit trail). If you're not sure which account to use for the offset posting, ask your accountant.

Perform the Reconciliation

To begin the reconciliation process, select Tools Menu (gear icon) | Tools | Reconcile to open the Register window seen in Figure 8-15. Here you'll find a drop-down list from which you can select the account to reconcile. When you select an account, a listing of recent reconciliations appears. Clicking on a listing displays the reconciliation report.

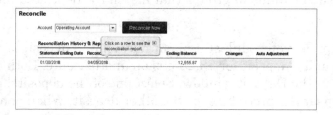

Figure 8-15: The Reconcile window provides access to previous reconciliations.

ProAdvisor TIP: *You can bypass the Reconcile window and begin the reconciliation by opening the bank register and clicking the Reconcile button found in the bottom left corner of the register window.*

Select the account to reconcile and click the Reconcile Now button to open the Start Reconciling dialog. What you see depends on the online banking status of the account selected. Online banking-connected accounts will see the dialog shown in Figure 8-16.

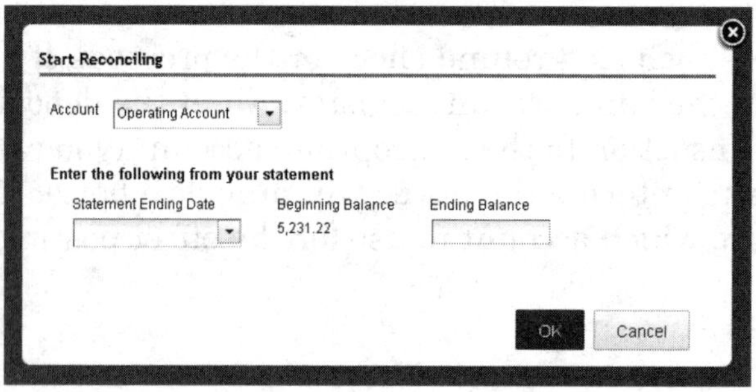

Figure 8-16: Online banking accounts will have fewer options.

Bank accounts not connected to online banking will see the dialog shown in Figure 8-17.

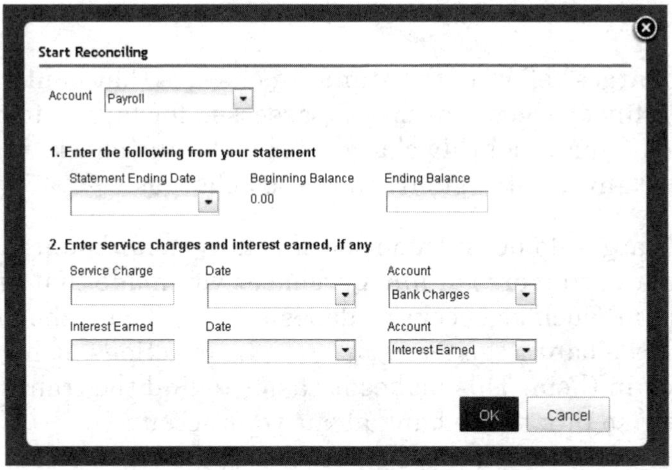

Figure 8-17: Non-online banking connected accounts have additional
fields for interest and service charges.

The reason for the different dialogs is the fact that downloaded transactions from online banking accounts will include service charges and interest earned. By eliminating those fields, QuickBooks Online minimizes the risk that those transactions will be duplicated by being entered manually.

Enter the statement ending date. Next, check the Beginning Balance field in the window against the beginning balance on the bank statement. (Your bank may call it the starting balance.) If the beginning balances don't match, see the section "Resolving Differences in the Beginning Balance."

If your beginning balances match, enter the ending balance from your statement in the Ending Balance field and enter the statement date.

Entering Interest Income and Service Charges

If the account is not connected to online banking, enter any interest earned and/or service charges incurred. Your statement shows interest and bank service charges, if either (or both) are applied to your account. Enter those numbers in the Start Reconciling window and choose the appropriate account for posting – usually Interest Earned and Bank Charges.

Bank Charges refers to the standard charges that banks assess, such as monthly charges that may be assessed for failure to maintain a minimum balance, monthly charges for including checks in your statement, or any other regularly assessed charges.

Bank Charges do not include special charges for bounced checks (yours or your customers') or any purchases you made that are charged to your account (such as checks or deposit slips). Those should be entered into the bank register as discrete transactions, using the Memo fields to explain them. This makes it easier to find the transactions in case you have to talk to the bank about your account.

Reconcile Transactions

After you've filled out the information in the Start Reconciling dialog, click OK to open the Reconcile window, shown in Figure 8-18.

Figure 8-18: The Reconcile window displays unreconciled transactions.

If, after opening the Reconcile window, you realize that you entered the wrong date, ending balance, or interest and service charge data you can make the correction(s) from within the Reconcile window. Click the Edit Information From Statement link located at the bottom left of the window.

Eliminating Future Transactions

If the transaction list in the Reconcile window has a great many entries, select the option Hide Transactions After The Statement's End Date.

Theoretically, transactions that were created after the statement ending date couldn't have cleared the bank. Removing those listings from the window leaves only those transactions likely to have cleared.

If you select this option and your reconciliation doesn't balance, deselect the option so that you can clear the transactions, in case you made a mistake when you entered the date of a transaction. You may have entered a wrong month, or even a wrong year, which resulted in moving the transaction date into the future.

Clearing Transactions

All of the transactions that are printed on your bank statement are cleared transactions. If the transactions are not listed on the statement, they have not cleared as of the statement date.

In the Reconcile window, click the check box to the left of each transaction that cleared. A check mark appears in the box to indicate that the transaction has cleared the bank. If you clear a transaction in error, click again to remove the check mark—it's a toggle. To check (or uncheck) all of the transactions in the list, click the checkbox to the left of Date in the header section of the list.

To facilitate the clearing process you can click a column name in the header section of the list to resort the list by that column/field.

As you check each cleared transaction, the Difference amount in the lower-right corner of the Reconcile window changes. Your goal is to get that figure to 0.00.

Viewing Transactions During Reconciliation

If you need to look at the original transaction window for any transaction in the reconcile window, click its listing. The original transaction opens in a window that slides down over the Reconcile window. When you're done, click the Close button (X) to return to the Reconcile window.

Adding Transactions During Reconciliation

When you're working in the Reconcile window, if you find a transaction on the statement that you haven't entered into your QuickBooks software (probably one of those ATM transactions you forgot to enter), you don't have to shut down the reconciliation process to remedy the situation. You can just enter the transaction into your register.

Open the bank account register and record the transaction. Then choose Tools Menu (gear icon) | Tools | Reconcile to return to the Reconcile window. Click Resume Reconciling to return to the reconciliation, exactly where you left off. The new transaction is now listed (QuickBooks Online automatically updates the Reconcile window). Mark the transaction as cleared, because it was on the statement.

Deleting Transactions During Reconciliation

Sometimes you find that a transaction that was transferred from your account register to the Reconcile window shouldn't be there. This commonly occurs if you entered an ATM withdrawal twice. Perhaps you forgot that you'd entered a bank charge, or even a deposit, and then entered it again.

To delete a transaction return to the account register, select the transaction, and click Delete. QuickBooks Online asks you to confirm the deletion. When you return to the Reconcile window, the transaction is gone.

Editing Transactions During Reconciliation

You may want to change some of the information in a transaction. For example, when you see the real check, you realize the amount you entered in QuickBooks is wrong. You might even have the wrong date on a check.

Whatever the problem, you can correct it by editing the transaction. Click the transaction listing in the Reconcile window to open the original transaction window. Enter the necessary changes and click Save And Close. You're returned to the Reconcile window, where the transaction list has been updated to reflect the change(s).

Resolving Missing Check Numbers

Most bank statements list your checks in order, and indicate a missing number with an asterisk. For instance, you may see check number 1234, followed by check number *1236 or 1236*. When a check number is missing, it means one of three things:

- The check cleared in a previous reconciliation.
- The check is still outstanding.
- The check number is unused and may actually be missing.

If a missing check number on your bank statement is puzzling, you can check its status. To see if the check cleared previously, check the bank register, which shows a check mark in the Reconciled column if a check cleared.

To investigate further, choose Reports | All Reports | Business Overview | Audit Log to run the Audit Log report. While not as convenient as the Missing Checks report found in QuickBooks Desktop applications, the Audit Log report does keep track of checks that have been deleted.

Finishing the Reconciliation

After all of the transactions that cleared are marked, the Difference figure at the bottom of the Reconcile window should display 0.00 (if it doesn't, read the following section). Click Finish Now to complete the reconciliation and return to the original Reconcile window, where the latest reconciliation is now listed. Click the listing to view a reconciliation report.

Resolving Reconciliation Problems

If the Difference figure at the bottom of the Reconcile window isn't 0.00, try the following to locate the problem:

Count the number of transactions on the bank statement, then look in the lower-left corner of the Reconcile window, where the number of items you have marked "cleared" is displayed. Mentally add another item to that number for each of the following:

- A service charge you entered in the Start Reconciling box

- An interest amount you entered in the Start Reconciling box

If the number of transactions now differs, the problem is in your QuickBooks records; there's a transaction you should have cleared but didn't or a transaction you cleared that you shouldn't have. Find and correct the problem transaction.

Check the totals for deposits and withdrawals on the bank statement and make sure they match the deposit and withdrawal totals in the Reconcile window. If they don't match, do the following:

- Check the amount of each transaction against the amount in the bank statement.

- Check your transactions and make sure a deposit wasn't inadvertently entered as a payment (or vice versa). A clue for this is a transaction that's half the difference. If the difference is $220.00, find a transaction that has an amount of $110.00 and make sure it's a deduction if it's supposed to be a deduction (or the other way around).

- Check for transposed figures. Perhaps you entered a figure incorrectly in the register, such as $549.00

when the bank cleared the transaction as $594.00. A clue that a transposed number is the problem is that the reconciliation difference can be divided by nine.

When (or if) you find the problem, correct it. When the Difference figure is 0.00, click Reconcile Now.

ProAdvisor TIP*: If you can't immediately get the reconciliation difference to 0.00, go to another task and then come back to the reconciliation (you may be staring right through the error and not recognizing it) or let somebody else check over the statement and the register, because sometimes you can't see your own mistakes.*

Pausing the Reconciliation Process

If the account doesn't reconcile (the Difference figure isn't 0.00), and you don't have the time or the will to track down the problem at the moment, you can stop the reconciliation process without losing all of the transactions you cleared.

Click the Finish Later button in the Reconcile window and go about your business. When you're ready to work on the reconciliation again, restart the process and everything will be exactly the way you left it.

Creating an Adjusting Entry

If you cannot find the problem, you can have QuickBooks make an adjusting entry to force the reconciliation to balance. The adjusting entry is placed in the bank account register and is offset in the Reconciliation Discrepancies other expenses account (which is created the first time you make an adjusting entry). If you ever figure out what the problem was, you can make the proper adjustment transaction and delete the adjusting entry.

To force a reconciliation, click Finish Now even though there's a difference. A dialog appears offering the opportunity to make an adjusting entry (see Figure 8-19). Click Add Adjustment.

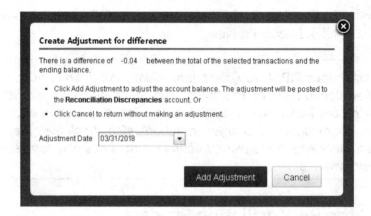

Create Adjustment for difference

There is a difference of -0.04 between the total of the selected transactions and the ending balance.

- Click Add Adjustment to adjust the account balance. The adjustment will be posted to the **Reconciliation Discrepancies** account. Or
- Click Cancel to return without making an adjustment.

Adjustment Date 03/31/2018

Add Adjustment   Cancel

Figure 8-19: When all else fails, make an adjusting entry.

Resolve Differences in the Beginning Balance

The beginning balance that's displayed on the Begin Reconciliation window should match the beginning balance on the bank statement. That beginning balance is the ending balance from the last reconciliation, and nothing should ever change its amount.

If the beginning balance doesn't match the statement, you probably performed one of the following actions, all of which are major mistakes and should never happen:

- You changed the amount on a transaction that had previously cleared.
- You voided a transaction that had previously cleared.
- You deleted a transaction that had previously cleared.
- You removed the Cleared check mark from a transaction that had previously cleared.

These are all things you should never do but if you did, you must figure out which one of those actions you took after you last reconciled the account.

CHAPTER 9:

Running Payroll in QuickBooks Online

- Subscribing to QuickBooks Online Payroll
- Preparing for Payroll
- Setting Payroll Preferences
- Using Time-Tracking
- Running QuickBooks Payroll
- Managing Payroll Liabilities

Running payroll is one of those chores faced by all small businesses that have employees. Many businesses, especially the larger ones, will frequently outsource payroll to facilitate the process. However, businesses with smaller numbers of employees usually opt to handle payroll in-house. In that case, QuickBooks Online Payroll – which integrates with QuickBooks Online – is the ideal solution.

First, the payroll service is available with all versions of QuickBooks Online (i.e., Simple Start, Essentials, and Plus). Next, the online service is so flexible that you can run payroll from anywhere, even from your iPhone or Android. Using online payroll is relatively simple, but does involve a number of processes:

- Subscribing to the service
- Gathering your payroll data
- Setting payroll preferences
- Adding employees
- Running payroll
- Paying payroll tax liabilities

Subscribing to QuickBooks Online Payroll

If you have employees, you have to create paychecks, track the liabilities and employer expenses related to those paychecks, and remit those liabilities and employer expenses. A great many postings to your general ledger take place as you perform these tasks. Even if you don't do your own payroll, you have to track those postings in your books (using the reports from your outside payroll company).

QuickBooks offers three payroll solutions, one of which should fit your needs.

- Basic. This is the bare-bones payroll service from Intuit that provides current tax tables so that you can create paychecks without having to do your own calculations. It creates paychecks, but does not fill out the payroll liability forms for you. You have to generate reports on the liabilities and then fill out and submit the forms yourself.

- Enhanced. To create paychecks, fill out the tax forms for payroll liabilities, and file those forms online, you'll have to sign up for the Enhanced Payroll subscription.

- Full Service. If you prefer to outsource your payroll, this is the plan for you. You keep track of your employees' hours and submit them to Intuit, and Intuit creates the paychecks and remits the payroll taxes for you.

To sign up for one of these plans independently visit http://payroll.intuit.com/ and follow the instructions there.

ProAdvisor TIP: *Unless you sign up for the Enhanced payroll plan from within QuickBooks Online (see the instructions later in this chapter), the plan will not seamlessly integrate with QuickBooks Online. This means that if you sign up for it on the Intuit site, you'll have to import the payroll data into QuickBooks Online. Neither the Basic nor the Full Service plans are available from within QuickBooks Online, so you have no choice but to sign up for them on the Intuit site and import the resulting payroll data into QuickBooks Online.*

Preparing for Payroll Setup

Before you jump in and start setting up payroll in QuickBooks Online, you should spend some time gathering the information you'll need to complete the setup.

- Employee Setup. Required information includes the employee's W-4 information (name, address, social security number, marital status, etc). Important information includes pay frequency and rate, vacation information, sick pay, overtime, deductions, and more.

- Compensation Information. Are your employees paid an hourly rate or a salary? What about bonuses, commissions, and tips—are they part of the compensation your employees receive? Do you offer health and retirement benefits? All of these things will have to be set up. If you have the information handy, the setup process will go a lot more smoothly.

- Taxes. QuickBooks needs to know which taxes (federal, state, local) apply, the agencies you file with, what the schedules are, and more.

- Year-To-Date Payrolls. Unless you're starting payroll on the first day of the year, you'll have to enter the historical payroll data into QuickBooks to ensure that your payroll information is accurate for the entire year.

Once you have this information pulled together, you're ready to start setting up payroll.

ProAdvisor TIP: *While you can start setting up payroll once you've gathered the necessary information, you'll save yourself some time and aggravation if you configure the payroll preferences first. This is especially true if you have a large number of employees with different schedules, deductions, and so on. If you do nothing else, I would suggest setting up payroll items, schedules, and deductions before starting the payroll wizard covered in the next section. For detailed instructions on configuring payroll preferences, see the section entitled "Setting Payroll Preferences" later in this chapter.*

Use the Get Started With Payroll Wizard

To subscribe to the integrated Enhanced payroll plan you must first log in to your QuickBooks Online account. Once logged in, select Employees from the left navigation bar to display the Employees center. Now, click the Get Started With Payroll button.

When you click the Get Started With Payroll button, QuickBooks Online automatically activates the integrated Enhanced Payroll subscription. In addition, it launches a wizard that takes you through all of the basic steps necessary for configuring payroll. While you can perform all of the steps independently using different features (Payroll Preferences, Add Employees, etc.), we're going to use the wizard since it offers an organized approach most users will find easy to use.

Payroll History

The first screen asks if you've paid any employees this year (or are you just starting payroll with your online subscription?). If you select No, only the two options appear. However, if you answer Yes, the additional fields shown in Figure 9-1 appear.

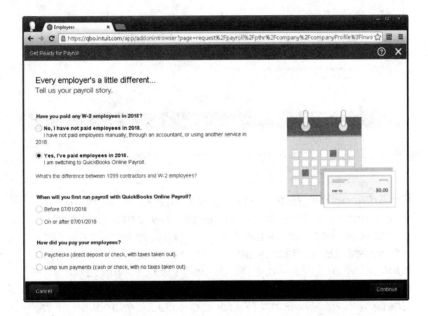

Figure 9-1: If you've already paid employees this year, QuickBooks Online needs more information.

Make your selection(s) and click Continue to proceed to the add employees section, where you can enter basic employee information.

ProAdvisor NOTE: *Don't worry, you'll get a chance to enter
historical payroll information during the payroll setup process.*

Add Employees

In this section (see Figure 9-2) you'll be able to add all of your employees.
Unfortunately, as of this writing, there is no way to import employee data
(current or historical) into QuickBooks Online – therefore it must all be
entered manually.

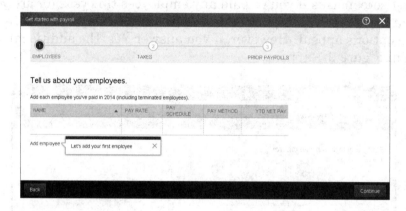

Figure 9-2: It's hard to run payroll without employees.

ProAdvisor TIP: *Before adding employees, be sure that
you understand the difference between an employee and
an independent contractor. Many employers think it may be
advantageous to classify an employee as an independent
contractor. Unfortunately, the decision is not a matter of
choice, but rather of strict definition as determined by the IRS.
Check IRS Publication 1779 for a detailed explanation of the
differences. Failure to include an employee (by IRS definition)
on the payroll can result in unpaid/overdue liabilities, along
with associated interest and penalties.*

1. Click the Add Employee link to open the Add Employee
   window (see Figure 9-3).

Figure 9-3: Enter the employee's basic information.

2. Fill in the first and last name of the employee. A middle initial is not required, but can be added if desired.

3. Move to step 1 and click the Enter W-4 Form button to display the W-4 form dialog shown in Figure 9-4.

Figure 9-4: Use the employee's original W-4 to complete this one.

4. Fill out the form using the original W-4 submitted by the employee.

5. Move to step 2 and select a pay schedule for the new employee. If no schedules exist (which they shouldn't since we're starting from scratch), a screen opens with a new schedule form. Fill it out accordingly. See the section entitled "Pay Schedules" later in this chapter for details on creating schedules.

6. From the step 3 drop-down list choose the pay type for this employee and enter the amount in the text box to the right.

7. Move to step 4 and click the pencil icon to add deductions for this employee (see Figure 9-5).

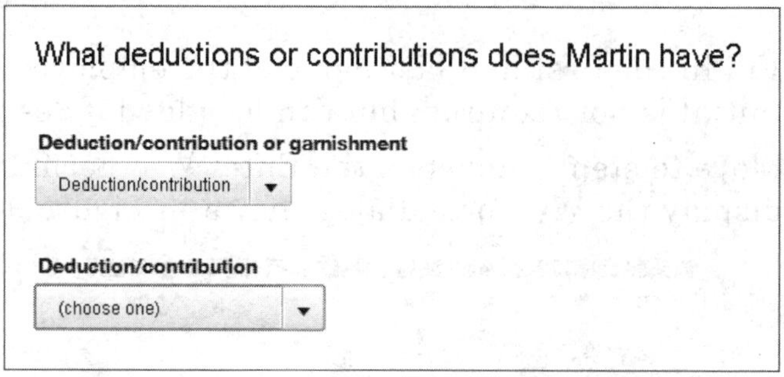

What deductions or contributions does Martin have?

Deduction/contribution or garnishment

Deduction/contribution ▼

Deduction/contribution

(choose one) ▼

Figure 9-5: You can add regular deductions and garnishments.

8. Choose the deduction type (deduction or garnishment) from the first drop-down list. Then choose (or add) the specific deduction from the second drop-down list. Click OK when you're done.

9. Move to step 5 and click the pencil icon to display the payment options seen in Figure 9-6.

10. From the drop-down list, choose the manner in which you want to pay the employee. Click OK when you're done.

Your choices, which are self-explanatory, include:

- Paper Check
- Direct Deposit
- Direct Deposit To Two Accounts
- Direct Deposit With Balance As A Check

11. Once the above steps are completed, step 6 displays a button entitled Enter <year> Prior Pay Details. If you don't see step 6 it means that when subscribing to payroll you stated that you did not have any historical payroll prior to the subscription date.

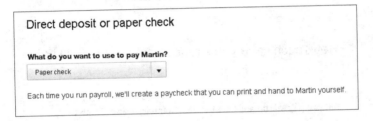

Figure 9-6: You can pay employees by check, direct deposit, or a combination of the two.

ProAdvisor TIP: *Keep an eye on the Sample Check preview on the right side of the Add Employee window. It changes to reflect the choices you make as you add the employee information.*

Entering Historical Employee Payroll Data

If, during your payroll plan subscription (or during this setup) you stated that you had paid employees prior to subscribing (and in the current year) you will find a step 6 in the Add Employee window that asks How Much

Did You Pay <employee first name> So Far This Year? In addition, there will be a button that opens the historical data entry wizard (see Figure 9-7).

6
How much did you pay Martin so far this year?
Enter 2018 prior pay details

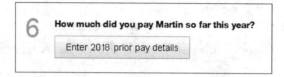

Figure 9-7: Click the button to enter historical payroll data for the employee.

Click the Enter <year> Prior Pay Details button to display the first screen of the historical data entry wizard shown in Figure 9-8.

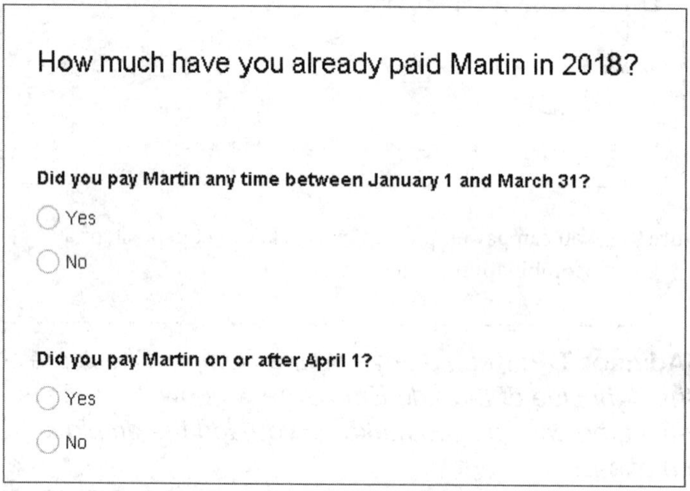

How much have you already paid Martin in 2018?
Did you pay Martin any time between January 1 and March 31?
Yes
No
Did you pay Martin on or after April 1?
Yes
No

Figure 9-8: During which period(s) did you pay the employee this year?

The first thing QuickBooks Online needs to know is you've paid the employee during the previous quarters of this year. Next it wants to know if you've paid the employee during the current quarter. If you answer yes to either (or both) questions, tables appear at the bottom of the window where you can enter the quarter-to-date and/or year-to-date totals (see Figure 9-9).

Fill out the table(s) with payroll data from your previous payroll system. Either run reports, or as the hints in Figure 9-9 suggest, get the data from old pay stubs. When you've entered the information, click Continue to return to the Add Employee window.

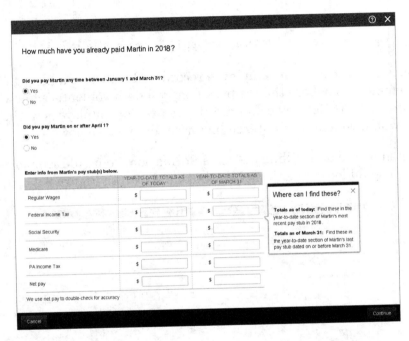

Figure 9-9: Use the data entry tables to add the employee's pay history.

ProAdvisor TIP: *If you answered yes to both questions, be sure to note that even though the second question was directed at the current quarter, the table that appears asks for the Year-To-Date Totals. In other words, it will automatically calculate the current quarter totals by subtracting the previous quarter's numbers from the year-to-date numbers.*

When you return to the Add Employee window you'll see that the year-to-date totals have been added to step 6 (see Figure 9-10).

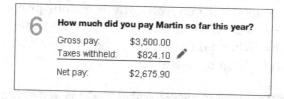

Figure 9-10: Year-to-date totals now appear in the employee record.

Click Done to save the employee record and return to a listing of active employees, where the historical payroll data you entered now appears in the YTD Net Pay column. If there are any employees in the listing for whom you haven't entered historical data, do so now.

When you're done filling out the information, your Add Employee window should look something like the one shown in Figure 9-11.

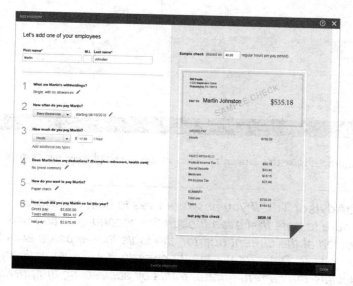

Figure 9-11: This employee is ready to be added.

ProAdvisor NOTE: *If any of the employee listings have a yellow exclamation point to the left, it means that required information is missing. Until you open the record (click the employee name) and enter the information, you will not be able to proceed. In the event that you close the wizard and try to run payroll, you'll find that QuickBooks Online balks and tells you that you have to enter the missing information first.*

Click Done and you're returned to the screen for adding employees. Repeat the process for all employees. When all of your employees are added, click Continue to move to the next step of the wizard.

Configure Payroll Taxes

The next section of the wizard deals with setting up your tax withholding and reporting information. The first screen is informational. Once you've read it, click Continue to view the Employee Details window (see Figure 9-12).

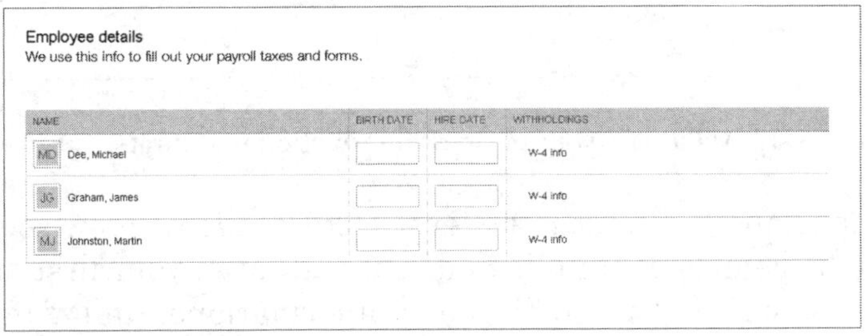

Figure 9-12: Enter important employee dates.

Enter each employee's hire and birth dates, and click the W-4 Info link to review (and modify if necessary) the employee's W-4 data.

ProAdvisor TIP: *Be sure to use the mm/dd/yyyy format when entering dates or you'll be staring at date boxes with red borders and no other indication of what is wrong.*

Click Continue to view the Business Details screen shown in Figure 9-13. Review the information and make any necessary changes. The last question about buying your business from a previous owner only appears if you answer yes to hiring your first employee within the last six months.

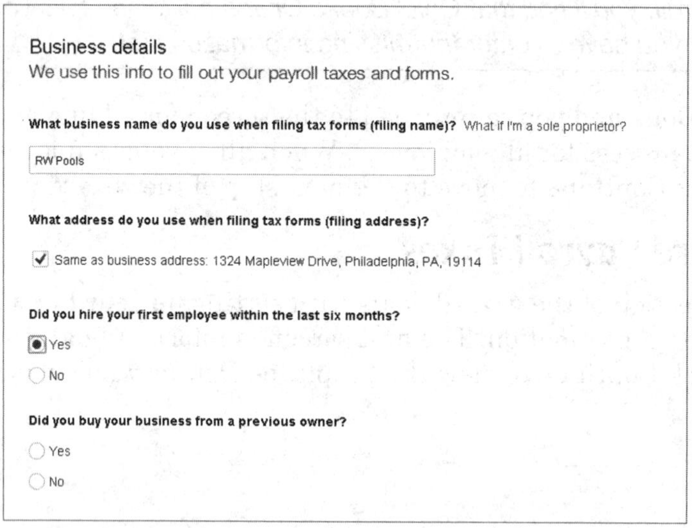

Figure 9-13: Make sure your business information is accurate.

Click Continue to open the Federal Tax Details window seen in Figure 9-14. If, by chance, you indicated that you hired your first employee within the last six months, you'll see an informational dialog indicating that QuickBooks Online has automatically configured some "New Employer Settings" for you.

Here again, most of the fields are self-explanatory. However, if you're not sure, you'll want to consult with your accountant to guarantee that you file the correct tax forms.

Click Continue to view the State Tax Details window (see Figure 9-15). Of course, the window you see will depend on the state in which you do business. Fill in the fields, consulting with your accountant when in doubt.

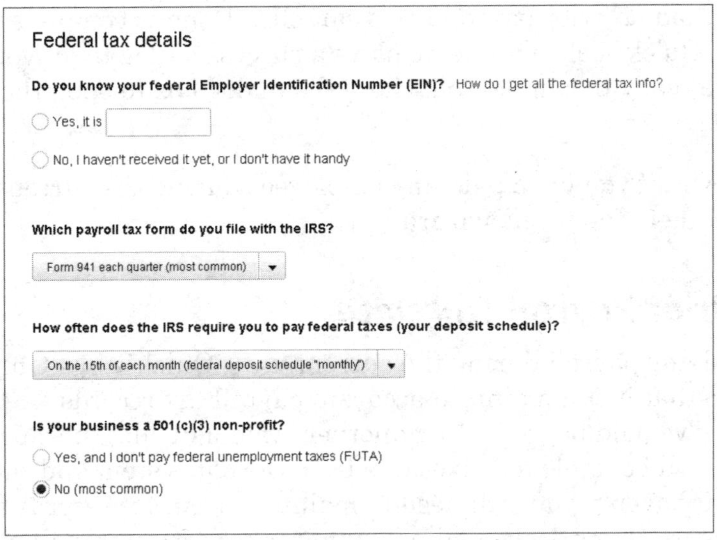

Figure 9-14: Time to add your EIN and other tax data.

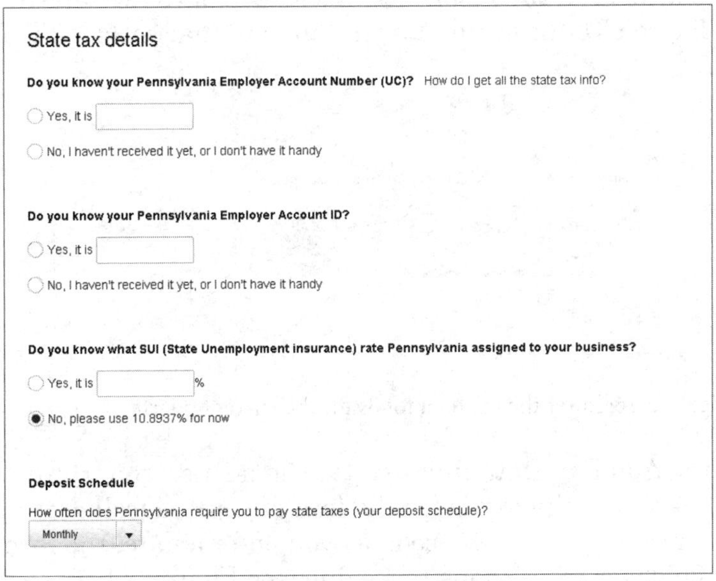

Figure 9-15: This window varies, depending on your work location state.

If you had no prior payroll this year, click Done to complete the payroll setup. QuickBooks Online displays a success dialog to let you know that you're ready to run payroll. Close the dialog box to open the Payroll Tax Center.

However, if you have paid any employees during the current year, there's another step to the wizard.

Enter Prior Payroll Tax Data

If you paid any payroll during the current year, QuickBooks Online needs to know so that it can maintain accurate payroll tax records for the entire year. If you've paid payroll using another system during the current quarter, you'll be liable for taxes due from the old system and the new. Even if you haven't, you still need to maintain accurate records for the year to ensure QuickBooks Online payroll takes certain tax limits into consideration and provides correct year-end reports.

Click Continue in the Prior Payrolls screen of the wizard to view the Company Payroll Totals screen for the current quarter (see Figure 9-16).

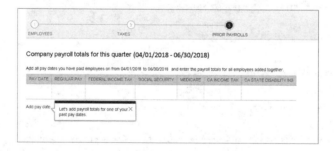

Figure 9-16: Enter the tax data totals for the current quarter.

Click the Add Pay Data link to open the next screen. Here, Quick-Books Online wants the totals for the first of your payroll dates that fell within the current quarter. As soon as you enter a date, the form expands to include fields for the various taxes due (see Figure 9-17).

Provide the payroll totals for one of your past pay dates this quarter

Past pay date (from 04/01/2018 - 06/30/2018)

| 04/04/2018 |

Enter the total amounts paid to all employees on this pay date

	TOTAL AMOUNT PAID ON 04/04/2018
Gross pay	
Regular Wages	$ _____
Taxes withheld	
Federal Income Tax	$ _____
Social Security	$ _____
Medicare	$ _____
CA Income Tax	$ _____
CA State Disability Ins	$ _____

Figure 9-17: QuickBooks Online wants to know the total payroll numbers
for one pay period during the current quarter.

Run a report from your previous payroll program for each pay period
(for the current quarter). Enter the totals from the first pay period in this
form. When you've entered the information, click Done to return to the
Prior Payrolls screen where the information from that first payroll is entered. If there were additional payroll runs this quarter from your previous payroll system, enter the totals for each one by clicking the Add Pay
Date link.

When all of the prior payroll data has been entered, click Continue
to complete the setup wizard. QuickBooks Online informs you that you're
ready to run payroll. If you want to run payroll right this minute, click
Run Payroll Now. To run it at another time, click the Run Payroll Later
button.

For this exercise we're going to tell QuickBooks Online to run it later
and return to the Employees center.

Setting Payroll Preferences

While you can start adding employees whenever you wish, you'll save yourself some time and aggravation if you configure the payroll preferences first. This is especially true if you have a large number of employees with different schedules, deductions, and so on.

To access the payroll preferences choose Tools Menu (gear icon) | Settings | Payroll Settings to display the Preferences page containing links to all payroll settings shown in Figure 9-18.

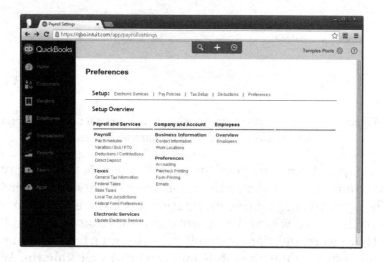

Figure 9-18: QuickBooks Online Payroll offers plenty of configuration options.

As you can see in Figure 9-18, the Preferences page has two sections – Setup: and Setup Overview. The two sections do not offer different preferences, but rather different avenues of accessing the same payroll settings. Therefore, we are only going to cover the Setup Overview section.

Payroll and Services

This is where you'll set up your payroll basics such as schedules, deductions, and direct deposit, as well as tax liabilities and agencies, and finally, electronic filing services.

Payroll

Unlike QuickBooks desktop applications, QuickBooks Online does not offer a group of employee defaults that you can pre-configure and automatically apply to new employees. With the exception of payroll schedules (which can be assigned as defaults), the other payroll items, once created here, will be available in drop-down lists when you add new employees.

Pay Schedules

Payroll schedules let you assign employees with the same pay frequency and other criteria to groups for which you can run separate payrolls. For example, if some of your employees are paid weekly and others are paid biweekly, you can create two payroll schedules and run each one at the appropriate time. If all of your employees are paid at the same frequency, but some receive a paycheck while others have their pay deposited directly into their bank accounts, you can create a schedule for each group and run one after the other on the day you generate payroll.

To set up a payroll schedule, follow these steps:

1. Open the payroll Preferences window and click the Pay Schedules link in the Payroll section. This opens the Edit Pay Policies screen seen in Figure 9-19.

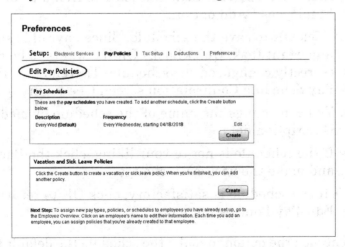

Figure 9-19: You can add pay schedules as well as vacation and sick leave policies here.

2. To create a new schedule, click the Create button to display the Pay Schedule dialog shown in Figure 9-20.

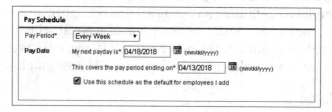

Figure 9-20: Setting up pay schedules is a snap.

3. Choose the payroll frequency from the Pay Period drop-down list.

4. Enter the date on which the paychecks for this schedule will next be issued (this is the day you actually hand out the paychecks).

5. In the next date field, enter the ending date of the pay period covered. In the example shown in Figure 9-20 the pay period ends on Friday (04/13) and the checks are handed out the following Wednesday (04/18).

6. If all (or most) of your employees are on this schedule, check the Use This Schedule As The Default For Employees I Add option.

7. Click OK to save the schedule. Since payroll is such an important task, QuickBooks Online wants to be sure you've correctly configured the schedule. Therefore, it displays a Pay Schedule Confirmation screen (see Figure 9-21).

8. You can change the name of the schedule by modifying the Description field.

9. If the schedule is not to your liking, click the Back button and make the necessary changes.

10. If the schedule is satisfactory, click OK to return to the Edit Pay Policies screen.

If you checked the option to make the schedule the default for new employees it will be marked as such. If you need to make any changes to the schedule, click the Edit link to the right.

Vacation and Sick Leave

If you offer your employees any type of paid time off (PTO), such as vacation or sick leave, you'll want to set it up ahead of time so that you can apply it to new and existing employees. To configure paid time off, open the payroll Preferences window and follow the steps below.

1. Click the Vacation/Sick/PTO link to display the Edit Pay Policies screen (refer back to Figure 9-19).

2. Click the Create button in the Vacation And Sick Leave Policies section to open the Create Vacation And Sick Leave Policies window shown in Figure 9-22.

Figure 9-22: How is paid time off accumulated?

3. From the Category drop-down list, choose the appropriate category (Sick or Vacation).

4. Enter a unique name for the policy in the Description field. Make it something easily recognizable for when you're selecting it from a drop-down list.

5. From the Accrual Frequency drop-down list, select the rate at which time for this category is accumulated. Your choices are:

   • At Beginning Of Year. If all employees automatically receive their vacation or sick time in a lump sum, at the beginning of the year, this is your choice.

- Each Pay Period. Some employers prefer that sick/vacation time is accumulated as the employee works to ensure it is earned. Use this option to add PTO as each paycheck is issued.

- Per Hours Worked. To be even more precise, use this option to calculate accrued time by linking it to the hours worked. One thing to note – this changes the next field from Hours Earned Per Year to Hours Earned Per Hour Worked.

- On Anniversary Date. If you want to assign sick/vacation time according to the employee's hire date use this option. When you add it to the Employee record QuickBooks Online will ask for the hire date.

6. Fill in the Hours Earned Per Year field. How many hours are accumulated during the course of the year? If the employee is entitled to two weeks of PTO per year, and your work week is 40 hours, enter 80. Remember, this field will change to Hours Earned Per Hour Worked if you select Per Hours Worked in the previous field. In that case you would calculate the time based on hours. For example, if you offer two (40-hour) weeks of PTO per year, you would set this to .04. Here's how we obtained the number. If the work week is 40 hours there will be a total of 2000 working hours in the work year (40x50). If the employee is entitled to 80 hours a year for vacation time, that is 1/25 or .04 of the total time worked (80/2000). Therefore, for each hour worked, the employee earns 1/25 or .04 of an hour vacation time.

7. Set the Maximum Available hours. If you do not want employees rolling over their accumulated paid time off from period to period, set a maximum number of hours that can be held by an employee at any given time.

8. Click OK to save the policy and return to the Edit Pay Policies window.

To edit a PTO policy, click the Edit link to the right of the policy.

Deductions and Contributions

This is where you configure deductions (other than taxes) that are taken out of employee paychecks. For example, if you offer a health plan, part or all of which is paid for by the employee, you need a deduction item for it. The same goes for a retirement plan. You might also need additional deduction items for such things as employee advances or voluntary charitable contributions. In addition, you might be required by law to make involuntary deductions called garnishments (e.g., alimony, child support).

> **ProAdvisor NOTE**: *Some deductions require a contribution from both the employee and the employer. This is the case where a health or retirement plan is offered, and both the employer and the employee share the cost. These are the only two types of deductions for which QuickBooks Online will create a Company-Paid Contribution field when adding the deduction to an employee record.*

1. To begin, choose Tools Menu (gear icon) | Settings | Payroll Settings to open the payroll Preferences window.

2. Click the Deductions/Contributions link to display the Create Deductions/Company Contributions screen shown in Figure 9-23.

Figure 9-23: Non-tax deductions are created here.

3. For a voluntary deduction, click the Add A New Deduction/Contribution link to display the New Deduction/Contribution screen (see Figure 9-24).

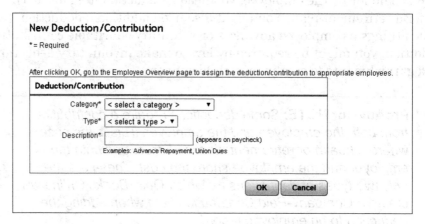

New Deduction/Contribution

* = Required

After clicking OK, go to the Employee Overview page to assign the deduction/contribution to appropriate employees.

Deduction/Contribution

Category* < select a category > ▼

Type* < select a type > ▼

Description* _____ (appears on paycheck)

Examples: Advance Repayment, Union Dues

OK Cancel

Figure 9-24: Provide basic information for the deduction here, and enter the details in the employee record.

4. From the Category drop-down list, choose the general type of deduction. If one of the preconfigured categories doesn't fit, select Other Deductions.

5. Make a selection from the Type drop-down list to further refine the deduction type.

6. Enter a description to identify this deduction. If it's for a health plan, you can enter the name of the insurance provider.

7. Click OK to save the deduction. QuickBooks Online asks if you want to assign it to employees now. Click Yes to open the Employees center or No to return to the Edit Deductions/Company Contributions window.

You enter the amount of the deduction when adding it to the individual employee record. If it's a shared health or retirement plan you'll have the opportunity to add an employer contribution as well as the employee contribution.

To add a garnishment, choose the employee from the Add Garnishment For drop-down list in the Employee Garnishments section (refer back to Figure 9-23). This opens the Edit An Employee screen. Choose Garnishment from the first drop-down list, and the garnishment type from the second (Garnishment Type). Fill in the fields that appear, and click OK when you're done.

Direct Deposit

If you want to utilize the free direct deposit feature that comes with all of the payroll plans, open the payroll Preferences window and click the Direct Deposit link in the Payroll section. In the next screen, click the Yes! Let's Get Started button and follow the online instructions.

ProAdvisor TIP: *Be sure to get signed authorization from your employees before setting them up for direct deposit. In the Direct Deposit window, click the Direct Deposit Authorization Form and print copies of the form for your employees to fill out and sign.*

Taxes

Taxes, the bane of both employers and employees, are a fact of life that everyone running or working in a business must deal with. The settings in this group of options enable the employer to provide the basic tax data for the company. This includes the company type, EIN number, and state tax information.

General Tax Information

Click this link to open the Company General Tax Information screen shown in Figure 9-25.

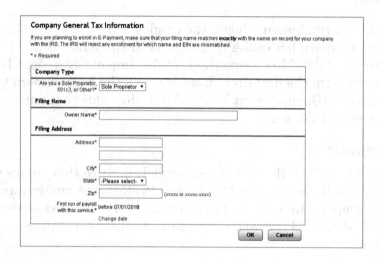

Figure 9-25: Enter (or edit) basic company information in this screen.

The fields are self-explanatory, and may already be filled in for you.

Federal Taxes

This is where you enter your Employer Identification Number (EIN) and your filing schedule (see Figure 9-26).

An EIN is free and easy to obtain. Simply go to the IRS website (https://sa.www4.irs.gov/modiein/individual/index.jsp), and fill out the form. You'll receive your EIN as soon as your information is confirmed online. While you can use it immediately for most common purposes, you'll have to wait until it is incorporated into the IRS system before filing electronic returns or payments. That should be within a couple of weeks of applying for and receiving it.

State Taxes

What you see when you click this link depends on the state that you do business in. If, like Pennsylvania, it has a state income tax, you'll see something similar to the screen shown in Figure 9-27.

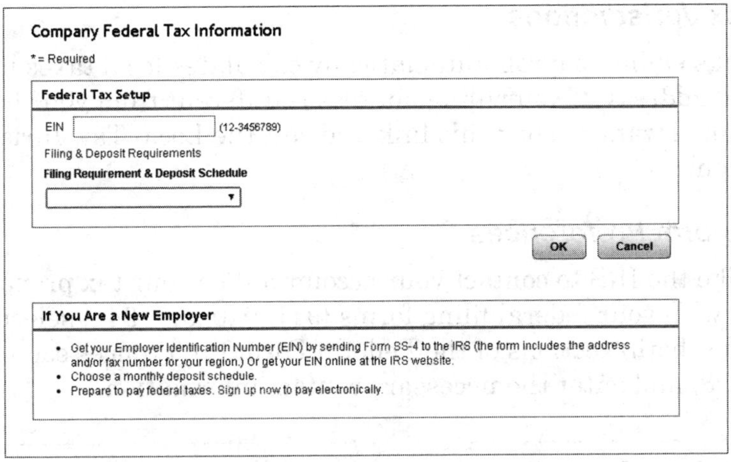

Figure 9-26: You need an EIN for running payroll.

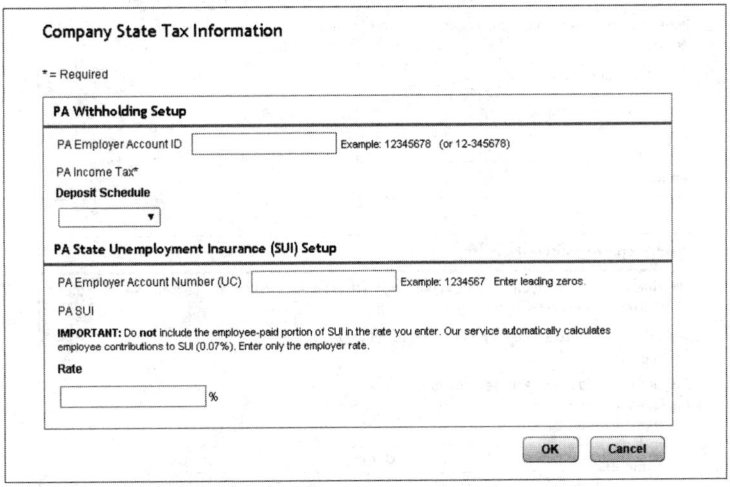

Figure 9-27: This state has withholding for both the state income tax and
the state unemployment insurance.

If you're in a state like Florida that has no income tax, you'll only see
the unemployment insurance section.

Here again, the fields are self-explanatory. Fill them in and click OK
to save the data.

Local Tax Jurisdictions

QuickBooks Online payroll automatically calculates local taxes based on your filing address. If your filing address is different from your business address you'll want to click this link and edit the Local Tax Jurisdiction information.

Federal Form Preferences

If you'd like the IRS to contact your accountant or your tax preparer about problems with your federal filing forms (941, 940, and 944) select Yes in either (or both) sections of the Federal Form Preferences screen (see Figure 9-28) and enter the necessary contact information.

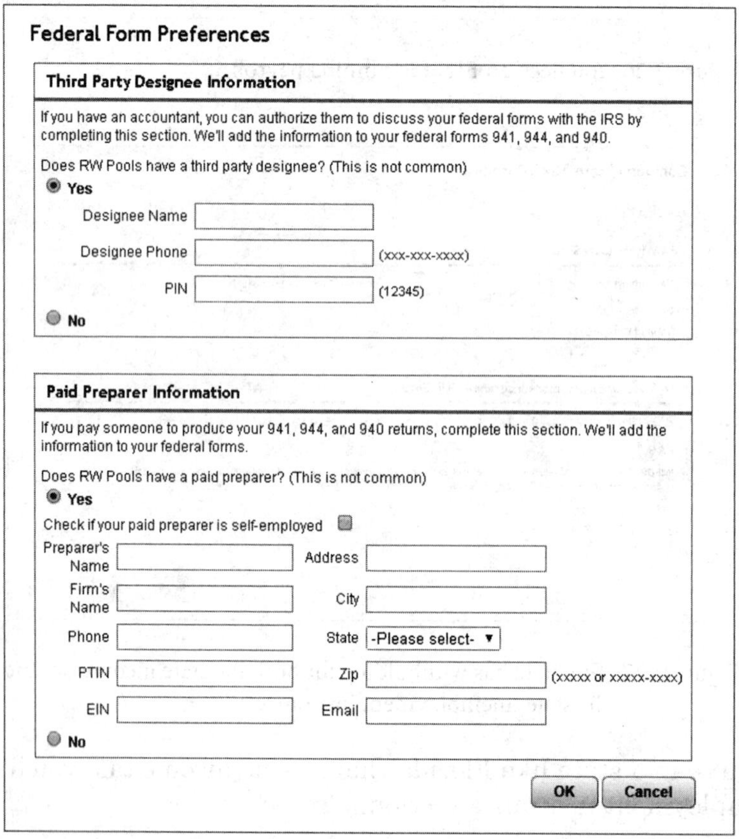

Figure 9-28: You can let your accountant deal with IRS inquiries.

Electronic Services

If you're subscribed to the Enhanced Payroll plan the electronic filing feature is included. It enables you to both pay federal (and state, where needed) taxes, and file tax forms (940, 941, 944, and W-2s) online. This is a great time-saving feature. To use the feature you must first configure it by opening the payroll Preferences and clicking the Update Electronic Services link in the Electronic Services section. This opens the Electronic Services (E-Services) Enrollment screen (see Figure 9-29).

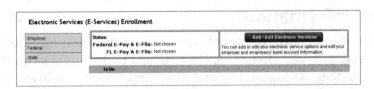

Figure 9-29: Paying taxes and filing tax forms is a snap with electronic filing.

Click the Add/Edit Electronic Services button to open an information window that explains the basics of electronic services. Next, click the Start button to display the first screen of the setup wizard. Select Yes, I Want To Electronically Pay & File My Payroll Taxes, and click Continue. In addition to your EIN number, you'll need bank account information, including the account number, routing number, and birth date and social security number of the principal account holder (see Figure 9-30).

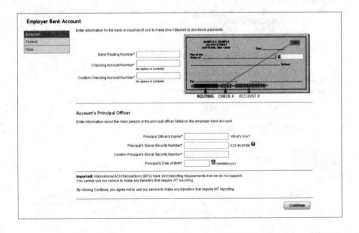

Figure 9-30: QuickBooks Online needs your account information.

Follow the on-screen instructions to complete the wizard and configure the electronic services.

Company and Account

The settings found in this section provide the opportunity to review and modify company contact information, as well accounting and printing preferences.

Business Information

It's important to ensure that all of your contact information is accurate when running payroll. Therefore, QuickBooks Online offers two different configuration options for adding and modifying contact information.

Contact Information

Click the Contact Information link to open the Edit Contact Information screen shown in Figure 9-31.

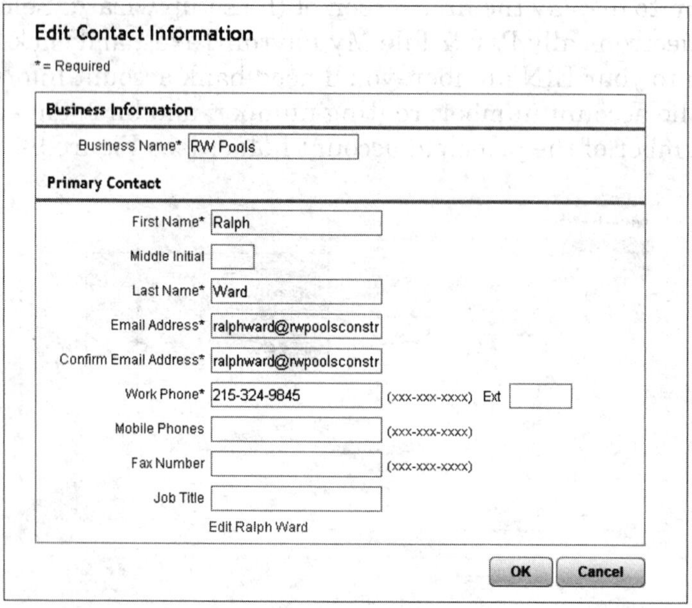

Edit Contact Information

* = Required

Business Information

Business Name* `RW Pools`

Primary Contact

First Name* `Ralph`

Middle Initial

Last Name* `Ward`

Email Address* `ralphward@rwpoolsconstr`

Confirm Email Address* `ralphward@rwpoolsconstr`

Work Phone* `215-324-9845`   (xxx-xxx-xxxx) Ext

Mobile Phones   (xxx-xxx-xxxx)

Fax Number   (xxx-xxx-xxxx)

Job Title

Edit Ralph Ward

`OK`   `Cancel`

Figure 9-31: Make sure your contact information is up-to-date.

As you can see in Figure 9-31, the existing contact information is carried over from the company information section. If anything needs to be added or modified you can do it here.

Work Locations

This is very handy if you have multiple business locations. For example, if you have warehouses or retail stores in different tax districts – or even in different states – you'll have to be sure to take them into account when running payroll. If employees live in one area but work in another, you'll want to assign each worker to the correct work location.

QuickBooks Online assumes that your primary business location is your work location as well. In most cases it probably is. However, if you need to change it, or if you need to add additional work locations, you can do so here. Click the Work Locations link to open the Edit Work Location window. To add a new location, click the Add A work Location link at the bottom of the dialog box. This opens the Add Work Location screen shown in Figure 9-32.

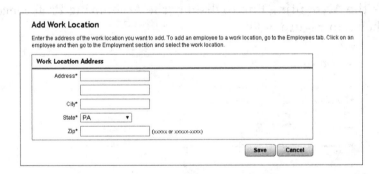

Figure 9-32: QuickBooks Online assumes your new work location is in the same state as your primary business location.

Complete the fields in the dialog box and click Save to create a new location. After confirming the address data, QuickBooks Online opens the Company Local Tax Information screen where you can modify the local tax jurisdiction information. Make any necessary changes by clicking the Edit button. When you're done, click Continue to return to the payroll Preferences window. Repeat the process if you need to create additional work locations.

Preferences

To ensure that payroll runs smoothly and according to your needs, you can set a number of options that determine the accounts used and the manner in which checks and forms are printed.

Accounting

Since maintaining accurate payroll records is essential, this is the place to start. You have to let QuickBooks Online know which account to use for writing payroll checks, and to which expense accounts you want the various payroll liabilities posted.

ProAdvisor TIP: *If you plan to use custom expense accounts for payroll (e.g., separate wage expense accounts for sales and service personnel) you'll want to add them prior to setting the accounting preferences. You can select existing accounts, but cannot create any new accounts during this process.*

Click the Accounting link to display the Accounting Preferences screen shown in Figure 9-33.

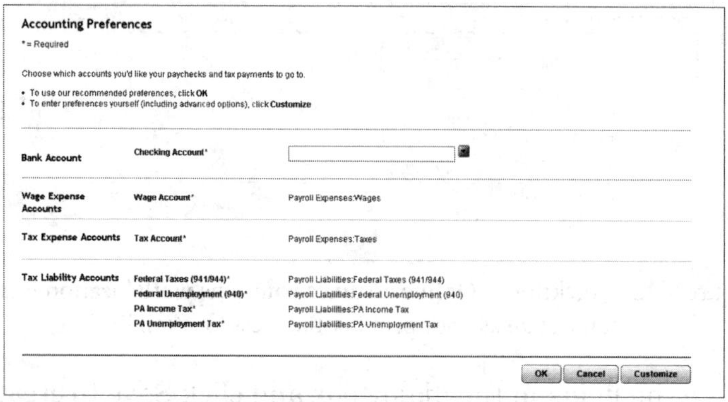

Figure 9-33: Setting up your payroll accounts correctly is essential.

If you only have one bank account configured, QuickBooks Online uses it. However, if you have multiple bank accounts (see Figure 9-33), a Bank Account drop-down list is provided so that you can select the correct account. When you click the arrow next to the drop-down list, a pop-up window appears with a list of existing bank accounts.

ProAdvisor TIP: *While many small businesses prefer to avoid the hassle of opening and managing multiple accounts, it is strongly advised that you open a separate bank account for payroll. Not only is it cleaner; it's also easier to ensure that payroll liabilities don't get accidentally spent, which frequently happens when they're mixed with operating funds.*

Select your payroll bank account from the list, and review the expense and liability accounts QuickBooks Online is suggesting you use. The recommended accounts should work for most businesses. If you prefer other accounts, create them in the Chart Of Accounts window and then return here and click the Customize button. A new Accounting Preferences window opens with drop-down lists and some new options (see Figure 9-34).

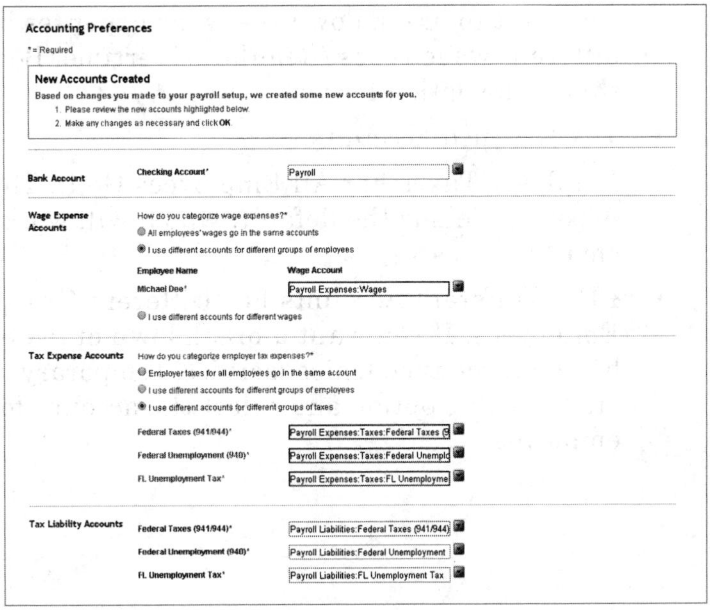

Figure 9-34: You can fine-tune your payroll expense accounts.

Here you can select the custom expense accounts you created in the Chart Of Accounts window. In addition, you can elect to use different accounts for different employees or for different types of wages and/or taxes. The available options include:

- Wage Expense Accounts
- All Employees' Wages Go In The Same Accounts. This is the default, and works for most small businesses.
- I Use Different Accounts For Different Groups Of Employees. If you want a break down of wage expenses by employee groups (such as sales employees and service employees) you would use this option. Unfortunately, QuickBooks Online doesn't offer the option to create wage groups. Therefore, you have to assign each employee to a specific wage expense account.
- I Use Different Accounts For Different Wages. If you want to break down the wage expenses by the different wage types (Regular, Overtime, Bonus, etc.) this is the option for you.
- Tax Expense Accounts
- Employer Taxes For All Employees Go In The Same Account. This is the default, which will work for most small businesses.
- I Use Different Accounts For Different Groups Of Employees. If you want a breakdown of tax expenses by employee type (sales, service, temporary help, etc.) use this option and select the account for each employee.

- I Use Different Accounts For Different Groups Of Taxes. This is actually a good option to select for any business, since it provides more detailed information in your Profit & Loss report. Instead of just showing Payroll taxes, it breaks them down into Federal Taxes, Federal unemployment, and state unemployment.

When you're done customizing the expense and liability account options, click OK to save the changes. If you opt to use the default expense accounts found in the various drop-down lists, QuickBooks Online waits until you run your fist payroll before creating those accounts in the Chart Of Accounts list (see Figure 9-35).

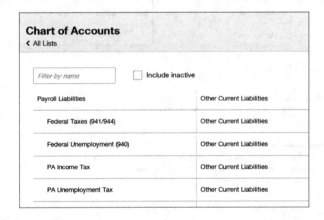

Figure 9-35: Payroll expense and liability accounts are created when you run your first payroll.

Paycheck Printing

If you plan to print some or all of your paychecks, you'll want to configure the printing options first. To do so, click the Paycheck Printing link to display the Paycheck Printing Settings screen shown in Figure 9-36.

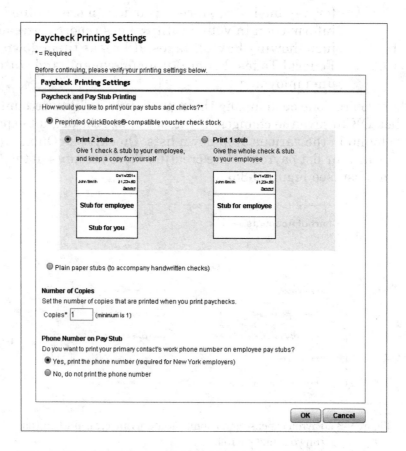

Figure 9-36: Let QBO know what kind of checks you're using.

As you can see in Figure 9-36, you have three different options to set.

- Paycheck And Pay Stub Printing. If you're using QuickBooks compatible checks that include a voucher, select the first option. This displays two additional options – to print one or two copies. If you want to

print the pay stubs on plain paper and include them
with handwritten checks from your checkbook, choose
the second option.

- Number of Copies. This is a no-brainer. How many
  copies do you want?
- Phone Number On Pay Stub. Some states require the
  phone number of the business' primary contact to
  be printed on the pay stubs. If yours is among them,
  check the first option.

Make your selections and click OK to save them. This opens the
Printer Setup window (see Figure 9-37).

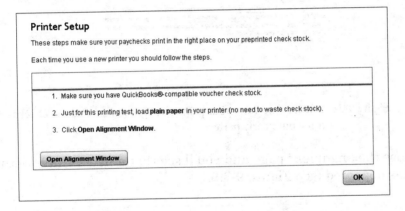

Figure 9-37: Don't waste expensive, preprinted checks. Be sure to run a test
first!

If you're using preprinted checks, you'll want to make sure that the
payroll information (names, amounts, etc.) line up on the checks before
printing. In that case, click the Open Alignment Window button to display
the sample check with voucher. Right-click the sample and choose print.
Print a copy using your default printer. Now, hold it up against a real
check and see if everything lines up. Close the sample check window, click
OK, and you're done.

If the check and the sample don't line up, click the Align Checks button to display an alignment page shown in Figure 9-38.

Print this form on your QuickBooks-compatible check stock, and follow the instructions below.
After you have printed this form, close this Acrobat window.
In the Printer Setup window:
- Enter the letter that is just above the "Pay to the Order of" line on your check.
- Enter the first number that is completely to the right of the dollar sign on your check.
- Click the "Update Settings" button on the Print Setup screen and reprint the sample check to test your alignment settings.
- When the alignment is correct, click the OK button.

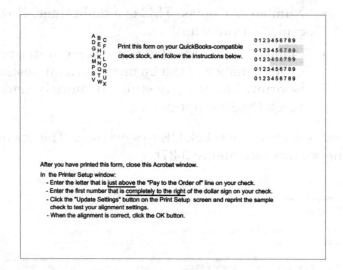

Figure 9-38: You can fine-tune your printer's alignment so that the checks come out nearly perfect.

Close the alignment page and you'll see that a new Printer Setup page has appeared (see Figure 9-39).

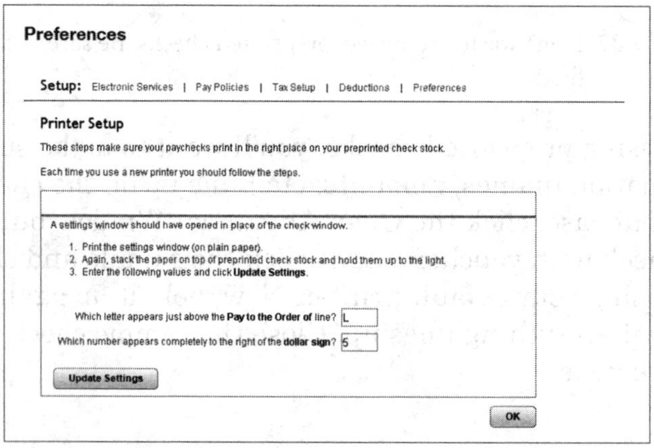

Preferences
Setup: Electronic Services | Pay Policies | Tax Setup | Deductions | Preferences
Printer Setup
These steps make sure your paychecks print in the right place on your preprinted check stock.
Each time you use a new printer you should follow the steps.
A settings window should have opened in place of the check window.
1. Print the settings window (on plain paper).
2. Again, stack the paper on top of preprinted check stock and hold them up to the light.
3. Enter the following values and click Update Settings.
Which letter appears just above the Pay to the Order of line?
L
Which number appears completely to the right of the dollar sign?
5
Update Settings
OK

Figure 9-39: Follow the instructions on the printed alignment page.

Review and follow the instructions on the page you just printed. When you're done, click the Update Settings button to display a new sample check to print and match with a preprinted check. Repeat the process until the sample and preprinted check match satisfactorily. Then click the OK button to save the alignment settings.

Form Printing

Click the Form Printing link to open the Form W-2 Printing Settings window seen in Figure 9-40.

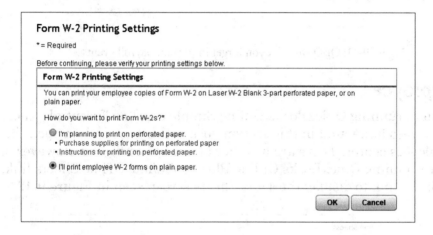

Figure 9-40: Let QuickBooks Online know how you plan to print your year-end W-2s.

At the end of every year (actually, at the beginning of the next year) every employer must file a W-2 form (wage and tax statement) for each employee. If you plan to print and mail the forms, you have to let Quick-Books Online know whether you're using preprinted forms or plain paper. Just make your selection and click OK.

Emails

The settings in this section are for reminders sent via e-mail. To ensure that you don't forget important payroll events, QuickBooks Online will alert you when it's time to run payroll, make tax payments, and/or file tax forms. Simply check the alerts you want to activate and deselect those you want to turn off. For Payday Reminders you can choose when you want the alert sent by making a selection from the Send The Payday Reminder drop-down list (see Figure 9-41).

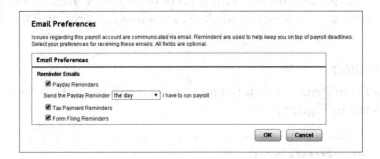

Figure 9-41: QBO won't let you forget important payroll events.

Employees

If you're running QuickBooks Online Simple Start or Essentials, the Employees link found in this section does nothing more than open the Employees center. There are no other options to configure. However, if you're running QuickBooks Online Plus you'll find a Time Sheets link. Click the link to display the Time Sheets screen seen in Figure 9-42.

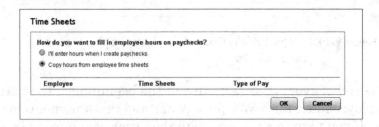

Figure 9-42: Let QuickBooks Online payroll know if you plan to use employee time sheets.

If you don't plan to use the timesheets feature to keep track of employee hours, check the first option, I'll Enter Hours When I Create Paychecks. If you are going to use the QuickBooks Online Plus timesheets feature, select the second option, Copy Hours From Employee Time Sheets. When you run payroll, QuickBooks Online Payroll checks for time sheets (single activity and weekly), and automatically ports the hours over to use in the paycheck calculations.

Using Time-Tracking (Plus Only)

If you're running QuickBooks Online Plus you have the added ability to link your payroll to your time-tracking feature. Time tracking enables you to keep a daily or weekly record of employees' hours worked. One of the nice things about the QuickBooks Online Plus time-tracking feature is that you can have an unlimited number of users whose access to QuickBooks Online is limited to timesheets. This means that each employee can be set up as a user with no privileges other than filling out online timesheets. See the section entitled "Adding Time-Tracking Users" in Chapter 3 for details on creating users with time-tracking permissions.

Once you've added time-tracking users, each one logs into Quick-Books Online and fills out either a single activity timesheet or a weekly timesheet. While time-tracking users do not have to be employees (you can allow independent contractors to use the feature also), for payroll purposes they must be employees.

To use the time-tracking feature an employee would first Log into QuickBooks Online to display the time-tracking screen shown in Figure 9-43. As you can see, the user has the option to fill out a single activity timesheet, a weekly timesheet, or to view the user's time report.

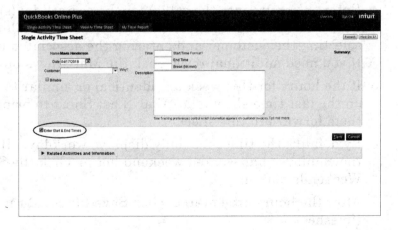

Figure 9-43: Check the Enter Start & End Times option to display additional fields.

To use a Single Activity Time Sheet, which is selected by default, follow these steps:

1. Enter the date for the activity and select a customer from the Customer drop-down list, if you're tracking work done for customers.

2. If the customer is going to be billed for the time, check the Billable checkbox.

3. Enter the time in the Time field or click the Enter Start & End Times option to have QuickBooks Online automatically calculate the time. In that case, two new fields appear for the start and end time.

4. Use the Description field to indicate what work was done.

5. Click Save to record the time.

Filling out the weekly timesheet is a little different:

1. Click the Weekly Time Sheet tab to enter hours for an entire week (see Figure 9-44).

2. From the Customer drop-down list select the customer for whom the work was done.

3. Check the Billable box to bill the customer for the time.

4. Enter the hours into the cell(s) for the correct day(s). If work was done for multiple customers, use multiple rows, selecting the customer and entering the associated hours. If you need additional rows, click the More Rows button.

5. If the hours for this week are identical or similar to those on the last time sheet, click Copy Last Sheet to bring them forward to this sheet.

6. By default, the timesheet only displays workdays. If the employee has worked weekend hours, click the Show Weekends option.

7. After the hours are entered, click Save to record the timesheet.

Click the Related Activities And Information link to display additional links and help (refer back to Figure 9-44).

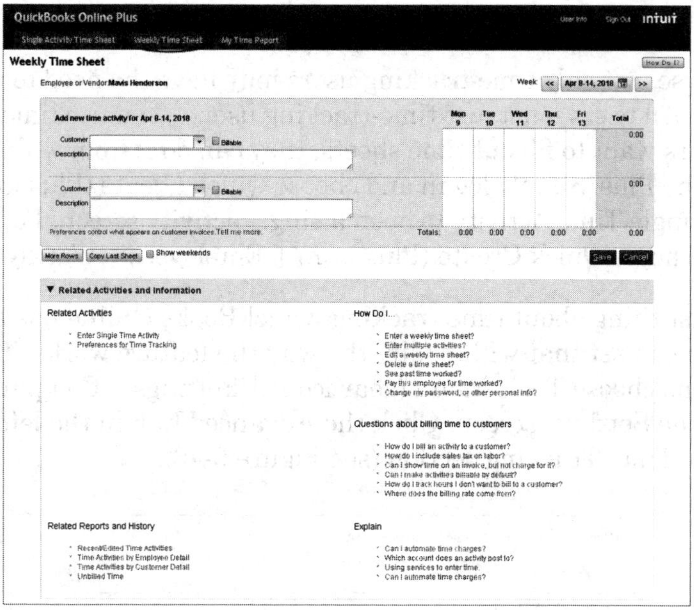

Figure 9-44: Enter a week's worth of hours in one fell swoop.

To view the hours entered (either now or previously), click the My Time Report tab, enter the dates you want to view, and click Run Report. A Time Activities By Employee Detail report is run for the employee logged in (see Figure 9-45). The buttons above the report allow the user to print, e-mail, or export the report. To fine-tune the report, click the Customize button.

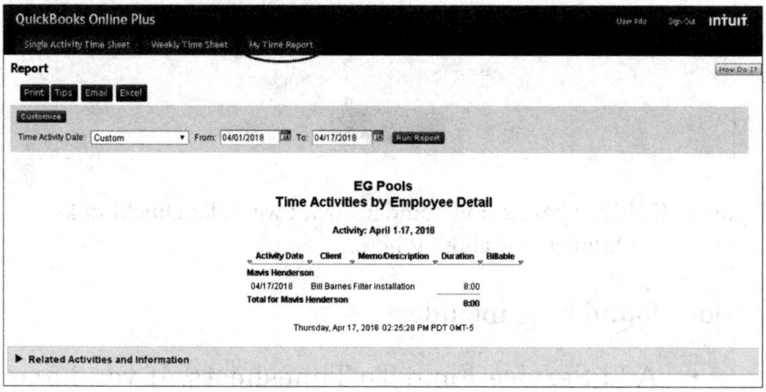

Figure 9-45: Use the My Time Report tab to review past and current hours.

Click Sign Out when finished working with timesheets.

Of course, not only time-tracking users may have the need to fill out timesheets. All users – not just time-tracking users – can use timesheets. If other users want to fill out time sheets, they can do it from within Quick-Books Online Plus. Simply log in and choose Quick Create (Plus icon) | Employees | Single Time Activity to open a single activity screen. For a weekly timesheet, choose Quick Create (Plus icon) | Employees | Weekly Timesheet.

One last thing about time tracking. QuickBooks Online has a couple of options you can set that will modify the way the feature works. To configure these options choose Tools Menu (gear icon) | Settings | Company settings to display the Settings screen. Click the Advanced link in the left pane and move to the Time-Tracking section (see Figure 9-46).

Figure 9-46: Decide which additional fields to enter to timesheets.

At first glance there appear to be two options – to add Service fields and Customer fields to the timesheets. However, when you click the pencil icon for either option, the available settings expand (see Figure 9-47).

Time tracking	
☐ Add Service field to timesheets ⑦	Off
☑ Add Customer field to timesheets ⑦	On
☐ Show billing rate to users entering time ⑦	
First day of work week	
Sunday ▾	
Cancel Save	

Figure 9-47: If you have a non-standard work week, let QuickBooks Online know about it here.

The options found here include:

- **Add Service Field To Timesheets.** If you have service items for which you bill customers (e.g., installation, repairs, maintenance) you can add a field to the timesheets so the employee (user) can link the service to the time spent.

- Add Customer Field To Timesheets. This option is turned on by default. It adds the customer (and billing) fields to timesheets. Even if you don't bill the customer for time, you may want to track it for job costing purposes.

- Show Billing Rate To Users Entering Time. This option is best left off unless you charge the same rate to the customer that you pay the employee (user). For example, if you pay the employee $20/hr for a service, but charge the customer $50/hr, you probably don't want the employee seeing the billing rate.

- First Day Of Work Week. Tell QuickBooks Online on which day your work weeks starts.

After the options are set, click Save to record the changes.

Running QuickBooks Payroll

Once you have all of your employees, payroll items, and preferences configured, the hard work is done. Now, you're ready for the easy part – running payroll.

Processing Payroll

For your first payroll run you'll want to start in the Employees center. Click the Employees link in the Left Navigation Bar, and click the Run Payroll button to display the Enter Employee Pay Details screen shown in Figure 9-48.

ProAdvisor NOTE: *If you still see a Get Started With Payroll button it means you haven't finished the setup. Click the button and finish the payroll configuration.*

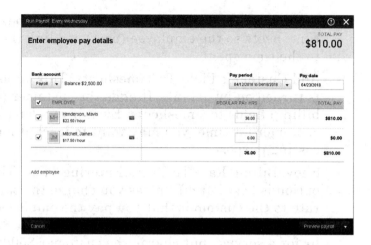

Figure 9-48: If the hours aren't entered automatically from timesheets, you can enter them now.

If you have more than one bank account, be sure to select the payroll bank account from the Bank Account drop-down list.

If you refer back to Figure 9-48 you'll see that the hours for Mavis Henderson have been pulled from her most recent timesheet and entered automatically here. James Mitchell, on the other hand, has not filled out a timesheet (or had one filled out for him). Therefore, his hours have to be entered manually. If an employee has a current timesheet with hours, but they don't appear here, that means you forgot to turn on the setting to use timesheet data for payroll. To enable the option choose Tools Menu (gear icon) | Settings | Payroll Settings and click the Time Sheets link in the Employees section. Then click the employee name and enable the option.

If you need to add an employee during a payroll run, click the Add Employee link to open a new Add Employee window. Fill out the form and click Done. The employee is added to this payroll run. Enter the hours and continue to process payroll.

When all of the hours have been entered, click the Preview Payroll button to open the Review And Submit screen shown in Figure 9-49.

Each paycheck is listed with totals. To review the current and year-to-date totals for a particular employee, click the Net Pay total which opens a Payday Info window for the employee (see Figure 9-50).

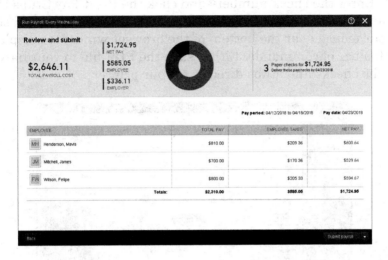

Figure 9-49: Double-check the numbers before printing the checks.

Payday info

Employee: **Mavis Henderson**
1495 Oaktree Avenue
Glendora , CA 91741

	Current payday (Apr 23, 2018)	YTD (2018)
Compensation	**$810.00**	**$1,710.00**
Regular Pay	$810.00	$1,710.00
Rate	$22.50/hr	-
Hours	36.00	-
Taxes	**$209.36**	**$456.43**
Federal Income Tax	$112.00	$246.50
Social Security	$50.22	$106.02
Medicare	$11.75	$24.80
CA Income Tax	$27.29	$62.01
CA State Disability Ins	$8.10	$17.10
Total pay	$810.00	$1,710.00
Taxes and deductions	$209.36	$456.43
Net pay	**$600.64**	**$1,253.57**

Figure 9-50: Check the details if you have any concerns.

If everything looks good, click the Submit Payroll button to process the payroll and open a summary page similar to the one shown in Figure 9-51. Enter the check numbers and click the Print Pay Stubs button to open a new browser tab with a PDF preview of the checks and stubs. Hover your mouse near the bottom of the browser window to display a floating toolbar of commands. Either save the PDF file to your hard drive or print the checks and stubs directly to your printer.

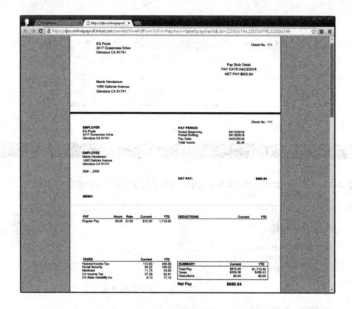

Figure 9-51: It's always a good idea to view the check and stub before printing.

That's all there is to it. When you're satisfied, close the browser tab and return to QuickBooks Online.

Payroll Liabilities

Payroll liabilities, like other liabilities, are monies that are being held for a third party. They're in your possession, but they belong to someone else. Payroll liabilities usually fall into three major categories:

- Tax withholding liabilities. This includes federal and state income tax withholdings, as well as social security and Medicare. These items are posted to the appropriate liability accounts in your general ledger. The employer's share of such things as social security, Medicare, federal unemployment tax, etc. is considered a business expense and posted to the appropriate expense account in your general ledger. However, always remember, it is not only a business expense, but also a liability (you're holding it for the designated tax agency). In other words, don't spend it.

- Employee benefit liabilities. Any amounts deducted from an employee's check to pay for health or retirement plans are included in this category.

- Miscellaneous liabilities. Less common deductions, such as charitable contributions or garnishments, make up this final category.

ProAdvisor TIP: *One of the traps many small businesses fall into is thinking that they can use the payroll liabilities money to pay regular business expenses, and replace it when the liabilities come due. It rarely works out as planned. To avoid that trap, open a separate payroll bank account, and always deposit the total payroll amount (net pay plus all employee and employer contributions) into the account.*

Paying Payroll Liabilities

How you remit your payroll liabilities will depend on the payroll plan to which you are subscribed. For this exercise we are assuming you've signed up for the integrated Enhanced payroll plan.

1. From the Left Navigation Bar choose Taxes | Payroll Tax to open the Payroll Tax Center shown in Figure 9-52.

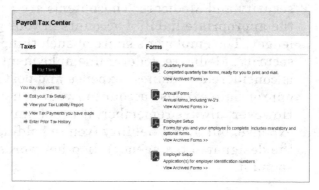

Figure 9-52: You can do more than pay taxes in the Payroll Tax Center.

2. Click the Pay Taxes button to open the Pay Taxes window seen in Figure 9-53.

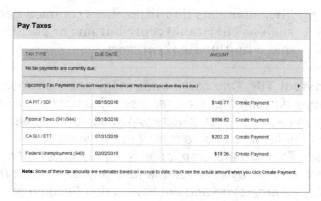

Figure 9-53: Here you'll find all payroll tax liabilities and their due dates.

3. Choose a tax that is due and click Tax Type to view the details. In the details windows that opens, you can click the Create Payment button to create a payment, or click the Pay Taxes link to return to the original Pay Taxes window.

4. If you don't need to see the details (and the payment is due) click the Create Payment link to create the payment and open the Approve Payment window (see Figure 9-54).

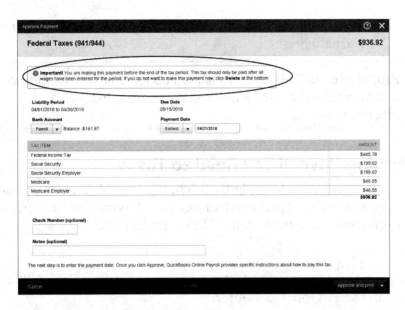

Figure 9-54: Keep an eye out for QuickBooks Online warnings. In this
case, the payment is not yet due.

5. Review the payment and enter a check number if
   applicable, and an optional note if desired. If the payment
   is correct, click the Approve And Print button and follow
   the online instructions (see Figure 9-55).

Figure 9-55: Even if you haven't enrolled in Electronic Services you can
still file electronically by clicking the link to the EFTPS
website.

6. Click View And Print Form to create a PDF copy of the worksheet.

ProAdvisor NOTE: *If you've signed up for QuickBooks Online Electronic Services you'll be able to complete the e-File process here.*

Performing Payroll Tax Related Tasks

As you can see (refer back to Figure 9-52), the Payroll Tax Center offers a lot more than just the opportunity to pay your payroll tax liabilities. The center is divided into two sections – Taxes and Forms.

Taxes

In addition to paying your payroll taxes, you can perform the following functions in the Payroll Tax Center:

- Edit Your Tax Setup. Click this link to visit the Tax Setup Overview window where you can review (and modify, if necessary) your current payroll tax settings.

- View Your Tax Liability Report. If you want to see the state of your current payroll tax liabilities, click this link to display a Tax Liability Report of all of your current payroll tax liabilities. You can modify the Date Range field to view past and future liabilities as well.

- View Tax Payments You Have Made. Clicking this link takes you to the Tax Payments window where you can view all of the payments for payroll taxes that you have made. Use the Date Range drop-down list to determine which payments to see.

- Enter Prior Tax History. This is a very important link. If you're just starting out with QuickBooks Online payroll and it's not the first day of a new year, you'll need to enter all historical payroll data to ensure your liabilities records and payments are up-to-date. Click the link to open the Prior Tax Payments window and enter any payments you have made this year. You can enter prior payments for other years, but you must enter them for the current year.

Forms

This section provides quick access to forms for the current period and forms that you've already submitted. To view the current form, click the form name. To view the submitted forms, click the View Archived Forms link.

CHAPTER 10:

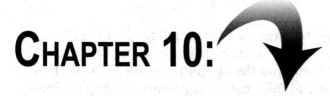

Running QuickBooks Online Reports

- Report Differences by Plan
- Understanding Standard Financial Reports
- Running Reports
- Customizing Reports
- Saving Customized Reports

One of the most important reasons for spending all of the time and effort it takes to enter your financial data into QuickBooks Online, is that it affords you the ability to produce robust, detailed reports. Accumulating financial information is essential to any business. However, information on tap is only as useful as the means you have to massage, review, and analyze it. That's where the QuickBooks Online reporting features come in.

Report Differences by Plan

All QuickBooks Online plans offer many useful financial reports. However, the number and type of reports available depends on the plan to which you're subscribed. Standard financial reports such as Profit & Loss, Balance Sheet, A/R, sales, and customer reports are available in all three plans.

Simple Start Reports

Simple Start users will find that they have fewer reports in number and in depth. For example, all subscribers have both Profit & Loss and Balance Sheet reports. However, Simple Start users are limited to standard reports, while Essentials and Plus users have standard and detail reports of each (P&L and Balance Sheet). The bottom line for Simple Start subscribers is that they have access to reports that will enable them to perform rudimentary reporting and analysis. As of this writing there are twenty seven basic financial reports in six different categories, plus sixteen payroll reports for those users running payroll.

Essentials Reports

The Essentials plan adds some very important reports, such as the Profit & Loss Detail report, the A/R Aging Detail report, and the Company Snapshot report. Essentials subscribers will find that within the same six report categories they have an additional twenty two reports.

Plus Reports

As you would expect, the Plus plan offers the widest array of financial reports. Since it offers more features than any of the other two plans it also provides additional categories as well as more reports. Plus users have a total of eight report categories, containing seventy one different reports. The additional categories include accounts payable reports and inventory reports. Most of the other categories are expanded to offer additional reports, some of which are related to the additional features found in Plus.

For example, the Business Overview category includes a Profit and Loss by Class report and a couple of budget reports. Only the Plus plan supports class tracking and budgeting. The Review Expenses and Purchases category includes a purchase order report and reports by class and by location – features only found in QuickBooks Online Plus.

ProAdvisor NOTE: *Some reports appear in more than one category, which means that the total number of unique reports is smaller than the numbers presented here.*

Understanding Standard Financial Reports

Small businesses are fragile, especially in the early years. Therefore, it is vital that business owners keep an eye on the financial health of the business. Maybe the business is bringing in a lot of revenue on the books, but is the money being collected? Keep an eye on the A/R aging report every day, and nudge those customers who are late. Check the Profit & Loss and Balance Sheet reports on a regular basis, to stay abreast of changes in financial positions. Monitor the sales and expense reports to ensure that all products and all departments are profitable.

It's not enough to just run the reports and glance over them. To analyze the numbers you're seeing, you need to understand what the numbers represent. To that end, we're going to go over some of the standard financial reports you should be familiar with.

Cash vs. Accrual Reports

Before we begin discussing individual report types and reports, it's important to understand the difference between cash-basis reports and accrual-basis reports. Reports that include income and/or expenses can be run on one or the other – cash or accrual-basis. Well, that's not quite accurate. Accrual basis reports can only be run if you have accounts receivable and/or accounts payable.

The reason for that is simple. Accrual basis reports display both income and expenses as of the dates they have been incurred (e.g., invoices created, bills received and entered) In other words, accrual-basis reports include outstanding sums owed to you as income, even though you haven't yet received the money. They also include bills that you've received and entered into QuickBooks Online (but that you haven't yet paid) as expenses. Consequently, you cannot run an accrual based expense report if you don't have accounts payable, which is the case with Simple Start users. Any reports that include expenses will show those expenses on a cash-basis (even if the report is run on an accrual-basis) since Simple Start doesn't support bills/accounts payable.

Cash basis reports, on the other hand, display income received as of the dates for which the reports are run. In other words, monies that you have physically collected (e.g., cash sales, invoice payments, refund checks) are included in the report. Expenses that you have paid (e.g., sent a check, paid online, wired the money) as of the dates of the reports are shown in the cash-basis report.

Profit and Loss Report

The most often run (and used) report is the Profit And Loss report, seen in Figure 10-1. This report includes all of your income and expense accounts and their balances. In addition, it shows your net profit or loss, which is determined by the formula, [Income – Expenses = Net Profit/ Loss].

Of interest to both business owners and accountants is the last entry – Net Income. There's a reason that financial professionals call it the "bottom line." It literally is the bottom line, and it is a critical number for the business owner. One other thing to note is that the Net Income figure is also included in the Equity portion of your Balance Sheet report, which I'll cover in the next section.

Figure 10-1: The Profit & Loss report is sometimes referred to as the
income statement.

The Profit And Loss report is a useful tool in analyzing the profitability of your business. It enables you to scrutinize your income, your
expenses, and the relation between the two. You can see an overview of
the source of your income, as well as the expenses incurred in the earning
of that income.

To do a sound analysis of your business you should review the Profit
And Loss report to determine if there are ways to increase the income
and/or decrease the expenses. The report also can help compare your
actual profit to your projected profit, and help you estimate your future
profit. It's also a good place to spot problem areas in your operation.

Balance Sheet Report

The Balance Sheet report shown in Figure 10-2 is the report you use to
gauge your business's overall financial health. It's the report that bankers
and investors want to see. It displays all of your balance sheet accounts
(i.e., assets, liabilities, and equities) and their balances. Like the Profit

And Loss report, the Balance Sheet report uses a formula to determine the bottom line – [Assets = Liabilities + Equity].

Figure 10-2: The Balance Sheet report offers a snapshot of your company's financial health.

Simple Start users will find that the only balance sheet report available to them is a standard Balance Sheet report, which is a cross between a summary report and a detail report. It provides totals for all of the individual accounts that are included in the report. However, unlike the Balance Sheet Detail report, it does not display all of the transactions for each account. Essentials and Plus plan subscribers have both a standard Balance Sheet report and a Balance Sheet Summary report.

Accounts Receivable Reports

Accounts Receivable (money that is owed to you) is an asset, and therefore an important part of your business's financial health. The accounts receivable total is not *just* an asset; it's sometimes the basis of a line of credit (a lender assumes the money, or most of it, will be collected).

Unfortunately, the fact that receivables are assets doesn't help your actual (as opposed to theoretical) financial health. You can't write checks against the receivables balance, you need the cash. A high receivables total often indicates a poor cash position.

To see the general state of your receivables, you'll want to run an A/R Aging report (see Figure 10-3). This report displays each customer and job that has an A/R balance, and shows both the current balances and the overdue balances. Overdue balances are sorted in columns by the amount of time the balance is overdue (1-30 days, 31-60 days, 61-90 days, and >90 days). This report is a good way to get a quick look at the amount of money "on the street" (accounting jargon for uncollected receivables).

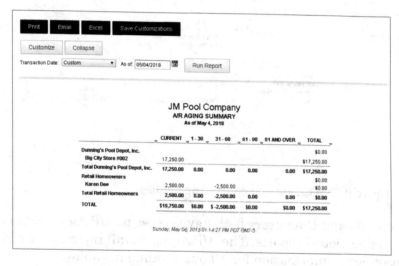

Figure 10-3: How much money do you have "on the street"?

Simple Start users are limited to an A/R Aging Summary report, while Essentials and Plus subscribers have an A/R Aging Summary and an A/R Aging Detail report.

Accounts Payable Reports

You have to keep an eye on your payables to avoid problems with vendors, late charges, or fines. This, of course, only applies to Essentials and Plus users, since Simple Start does not support accounts payable. The best Simple Start users can do is run reports to see what they've paid so far, but not what expenses are coming due in the future.

The most commonly used A/P report is the Aging Summary Report, which provides a quick look at the state of your payables. The report lists each vendor for which unpaid bills exist, and displays the totals by 30-day intervals (see Figure 10-4). You can double-click any total to drill down to see the original transactions.

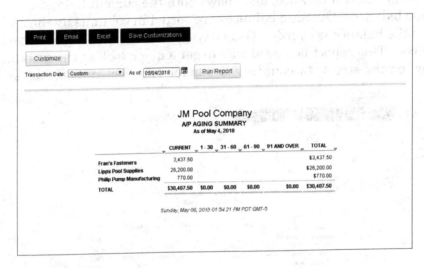

Figure 10-4: What are your outstanding payables?

Essentials and Plus users both have access to A/P Aging Summary and A/P Aging Detail reports. The A/P Aging Detail report provides transaction-level information for all outstanding payables.

Running QuickBooks Online Reports

Now that you've got the basic reports under your belt, let's see how you actually run them. The task is quite simple, and begins in the Reports center shown in Figure 10-5. Click the Reports button on the Left Navigation Bar to open the center.

As you can see in Figure 10-5, the Reports center is comprised of a number of elements:

- **P&L Graph.** The Profit And Loss graph displays the results of the current P&L report in a bar graph. It's just a quick, visual reminder of how you're doing.

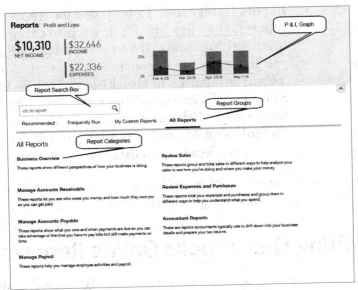

Figure 10-5: Simple Start & Essentials users have seven report categories to choose from.

- Search Box. If you know the name of the report and don't want to bother slogging through all the categories to find it, use the search box. As soon as you click in the field, QuickBooks Online presents an alphabetical drop-down list of existing reports. Start typing, and QuickBooks Online searches for reports that match the text you're typing. All reports, including custom reports are included.

- Report Groups. To better organize your reports, QuickBooks Online offers four distinct groups. The Recommended group is for reports that are most commonly used by small businesses. The Frequently Run group contains the reports that you run most often. My Custom Reports is where you'll find the reports that you have customized (and saved). The last group, All Reports, takes you to the main screen of the Reports center where all of the categories are listed.

- **Report Categories.** To help you easily locate reports, they are broken down into categories of financial functions. If you refer back to Figure 10-5 you'll see that the reports are separated into seven logical categories in QuickBooks Online Simple Start and Essentials. Plus users will find that they have two additional categories – Manage Accounts Payable and Manage Products And Inventory. Click a category heading to display the related reports.

To run a report, locate it either by group or category, or search and click the report name. It doesn't get much easier.

Customizing QuickBooks Online Reports

By default, the reports in QuickBooks Online are configured to display frequently requested information. However, it's the rare user who only needs the data supplied by the default reports. Fortunately, QuickBooks Online reports can be modified to present the information needed, in the manner required, by most users.

ProAdvisor NOTE: *All three versions of QuickBooks Online contain payroll reports. However, unlike the other QuickBooks Online reports, payroll reports cannot be customized.*

Before moving on to the Customize dialog box options, it should be noted that all reports (in all versions) have a number of common tools located on the report screen (see Figure 10-6).

On the top row of buttons, the first three – Print, Email, and Excel – are self-explanatory. The Save Customizations button is used to store a report that you've modified for future use. After you've made changes to the report using the Customize dialog box, return to the report and click the Save Customizations button. Enter a new name and add it to a report group to better organize your customized reports.

Figure 10-6: You can make minor changes to the report using these tools.

The Customize button opens the Customize <report name> dialog box where you can make your modifications. If a Collapse button appears, it means that you can reduce the number of elements showing on the report by collapsing some of the categories. For example, a Profit And Loss statement may be displaying multiple expense category subaccounts, that you don't really want to see. Click Collapse, and only the parent accounts remain on the report.

The Transaction Date field lets you select a pre-configured date range (e.g., This Year, Last Month, Next Quarter). To enter your own date range, select the appropriate dates from the From and To fields – a calendar pops up when you click the icon to the right of the fields.

Finally, click the Run Report button to refresh the report once you've made any changes to it.

Tweak Reports in QuickBooks Online Simple Start

I want to cover Simple Start separately, since the plan provides far fewer customization options than either the Essentials or Plus plan. While Simple Start does contain a couple of detail reports, the bulk are summary and standard.

Modify Summary and Standard Reports

Summary reports are those that, as you might have guessed, only provide a brief overview of the data. They generally include data from parent accounts only. Standard reports provide more detail by including subaccount data. The detail reports include everything found in the summary and standard reports, with the addition of transaction-level data.

Most of the Simple Start reports are of the summary and standard variety, so let's go over those options first. As you can see in Figure 10-7, the customization options for a standard Profit And Loss report are pretty bare bones.

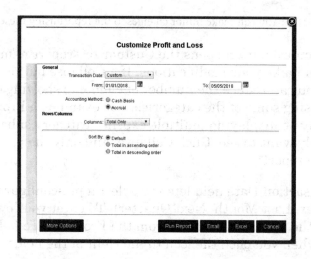

Figure 10-7: If you click the More Options buttons, you'll be told to upgrade your version of QuickBooks Online.

To customize a report, open it and then click the Customize button located above the Transaction Date field. The customization options will vary depending on the report type and coverage. Most of the reports will have some combination of the customization options described here.

- General. All reports include the General section in the Customize dialog box. There you'll find the Transaction Date field, which offers a drop-down list of pre-configured date ranges. If none of the date ranges suits your needs you can create your own by entering From and To dates in the fields provided.

- Accounting Method. Any reports that include income and/or expenses will offer the Accounting Method field. You can choose Cash-Basis or

Accrual. See the discussions earlier in this chapter for an explanation of both.

- Aging. This section only appears in A/R-related reports, such as the A/R Aging Summary and Collections reports.

    o Aging Method. By default, Report Date is selected, meaning that the past due status of invoices is determined using the date of the report, and not today's date (if they are different).

    o Days Per Aging Period. This changes the number of days displayed in the aging report columns. By default, it's set to 30 – which means that the columns display data for 1-30 days, 31-60 days, and so on.

    o Number of Periods. How many columns of aging periods do you want? The default is four, but you can reduce or increase it to suit your needs. Remember, the Current column always appears and is not affected by your choice here.

    o Min. Days Past Due. This field appears on the collections report and allows you to determine the number of days overdue invoices have to be before they are shown on the report. The default is one, which means that all overdue invoices show. However, if you only want to see seriously overdue invoices (especially for a collections report), you can change it to 30, 60, or even 90.

- Rows/Columns. A Row/Columns section appears in all reports. Some reports have more options in this section than others.

    o Change Columns. Click the Change Columns button to display the Select And Reorder Columns dialog shown in Figure

10-8. Here you can dictate which columns appear in the reports. Select a column in the Available Columns pane and click Add to move it to the Selected Columns pane. Any column that appears in the Selected Columns pane also appears in the report. The order of the columns in the report corresponds to the order in the list. Items at the top of the list appear to the left in the report.

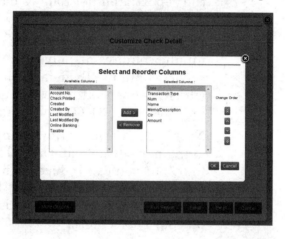

Figure 10-8: Show only the data you need.

- o Columns. This is another field that lets you change the columns that appear. It allows you to break down a report by dates or by list names (e.g., customers, vendors)

- o Sort By. How do you want the report data sorted?

- Lists. These fields let you filter the report results by narrowing the names (e.g., customers, vendors, products/services) for which the report data is shown. The number and type of lists depend on the report type.

- Status. Status sections are found in list reports and tax reports.

- o Customer Taxable. Use this list to filter the report by taxable customer or by non-taxable customers.

- o Product/Service Taxable. Same here, only it's by taxable or non-taxable products/services.

- o Deleted. Found in the Customize Account Listing dialog, Customize Vendor Contact List dialog, and others, this field lets you filter the data by including or eliminating deleted elements. Your choices are All, Not Deleted, and Deleted.

When you're done modifying the customizing options, click the Run Report button to close the dialog and refresh the report, to show the results based on the changes you just made. You can also e-mail the customized report by clicking the Email button, or export it by clicking the Excel button.

Customize Detail Reports

Detail reports are the ones that display the most information. They do not merely include totals, but individual transaction information as well. Currently, Simple Start only contains two detail reports – Check Detail and Deposit Detail. They both contain the same options (see Figure 10-9).

Figure 10-9: Detail reports have limited customization options.

As you can see, the detail report options are the same as the options provided for some of the standard and summary reports. See the previous section "Modify Summary and Standard Reports" for details on specific options.

Customize Essentials and Plus Reports

The customization process is the same regardless of the QuickBooks Online version you're subscribed to – it's the number of options that differs greatly. In general, the Essentials and Plus reports contain the same options found in the Simple Start reports, and more. Therefore, we're not going to go over the options already covered in the previous section on Simple Start reports – we'll only cover the additional options only found in Essentials and Plus reports.

Adjust Summary and Standard Reports

The definitions of summary and standard reports remain the same; summary reports display parent account data, while standard reports include data from both parent accounts and subaccounts.

The additional options found in summary and standard reports in the Essentials and Plus plans include the following.

- General. In some reports, the General section includes the option to Collapse or Expand subitems. In other words, show the subitems (Expand) or hide them (Collapse).

- Rows/Columns. Here you may find several options not included with Simple Start reports.
  - % Of Column. Check this option to add a new column to the report. It's called % Of Column, and it displays the percentage of the total for each row in the report.
  - Show Rows. Narrow the results displayed in the report rows by selecting Active (any fields with activity), All (all fields, regardless of activity), or Non-Zero (all

fields with totals that are either greater or less than zero).

- o Show Columns. Your options are the same, but applied to the columns rather than rows.

- o Group By. Found in some of the list reports, this field lets you group (and total) row data based on a particular criterion. Depending on the report, the criteria may include list type (customer, vendor, etc.), transaction type, day, week, month, and so on.

- o Add Subcolumns For Comparison. This option provides a group of different subcolumns that can be added to some summary reports. The columns are for comparison data (e.g., Previous Period, Previous Year) and percentage information (e.g., % Of Row, % Of YTD). Select (place a check mark next to) an item to include it in the report.

- Status. Some A/R related reports will add an A/R Paid field to the Status section. Use the field to filter the results by All invoices, Paid invoices, or Unpaid invoices. Transaction lists may display additional status fields such as Cleared, Check Printed, Sales Printed, and Sent.

- Numbers. This is a section only found in Essentials and Plus reports. It lets you determine how numbers appear in the report.

- o Show Negative Numbers. I don't know about you, but I frequently miss negative numbers unless they are in bright red. This option lets you decide how negative numbers are displayed on the report.

- o Show All Numbers. Scale back on large numbers and items with zero amounts. If business is booming and you're making way too much money, you might want the numbers divided by 1000 to make them more manageable (27,000,000 becomes 27,000). To leave off those annoying cents, check the Without Cents option. If you've got a lot of rows displaying zero amounts you can eliminate them with the Except Zero Amounts option.

- Header/Footer. This is another section only found in the Essentials and Plus plans. The options here let you customize the appearance as well as the information that appears at the top and bottom of the report.

  o Show In Header. Check the items you want to display in the report and modify (if necessary) the name and title fields. You can adjust the position of the header data by making a selection in the Header Alignment option (Left, Center, or Right). Check the little report preview in the bottom right of the dialog box to see how your selection affects the report.

  o Show In Footer. What do you want included in the report footer? Make your selections and choose the alignment for the footer data. The report preview displays the changes made to the Footer Alignment option.

- Dates. This section, which is not found in Simple Start, is another one that appears in some list reports. It lets you filter the report results by the creation, last modified, and due dates (if available) of the transactions.

- Match. Another section found in list reports, the Match section provides up to six fields into which you can enter text or numbers to filter out everything that does not match the information you insert in the field(s).

> **ProAdvisor TIP**: *If you find yourself customizing almost every report you open, save yourself a step and open the Customize <report name> dialog from the category list by clicking the Customize link found below the report description. It runs the report, but opens the Customize dialog first.*

Modify Detail Reports

Unlike Simple Start, Essentials and Plus have a ton of detail reports – from A/R Aging Detail to Vendor Balance Detail, and everything in between. Of course, Plus has more than Essentials. However, in neither plan are there additional options not found in the previous section on summary and standard reports.

> **ProAdvisor NOTE**: *The one thing you will find is that the options may vary depending on the company settings you have configured. For example, if you have shipping enabled you may see a Ship Via field as a choice in the Match section of a report. For Essentials users, there will be Class and Location options/fields in some reports if those features are enabled in the company file.*

Save Customized Reports

If you're familiar with memorized reports in QuickBooks desktop applications you'll be glad to know that they have their online equivalent in all QuickBooks Online versions. Even the process is similar.

1. Open the desired report.
2. Click the Customize button to open the Customize <report name> dialog.
3. Make your modifications.
4. Click Run Report to return to the report window.
5. Click the Save Customizations button to display the Save Report Customizations dialog (see Figure 10-10).

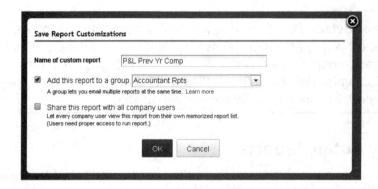

Figure 10-10: Don't forget to save customized reports that you use often.

6. Give the report a unique name that will easily identify the report the next time you go looking for it.

7. If you want to organize your reports into groups, click the Add This Report To A Group option and select a report from the list (or create an entirely new group by clicking Add New).

8. If you've got a great report that you think other Essentials and Plus subscribers would like to use, click the Share This Report With All option.

9. Click OK to save the customized report.

That's all there is to it. The next time you want to run the report, click the Reports button on the Left Navigation Bar and then click the My Custom Reports link to locate it (see Figure 10-11).

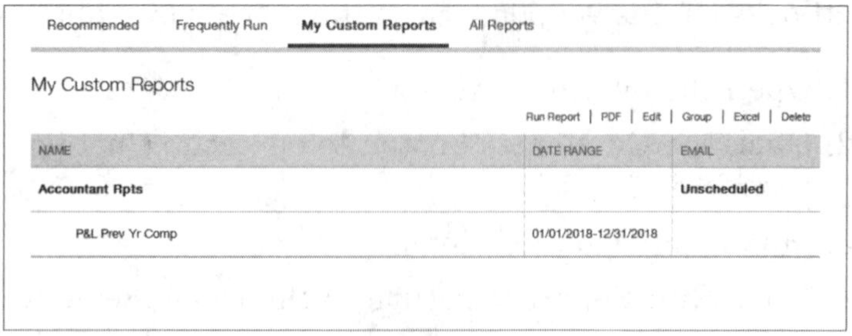

Figure 10-11: You can view and manage your customized reports here.

APPENDIX A: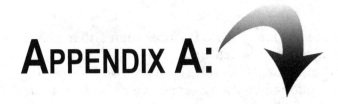

QuickBooks Online Plus Advanced Features

- Creating a Budget

- Working in the Budgets Window

- Running Budget Reports

- Understanding Inventory

- Adding Inventory Items

- Purchasing and Receiving Inventory

- Adjusting Inventory

QuickBooks Online Plus has many more features than either Simple Start or Essentials. Most of those features are covered in the first ten chapters of this book. However, there are two Plus plan features that deserve a little more in-depth coverage, which is the reason for this appendix.

Planning Ahead with QuickBooks Online Budgets

The whole idea behind budgets is not to restrict your spending, but to help you analyze and manage it. A budget is like a mini financial plan. You make your projections (create the budget), track them (run budget vs. actuals reports), analyze the results (use your brain), and make any necessary changes to your operations.

Create a Budget

The most common budget for any organization – one that's based on your income and expenses – is called a Profit And Loss (P&L) budget. Creating a P&L budget is quite easy, especially with the Create A Budget wizard (called a Mini Interview) to hold your hand during the process.

ProAdvisor TIP: *You cannot create accounts on the fly during the budget creation process. Therefore, if you wish to include new accounts in the budget, open the Chart Of Accounts and add them before starting the Create A Budget wizard.*

Getting started is easy.

1. Choose Tools Menu (gear icon) | Tools | Budgeting to launch the Create A Budget wizard. If you've already created at least one budget, the Budgets window opens instead. Click the New Budget button to open the wizard.

2. The initial screen is informational only. However, since it has good information, read it and then click Next.

3. The second screen (see Figure A-1) lets you decide what numbers you want to use in the creation of your new budget.

- Actual Amounts From. If you've been in business for a year or more, and you have that historical income and expense data in QuickBooks Online, you can use it to create the budget. From the drop-down list, select a fiscal year on which to base the budget.

- No Amounts. Choose this option to enter all numbers manually.

- Copy From An Existing Budget. If you have existing budgets, you can select one to use as the basis for the new budget.

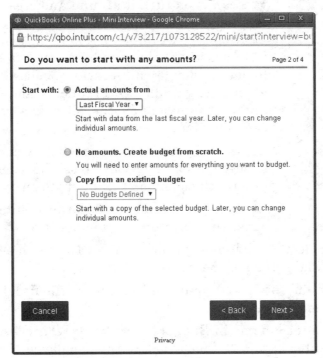

Figure A-1: Create the budget from scratch or use existing data.

4. Click Next to move to the third wizard screen. This is where you set additional criteria for this budget. Your choices are:

- Don't Subdivide. If all you need is a P&L budget by accounts, this is the right choice.

- Locations. If you are using the Locations feature this is a great option to create a P&L budget by location. Track each location to see if it is meeting its profitability targets, cutting expenses as planned, or increasing revenue. This budget presents the data by account, per period (i.e., month, quarter, or year), for the location you select. You can create a different budget for every location and sub-location in your company file. You can even turn it around and create a budget for every account in your Chart Of Accounts by location. For example, if you're only interested in forecasting sales numbers, you can set the budget to display all locations, choose a sales account (e.g., Sales Of Products), and then enter different numbers for the selected account, for each location.

- Classes. If you use class tracking you can subdivide the budget by class. The concept is exactly the same as the subdivision by locations.

- Customers. Reread the Locations bullet item and substitute "customers" for "locations."

5. Select a subdivide option and click Next to move on to the final screen of the wizard.

6. From the first drop-down list, choose the fiscal year for this budget.

7. Enter a name in Budget Name field. Whatever you enter here will appear before the Displayed Name that is created automatically (and cannot be modified by the user). As you can see in Figure A-2, the Displayed Name was "- FY19 P&L". When I entered By Customer in the

Budget Name field, the Displayed Name changed to "By Customer - FY 19 P&L"

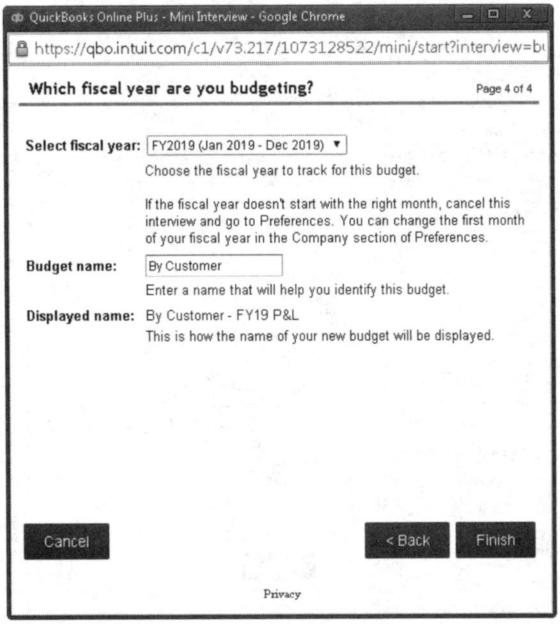

Figure A-2: Give the budget a unique name that will let you easily identify it in the future.

8. Click Finish to create the budget and open the Budgets window.

Once the Budgets screen appears, you can start entering (a "create from scratch budget") or modifying (a budget based on existing financial data) the numbers in the budget.

Work in the Budgets Window

All budgets are displayed and modified in the Budgets window. The window has a number of tools that make it easy to enter and manipulate the financial information. One thing to note is that the main budget display is just that – a display of the entered information. Unlike other budget applications, this one does not allow you to enter any data in the body of the budget. To enter or change budget data you have to use the

Edit - <budget name> section at the bottom of the window (see Figure A-3).

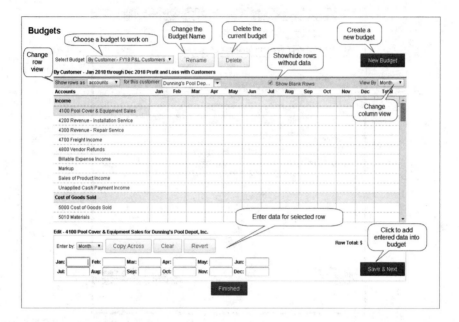

Figure A-3: This P&L budget by customer is going to be created from scratch.

The Budget window elements seen in Figure A-3 let you do two things – enter and modify data, and choose the way that information is displayed.

- Select Budget (drop-down list). If you have multiple existing budgets, choose the one that you want to view and/or modify.

- Rename button. Clicking this button opens a Rename Budget dialog box that lets you change the Budget Name you that entered in the wizard while creating the budget.

- Delete button. If you want to eliminate the currently displayed budget, click the Delete button and confirm that you want to delete it.

- New Budget button. Click this button to launch the Create A Budget wizard.

- Show Rows As (drop-down list). This option, which only appears on reports with subdivisions, lets you change the data displayed in the rows. For example, in the budget divided by customers (refer back to Figure A-3), the rows display accounts (the default). However, the Show Rows As drop-down list has a second choice – Customers. If you select Customers, all of the rows change to display every customer in the file.

- For This <customer, account, location, class – depending on the budget type> (drop-down list). The items displayed in the list change with the type of subdivisions used in the report. For example, in the P&L by Customer budget, this drop-down list displays all of the customers in the company file. By selecting a customer from the list you can create an entire P&L budget just for that customer. You can create as many different customer budgets as you wish. If you change the selection in the Show Rows As drop-down list, the choices in the For This list also change. For example, if you change the Show Rows As list from Accounts to Customers, the For This list displays Accounts instead of Customers. That means you can create a separate budget for every customer in the file for a single account.

- Show Blank Rows option. If you only want to create a budget for a handful of accounts there's no reason to scroll through the whole budget to see your results. Check this option, and only the rows containing data are displayed.

- View By (drop-down list). Here you can choose to display the columns by Month, Quarter, or Year.

- Enter By (drop-down list). You'll find this list in the Edit section at the bottom of the window. It allows you to change the data entry fields in the Edit section to match the way you want to display the data in the budget. If all that you want is quarterly information, why bother entering it by the month? If you do, QuickBooks Online will do the math for you, but it will be a lot quicker to enter quarterly information instead.

- Copy Across button. A very handy button indeed, if you want to enter the same data in multiple, consecutive fields/columns. For example, if you're entering monthly data and you want the first six months to contain 10,000 and the second six months to contain 15,000, use the Copy Across button. Enter 10000 in the first field (Jan if you're on a calendar year) and click the Copy Across button. It fills all twelve months with 10000. Now move to the Jul field, enter 15000, and click the Copy Across button. The result is that Jan through Jun contain 10000, while Jul through Dec have 15000.

- Clear button. Click this button to clear all of the fields in the Edit section. If you want to clear a row in the budget, highlight the row, click the clear button, and then click Save & Next.

- Revert button. This button returns the fields in the Edit section back to their original state. For example, if you highlight a row in the budget, click the Clear button, and then change your mind, you can click the Revert button to reinstate the original figures.

- Data fields. Named according to your choice in the Enter By drop-down list, these fields are the data entry fields.

- Save & Next button. Once you've entered numbers into the data fields, click this button to add them to the selected row in the budget.

- Finished button. To close the Budgets window and return to the last QuickBooks Online window you were working in, click the Finished button. If you've made changes without saving them, QuickBooks Online will ask if you want to save them before closing the Budgets window.

You'll notice that there are no Print, Email, or Export buttons in the Budgets window. That's because you have to run budget reports to display, customize, and output the budget information.

Run Budget Reports

Okay, now that you've created all those budgets what are you going to do with them? Analyze them, of course. The way you analyze your budget data is by running reports. QuickBooks Online Plus offers two budget reports – the Budget Overview report and the Budget vs. Actuals report – both found in the Business Overview category of the Reports section.

Budget Overview

The Budget Overview report is just that. This report presents the budget numbers in much the same format as the budget itself. It does, however, remove blank lines and add rows for totals (Total Income, Total COG, Gross Profit, Total Expenses, Net Operating Income, and Net Income).

If you have multiple existing budgets, the Customize Budget Overview dialog opens automatically so that you can select the budget you want to view in the report. While you're there you can make additional customizations – such as changing the date range, the sort order, and even the makeup of the rows and columns.

Budget vs. Actuals

This is the report that you use to analyze your progress in realizing your budgeting goals. It compares your budget numbers to the real numbers. For each account, it displays the amount posted, the amount budgeted, and the difference in dollars and percentage (see Figure A-4). By comparing the numbers you can see how well your forecast predicted the actual income and expenses incurred. It's a great tool for determining whether you need to adjust your spending, your marketing, or perhaps your budgets.

	JAN 2018			
	ACTUAL	BUDGET	OVER BUDGET	% OF BUDGET
Income				
4100 Pool Cover & Equipment Sales	34,500.00	20,000.00	14,500.00	172.50 %
4200 Revenue - Installation Service		8,000.00	-8,000.00	
4300 Revenue - Repair Service	168.00		168.00	
Total Income	**$34,668.00**	**$28,000.00**	**$6,668.00**	**123.81 %**

Figure A-4: Your budgeting skills in black and white.

Tracking Inventory in QuickBooks Online

I hate to start with the negative stuff, but it's extremely important to understand the limitations of the inventory tracking features in QuickBooks Online Plus. It's fine if you have a small number of inventory items and infrequently make inventory adjustments. However, if you have hundreds (or thousands) of inventory items, the features offered here are not going to work well for you. You'll have to look to third party add-ons, or revert to a QuickBooks desktop application.

QuickBooks Online inventory tracking limitations include the following;

- Inventory adjustments. There is no inventory adjustment tool in QuickBooks Online. You have to open each product/service item and manually "update" the quantity. Additionally, you cannot make value adjustments; they're done automatically when you make quantity adjustments.

- Receiving inventory items. There is no Receive Items procedure. The only way inventory items are received is by the creation of certain sales transactions (i.e., sales receipts, checks, or bills). This is especially dangerous since the simple act of entering a bill into QuickBooks Online automatically adds the items on the bill into inventory immediately. Of course, you may or may not receive the items, but they're already part of your inventory asset.

- Receiving partial orders. While you can easily convert a purchase order to a bill – and thereby receive the items into inventory – you cannot receive a partial order. In other words, if only half the items on the purchase order arrive, you'll have to turn the PO into a bill, change the items on the bill to match those received, and then create a new purchase order for the items that did not arrive.

- Inventory Assemblies. If you buy raw materials or parts from which you build inventory items you'll have to forego assembly items, which track the individual items that are included in the final product.

If you can work with the above limitations, then let's take a look at how inventory tracking works in QuickBooks Online.

Understand Inventory

Inventory is the collection of items that a business keeps in stock for the purpose of reselling. Inventory stock is an important asset, the value of which is determined by the cost of the goods rather their selling price. For many businesses (e.g., manufacturers, retail stores, distributors) inventory comprises a major portion (if not all) of their income. Therefore, managing inventory is a key task that must be performed diligently.

A business with a large inventory has a lot of money tied up in this asset, and must regularly turn over (sell) the inventory at a profit. Merchandise that sits in a warehouse is earning nothing, and may even be losing value. Therefore, it's essential to quickly restock good-selling items, and move out the slow movers. That's the purpose of inventory tracking.

QuickBooks Online Valuation Method

One of the nice things about QuickBooks Online is that it uses the FIFO (First In, First Out) method of determining the value of your inventory. This is the method used by QuickBooks Enterprise editions, and high-end inventory software. Unfortunately, you don't have a choice between valuation methods, so it's FIFO or nothing.

ProAdvisor NOTE: *Always remember that the value of inventory is determined by the cost of each item plus additional charges such as sales tax, shipping, handling charges, and so on. When accounting for those expenses you add them to the Account Details section of the transaction form, while the items themselves are listed in the Item Details section.*

The FIFO method is quite simple. It assumes that the oldest inventory items are the ones that are sold first. So, if you bought fifty widgets at $10/widget in May and fifty at $12/widget in July, QuickBooks Online is going to sell the $10 widgets first. Until all fifty of those $10 widgets are sold, QuickBooks Online is going to post $10 to the Cost of Goods Sold account every time you sell a widget. When the first fifty are gone, each widget sold will see $12 posted to the COGS account.

Turn Inventory Tracking On

Before you can add or track inventory in QuickBooks Online Plus, you have to first enable the feature. Choose Tools Menu (gear icon) | Settings | Company Settings to open the Settings window. Click Sales in the left pane and Products And Services in the right pane. Set the options that appear in the Products And Services section (see Figure A-5).

- Show Product/Service Column On Sales Forms. As long as you're selling products and/or services, you need to check this option. It adds the Product/Service column to sales receipts, invoices, and other sales forms, without which you cannot select a product or service to add to the transaction.

- Track Quantity And Price Rate. This is a must if you're tracking inventory. It adds the Qty and Rate fields to those same sales transaction forms.

- Track Quantity On Hand. You can't track inventory unless you know how many of each inventory item you have on hand. While you need all three options turned on to track inventory, this is the one that really enables the feature. When you check this option, the Track Quantity On Hand setting appears in the Product Or Service Information dialog you fill out to create a new inventory item.

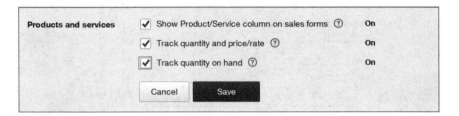

Figure A-5: You need all three options enabled to track inventory.

Add Inventory Items

If you have an existing inventory item list in Excel, or can get it into an Excel spreadsheet, that will be the easiest way to bring inventory items into QuickBooks Online. If not, you'll have to add each item manually.

Importing Inventory Items

The trick to importing inventory items is to correctly format the spreadsheet you're using for the import. Since importing and exporting are covered in Appendix B (where importing inventory items is used as an example) we're not going to cover it here. Suffice it to say that it will be a great time saver, especially if you have a large number of inventory items.

Creating Inventory Items Manually

Even if you are able to import your inventory items by using a spreadsheet, you'll still find yourself adding an occasional item by hand. If you have no way to get your inventory list into a spreadsheet, you'll have to add all your items by hand. Whatever the reason, here's how you do it.

1. Choose Tools Menu (gear icon) | Lists | Products And Services to open the Products And Services window.

2. Click the New button to open the Product Or Service Information dialog shown in Figure A-6.

Figure A-6: Inventory items require purchasing information.

3. Fill out the basic information (name, description, etc.).

4. Check the Track Quantity On Hand option to display addition fields. This is another of those fields, similar to Opening Balance fields, that I recommend you leave blank and enter historical transactions to create. (If you plan to follow my advice, enter zero in the field since you cannot leave it blank.) Like the others, it credits the Opening Bal Equity account, which tells you (or your accountant) nothing about the origin of the posting. If, instead, you enter the items by creating expense, check, or bill transactions, you will have correct expense (COGS) postings, as well as date and vendor data. The other thing that this field ignores is the true cost of the existing inventory. It uses the amount you enter in the Cost field to calculate the value. However, if the existing inventory

was purchased over time at different costs, they will not be reflected here.

5. Enter the As Of Date.

6. Choose the correct Inventory Asset Account. QuickBooks Online has probably already created (and selected here) an account called Inventory Asset. That should work for most small businesses.

ProAdvisor TIP: *You cannot create new inventory asset accounts on the fly when setting up inventory items. If you need to add an inventory asset account, you must do so in the Chart of Accounts window. The new account must be of the Other Current Assets type and of the Inventory detail type. This is extremely important. The only Other Current Assets type accounts that show up in the Inventory Asset Account drop-down list of the Product Or Service Information dialog are those designated as Inventory in the Detail Type field.*

---

7. Fill out the Purchasing Information fields that appeared when you checked the Track Quantity On Hand option.

8. Select the appropriate Cost Of Goods Sold (COGS) account from the Expense Account drop-down list. Although the name of the field is Expense Account, no expense accounts appear in the list. This is as it should be. The field name should really be changed to COGS Account. Cost Of Goods Sold accounts are expense accounts – they're just a specialized type used for tracking the cost of inventory items.

9. Click Save to record the information and create the new inventory item.

Purchase and Receive Inventory

As I mentioned at the beginning of the inventory section, there is no separate receiving procedure for inventory items. As soon as you make a purchase, QuickBooks Online records the purchased inventory items as received. Consequently, this section is really about purchasing inventory items. The receiving part is done automatically.

You have several ways to bring inventory into QuickBooks Online Plus.

- Convert a purchase order to a bill
- Create a bill
- Write a check for inventory items
- Create an expense for inventory items

Since bills, expenses, and checks (direct disbursements) are covered in other chapters, we're not going to duplicate those efforts here. However, purchase orders are only found in Plus, and are not addressed elsewhere in the book.

ProAdvisor NOTE: *Keep in mind that as soon as you write a check, create an expense, or generate a bill, the inventory items included in the transaction are immediately added to inventory.*

Creating Purchase Orders

Purchase orders are transaction forms used to record intended purchases from vendors. Some vendors require them, others don't. Some businesses use them, others don't. The nice thing about purchase orders is that they have no affect on your finances at all. No amounts are posted, no quantities are recorded. They simply let you know what you have on order.

Creating a purchase order is similar to filling out most other transaction forms. With the three inventory tracking options turned on (discussed earlier) your purchase order form will look something like the one in Figure A-7.

Fill out the fields in the form. Everything is self-explanatory. The only thing to be aware of is the Account Details section. This is where you can add such things as shipping charges, sales tax, and other assorted charges. You can use these fields to estimate what the final order will cost, but it's rare to have the exact numbers when creating the purchase order. In other words, when you convert the PO to a bill you're almost certainly going to have to change those numbers. Therefore, unless you're just looking to get a rough total, it's probably not worth using the Account Details section.

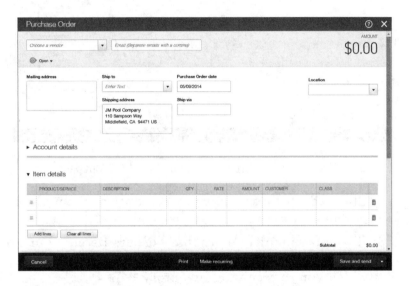

Figure A-7: Purchase orders are record-keeping devices that do not affect your financial data.

Converting Purchase Orders to Bills

When the goods finally arrive, you have to convert the purchase order to a bill. This accomplishes two things. First, it adds the amounts to your accounts payable. Second, it brings the items into inventory. Converting the purchase order to a bill is easy. However, it's not done from the purchase order screen, but rather the bill screen. I should probably call it creating a bill from a purchase order instead.

1. Choose Quick Create (Plus icon) | Vendors | Bill to open a blank Bill form, which displays any open purchase orders in a new pane on the right side (see Figure A-8).

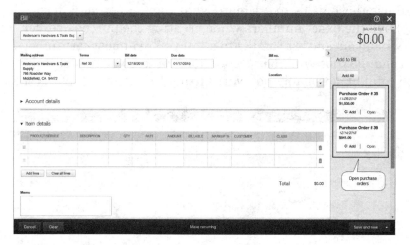

Figure A-8: Open purchase orders appear in the Add To Bill pane.

2. Click Add All if you have received items from all of the purchase orders listed.

3. If you have multiple purchase orders listed – but are only receiving items on one – click the Add link on the one for which you're receiving inventory.

ProAdvisor NOTE: *Remember, there's no way to receive a partial order. As soon as you add the purchase order to the bill and save it (the bill), all items on the bill are added into inventory. It doesn't matter how many items you actually received. For example, if the purchase order was for 50 widgets, but only ten arrived, all 50 are added to the bill. This means you have to change the number on the bill before saving it. It also means that you have to create a new purchase order for the items that failed to arrive.*

4. Adjust the quantities and prices if the actual numbers differ from those on the original purchase order.

5. Add taxes, shipping charges, and other miscellaneous charges to the Account Details section.

6. Click Save And Close to create the bill and add the items into inventory.

Adjust Inventory

One of the most important tasks in inventory control is taking a periodic count of your stock and making the necessary adjustments. The first thing to do is open the Products And Services window and check the Include Inactive option. You may still have stock on hand, even if the item has been made inactive. You need to include any such items in your count because they are still part of your inventory asset.

The next thing to do is click the Export button and send the entire list to an Excel spreadsheet. Open the list in Excel and delete the columns you don't need for an inventory count. Add a column all the way to the right for recording the physical count. You might want to go into the page setup and add grid lines to make the printed list easier to use. Finally, print the list and hand it out to the people doing the count.

When taking a physical inventory you should implement a few rules:

- Do not receive any new merchandise until the count has been completed.

- If you use a computerized cash register, record all sales transactions on paper and transfer them to the computer when the count is done.

- If you have multiple people involved in the count, put one person in charge.

- Decide what to do with damaged items encountered during the count.

When the count is over and you find that not all of the numbers match, it's time to make the adjustments in QuickBooks Online. Unfortunately, there is no inventory adjustment tool, so you'll have to make the adjustments manually.

Open the Products And Services window to begin. Locate the first inventory item that needs to be adjusted, highlight it, and click the Edit button to open the Product And Service Information dialog. Click the Update button to display the New Quantity On Hand, and Difference fields (see Figure A-9). Enter the true quantity from the physical count. QuickBooks Online automatically calculates the difference. Click the Save button to record the change.

Figure A-9: QuickBooks Online takes care of the math.

The first time you make an adjustment, QuickBooks Online creates a Cost Of Goods Sold account called Inventory Shrinkage. It uses this account to post inventory adjustment values. You cannot change it. If you make a negative adjustment (missing inventory), the Inventory Shrinkage account is debited (increased) and the Inventory Asset account is credited (decreased). If you make a positive adjustment (added inventory), the postings are exactly opposite – the Inventory Shrinkage account is credited and the Inventory Asset account debited.

If you want to track adjustments more closely you'll have to create your own COGS accounts for overages, breakage, theft, etc., and use a journal entry to move the amounts from the Inventory Shrinkage account into the appropriate COGS account.

APPENDIX B:

Importing & Exporting in QuickBooks Online

- Import from QuickBooks Desktop

- Use the Import Data Tool

- Export to QuickBooks Desktop

- Export to Spreadsheets

One of the most important features of any accounting application is the ability to import data from other sources, and to export data to other applications. QuickBooks Online has import and export tools to perform these functions. Unfortunately, they're somewhat limited. Some of the import and export features are covered elsewhere in the book. Here I'm going to deal with the rest.

Importing into QuickBooks Online

If you've ever entered accounting data into an application manually, you know what a pain it is. One of the most helpful features a data-intensive (especially accounting applications) programs can offer is a way to import information from other applications or files.

The most common method of importing (and exporting, on the other end) is the use of spreadsheet or delimited files. The common spreadsheet in use today is Excel, so if I refer to an Excel file I'm really talking about any Excel-compatible file, which includes TSV (Tab Separated Values) and CSV (Comma Separated Values) files. These are text files that have records separated by paragraph breaks, and fields separated either by tabs or commas. Most spreadsheet programs have no problem reading these files as long as they are properly laid out.

Importing into QuickBooks Online is accomplished in one of two ways – either you import data directly from an existing QuickBooks desktop company file, or you use the Import Data feature in QuickBooks Online to import from an Excel spreadsheet.

Import from QuickBooks Desktop

Since I covered the import process in detail in Chapter 3, I'm not going to go over it again here. However, I would like to say that importing data is not without its idiosyncrasies and problems. Depending on the version of QuickBooks Online to which you're subscribed, you may see more or fewer of these problems. For a good explanation of things you may encounter, check out this Intuit article https://qboe.custhelp.com/app/answers/detail/a_id/4095.

Use the Import Data Tool

QuickBooks Online provides a handy tool for importing list data (sorry, no transaction data). It's called, aptly enough, Import Data. To open it, choose Tools Menu (gear icon) | Tools | Import Data. As you can see in Figure B-1, it offers five choices.

- Customers
- Vendors
- Chart Of Accounts
- Bank Transactions
- Products And Services

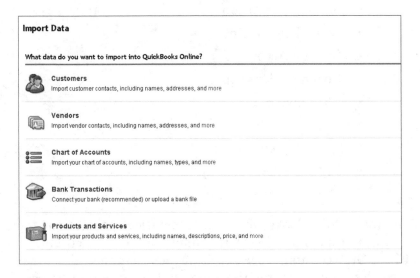

Figure B-1: Importing list data begins here.

With the exception of Bank Transactions, clicking any of the names launches an import wizard called Import <list name>. The wizard works the same way for all four lists that it accommodates. However, as you'd expect, the fields that appear in the Map Fields screen are different for each list. Rather than go through the wizard four times, I'm only going to cover the most complex list (Plus plan Products And Services) in detail.

Clicking Bank Transactions opens the Bank And Credit Cards window, where you can import bank accounts and download transactions. Both of these topics are covered extensively in Chapter 8.

Importing Inventory Items

The trick to importing inventory items is to correctly format the spreadsheet that you're using for the import. If the spreadsheet contains fields that QuickBooks Online neither recognizes nor has the capacity to import, those fields will be ignored. The only fields that will be imported are the following:

- Product/Service Name
- Sales Description
- Sales Price/Rate
- Income Account
- Purchase Description
- Purchase Cost
- Expense Account
- Quantity On Hand
- Inventory Asset Account
- Quantity as-of Date

If you want QuickBooks Online to automatically match the names, use the names in the bullet list (for accounts, use the exact name found in the Chart Of Accounts). However, if the header names don't match exactly, you'll be able to match them manually during the process. Just make sure that there are no cells above the header row, and that the data begins in the first column of the spreadsheet.

A couple of other things to keep in mind:

- Size. The list cannot be more than two megabytes in size, or contain more than one thousand rows. If your list is bigger, simply break it into multiple lists that meet the requirements.

- Subitems. The import process doesn't recognize subitems. So, they'll be imported as items. You'll have to edit each one to make it a subitem once it's imported.

- Duplicate items. If you import the same spreadsheet more than once, it will not overwrite existing items, it will add duplicates instead (The Products And Services list is the exception.) Therefore, be sure to only do the import once. You might want to do a test import of a small number of items first, to ensure that everything works as expected.

To import items from a spreadsheet follow these steps.

1. Choose Tools Menu (gear icon) | Tools | Import Data to open the Import Data Window.

2. Click the Products And Services (or whatever list you want to import) name to start the wizard. As you can see in Figure B-2, the wizard consists of four steps.

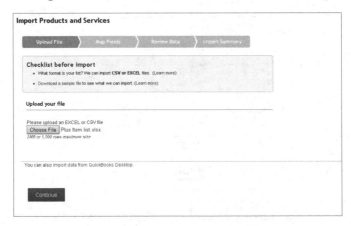

Figure B-2: This screen works the same for all lists.

3. Click the Choose File button to locate the spreadsheet file on your hard disk.

4. As soon as you've made your selection, click the Continue button to begin the upload process. When the file is

uploaded, the Map Fields screen opens. If you check out Figure B-3 you'll notice a few of things.

- A warning symbol next to the Product/Service Name field. This is the only field that is required. In this case, QuickBooks Online was unable to recognize the name in the uploaded spreadsheet.

- I Don't Have This. Some of the fields display I Don't Have This. What this means is that they couldn't make a match with any incoming fields.

- Non-exact matches. The four fields that are matched do not correspond with the field names exactly. However, they were close enough that QuickBooks Online was able to recognize them.

Figure B-3: Make sure your incoming fields match existing fields.

5. Go through the fields and select the correct field name from each drop-down list for those fields with missing or incorrect names.

6. Click Continue to display the Review Data screen (see Figure B-4). What you see here is what will be imported into QuickBooks Online. If there are any errors (a

warning symbol appears), you must fix them before continuing. For example, account names must be exact matches for existing Chart Of Accounts names. If there are mismatches, select the correct account from the drop-down list. Another error you might encounter is an invalid data type. As you can see in Figure B-4, the Quantity As-Of Date field is populated with numeric data, when date data is what's required.

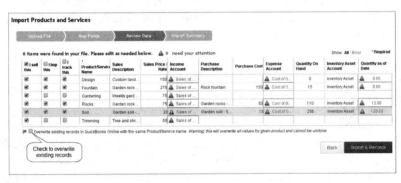

Figure B-4: The Product And Services import is the only one that offers an option to overwrite existing records.

7. You can edit any of the fields in this screen. Make all necessary changes.

8. Unlike the other three list imports, you can elect to overwrite existing records when importing products and services. If you want to overwrite existing records (including financial data) with the incoming information, check the Overwrite Existing Records ... option.

9. When you're satisfied (and there are no warnings), click Import <number> Records to begin the Import.

10. QuickBooks Online asks for confirmation. If you're sure, click OK to import the items.

When the import is completed, the Import Summary screen appears. It tells you how many records were imported and how many items (if any) were not. You can review the items not imported and either ignore them, or fix them and try again.

Remember, this is the most complex list of all to import – but the process is basically the same for the other lists. This exercise was done in Plus, which supports inventory items. If you import the Products And Services list in Simple Start or Essentials, you will see fewer fields.

Exporting from QuickBooks Online

Exporting data from QuickBooks Online is similar to importing, in that you have two choices; you can export data to a QuickBooks desktop application, or you can export certain lists and reports into Excel spreadsheets.

Export to QuickBooks Desktop

If you've decided that you need some of the more advanced features – such as multiple company support, sales orders, job costing, and/or enhanced inventory tracking – you certainly don't want to recreate your company file in the desktop application. Fortunately, QuickBooks Online offers a path for transferring much (not all) of your financial data to a QuickBooks desktop company file.

ProAdvisor TIP: *If you're not using Internet Explorer for accessing QuickBooks Online, you'll want to change for this exercise only. The reason is simple. The export to desktop procedure works in Internet Explorer exclusively. If you try it with any other browser, you're instructed to try it again using Internet Explorer.*

---

1. To begin, choose Tools Menu (gear icon) | Tools | Export to start the wizard.

2. The opening screen explains the steps of the wizard. Click the Get Started button to begin the export process.

3. Unless you've done this before, the next screen asks you to install the required ActiveX control. Click Install to display another screen requesting that you install the control.

4. Click the Install ActiveX Control Now button to really begin the installation. You may get a warning message. If so, tell Internet Explorer to install the control.

5. Finally, an Internet Explorer dialog appears (it's similar to a Save/Run dialog) that will really (I mean it this time) install the ActiveX control. Click Install to begin.

6. When the install is completed, a congratulations screen appears. Click Continue, and you're returned to QuickBooks Online home page.

7. After the ActiveX control is installed, start the export process again – Tools Menu (gear icon) | Tools | Export Data. You're back at the beginning of the wizard again.

8. Click Get Started to open the second screen, which informs you that the control has, indeed, been installed.

9. Click Continue to view the Step 2: Select Your Data screen (see Figure B-5), where you have two choices:

   • All Financial Data. Lists with balances (customers, vendors, accounts, etc) AND all transactions (invoices, sales receipts, checks, deposits, etc)

   • All Financial Data Without Transactions. All lists with balances but with no transactions. Products and services items are exported without quantity on hand numbers.

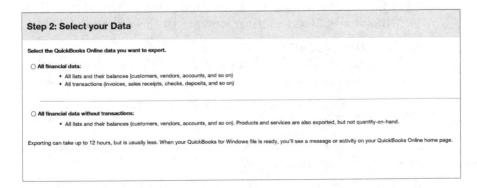

Figure B-5: Choose the second option if you don't need transaction detail.

10. Make your choice, and click Continue to open the Step 3: Request Your Data screen. Before you finalize your request, you are presented with some basic export limitations (no budgets, estimates, or customer credit card data). There's also a link that takes you to a detailed article on export limitations. It's worth reading.

11. Click Continue to open another Step 3: Request Your Data screen. This one asks you to confirm (or change) the name and e-mail address to which the e-mail notice of the completed export file will be sent.

12. Accept or change the contact information, and Click Continue to display yet another Step 3 screen informing you that an e-mail will be sent "shortly." If you haven't figured it out yet, there's an awful lot of redundancy built into this wizard.

13. Click Close to return to the QuickBooks Online home page.

Now you have to wait for the e-mail announcing that the file is ready to be downloaded. I wasn't really paying close attention, but I know it arrived within an hour (maybe less) of completing the export process. The next thing you have to do is download and import the file into your QuickBooks desktop application.

1. Log back into QuickBooks Online (using Internet Explorer). You'll see a flagged item in the Needs Attention section of the Activities pane on the right side of the Home Page. Mine reads "Take Action Download the Company File ... ".

2. Click the flagged item to open the Step 4: Create A QuickBooks For Windows Company File screen, which offers two options:

   • I'm Moving My Data To QuickBooks Desktop Edition.

   • I'm Creating A Local Copy To Keep On My Computer.

3. Make your selection and click Continue to view another Step 4 screen. It tells you to open QuickBooks desktop and close the company file that opens automatically.

4. Follow the instructions and click Download to begin downloading the exported file. Watch out for the status dialog. In my case, it opened in front of the Save dialog box and I thought the file was downloading. I finally realized that I had to select my location and file name, and then click Save to start the download.

5. When the file is downloaded, another (yep, another one) Step 4 screen opens. Read the instructions and click the Convert Now button. A Create New QuickBooks File dialog opens.

6. Choose a file name and location for the new QuickBooks file, and then click Save. When the file is converted, QuickBooks desktop becomes the active window (you DID open it, didn't you?) and sports an Application Certificate dialog that you have to fill out and accept.

7. Since you're creating a new company, select the last option, Yes, Always ... and click Continue. Confirm your choice by clicking Done in the dialog that appears. The company file is opened in QuickBooks desktop.

8. Meanwhile, back in Internet Explorer, the Step 5: Check Your Reports In QuickBooks For Windows screen appears. It tells you to run some reports in QuickBooks desktop to verify that the data has been transferred correctly.

9. Click the Finished button to return to the QuickBooks Online Home Page.

It's a good idea to follow the suggestion to verify that the data was transferred correctly, by running some reports.

Export to Spreadsheets

You can export a great deal of information from QuickBooks Online into an Excel spreadsheet. However, you are limited to exporting from QuickBooks Online lists and reports only.

Exporting QuickBooks Online Lists

While all QuickBooks Online lists offer a Print option, only a handful allow you to export data directly to an Excel spreadsheet. Those that do, provide an Export To Excel icon on the list window toolbar (see Figure B-6). You'll find the icon in the following windows: Customers, Vendors, Sales Transactions, and Expense Transactions. The Products And Services window doesn't have an icon, but an Export button instead.

Figure B-6: Lists that can be exported to Excel offer an Export To Excel icon.

Simply click the icon (or the button) to export the list. Depending on your browser settings, the list will either download automatically to your designated download folder, or a Save dialog will appear asking you where you want store the file on your computer.

Exporting QuickBooks Online Reports

This is another very simple process. All you have to do is open the report, make any necessary (desired) customizations, and click the Excel button. What happens next depends on your browser settings for downloads. If the download location is specified and no option to ask before saving is enabled, the file is automatically saved in the designated download folder. If the option to ask the user is enabled, a dialog box opens asking for a name and destination folder.

I didn't open every report to make sure that they can all be exported. However, I did notice that the neither the Company Snapshot, nor the Audit Log offers an Excel button. I imagine there are others.

Index